The Office
Interior Design Guide

Julie K. Rayfield, Principal, AI/Boggs

The Office
Interior Design Guide:
An Introduction for
Facilities Managers and Designers

JOHN WILEY & SONS, INC.
New York • Chichester • Brisbane • Toronto • Singapore

Library of Congress Cataloging-in-Publication Data:
Rayfield, Julie K., 1958–
    The office interior design guide : an introduction for facilities
  managers & designers / Julie K. Rayfield
      p. cm.
  Includes bibliographical references and index.
    ISBN 0-471-57286-1 (cloth)
    1. Office decoration—United States—Decoration. 2. Interior
  architecture—United States. I. Title.
NK2195.04R38   1994
725′ .23—dc20   93-21638

Printed in the United States of America

10 9 8 7 6 5 4 3 2 1

To my family

Preface

═══════

The importance of a high-quality workplace has never been more evident than in today's climate of rising real estate costs and increasing business competition. To attract and retain high-caliber employees, an organization must be able to offer a safe, comfortable, and stimulating work environment. To support those employees in executing their responsibilities and to maximize their contribution to the organization, the office must also be efficient, functional, and flexible. Meeting these objectives requires that an organization plan strategically and design facilities to meet the needs of the organization both now and in the future.

The intention of this book is to identify the major technical and design issues related to the office environment and to communicate those issues in terms that can readily be understood by the manager who does not have training in the interior architectural profession but is responsible for the planning and design of organizational facilities. The book also serves as an introduction to commercial office design for the design student, entry-level designer, and facilities management or real estate professional who desires a broad perspective of the process or the office environment.

The book is organized into two parts: Part One, Planning and Management, and Part Two, Design. In Part One I focus on issues related to long-term facilities planning as well as individual projects for the office. The text guides the reader through the strategic facilities planning process and explains in detail how to lay the proper groundwork for a specific interiors project by identifying clear objectives and selecting a qualified team. Finally, the project design process—from programming to move-in—is chronicled in a step-by-step approach.

In Part Two I concentrate on the various planning components of the office, building support systems, and elements of interior design. This section yields information about planning and design considerations with which every facilities manager and design student should be familiar: general office areas, support areas, ADA requirements, mechanical and electrical engineering systems, furniture, ceiling systems, lighting, color, acoustics, and finishes.

The book functions for the reader in two ways: first, as a comprehensive introduction to office planning and design, and second, as a reference on specific issues. It is a book to shelve within arm's reach at the office, providing ready clarification for day-to-day facilities issues as well as long-term strategic planning. It is a resource that I hope will serve to promote better understanding of the factors that constitute a high-quality workplace and the elements that combine to ensure successful implementation of any interiors project.

Julie K. Rayfield

Washington D.C.
September 1993

Acknowledgments

===============

Since its inception, this book has taken several forms. I would like to acknowledge those who have played a part in this evolving work. For their ongoing support, I would like to thank my partners. I would also like to thank the members of our staff at AI/Boggs and APM Engineering who added so much to my knowledge of the profession.

The credit for the graphic and illustrative work in this book belongs to Rick Laskowski of AI/Boggs, who was not only an artistic talent, but also a quieting and stabilizing influence for us all in the face of the impossible deadlines I set before him. I would also like to thank Sally Janin and Cyndi Clem who have also worked with Rick and me throughout the development of the book.

I would like to acknowledge the General Services Administration for providing me with the opportunity to take this book forward to publication and for its contribution to the first version of this book.

To my editor, Daniel Sayre, from whom I have learned so much, I express my gratitude for his guidance and patience.

Finally, I would like to thank the people who mean so much to me and who kept me going with their enthusiasm, support, technical expertise, and tireless work on this book: Rusty Meadows, Christine Hensel, and Katrina Dye. I relied upon them in so many ways: for advice, motivation, and support. Without them, I could not have completed this book.

Contents

PART TWO   DESIGN

Part One

Planning and Management

Chapter One

Strategic Facilities Planning

Strategic facilities planning is a proactive approach to the design, acquisition, and use of facilities as a means to support an organization's business plan or mission statement. Organizations of any size, with either leased or owned real estate holdings, can benefit from a strategic facilities planning effort as a means to achieve cost control for their facilities and to maximize employee productivity through the design of better facilities.

THE PURPOSE

The objective in conducting the strategic planning effort is to answer the following three fundamental questions:

- What does the organization have?
- What does the organization need?
- What is the approach for meeting the organization's long-term needs?

The goal is a coordinated plan clearly stating organizational objectives and the strategy for meeting those objectives. The strategy should define specific facilities actions, costs, and a schedule for implementing them. An effectively executed plan will enable the organization's management to work toward a common goal and function proactively rather than reactively in supporting the organization's needs. As a result, the organization's facilities will be properly sized, designed, and delivered cost-effectively as the organization needs them.

The ultimate planning objective is not an easy balance to achieve: developing a strategic facilities plan sufficiently specific in its approach to be effective but adequately flexible to respond to continual organizational changes.

THE FACILITIES PLANNING PROCESS

The strategic facilities plan should be developed by a professional strategic facilities planning consultant or an in-house real estate or facilities management professional with strategic planning experience. In either case, however, several areas of expertise must be available to the strategic planner:

- Facilities programming
- Real estate (sale, purchase, and lease of land and/or buildings)
- Architecture
- Engineering
- Financial analysis

The facilities programmer identifies the organization's needs. The real estate, architectural, and engineering professionals are responsible for defining the alternatives and recommending a physical solution. The financial analyst then evaluates the alternatives and makes a final recommendation from an economic perspective.

All members of the strategic facilities planning team should work under the direction of a single point of responsibility within the organization. Typically, that manager would be a member of the organization's real estate, facilities, or administrative department.

Although every strategic facilities plan can be approached in a similar way, the size and number of facilities that an organization leases and owns ultimately determine the complexity of the strategic facilities plan and, consequently, the specifics of the process. Developing a strategic facilities plan can take from three months to a year, depending on the amount of accurate information available on current and projected facility usage and organizational objectives. The planning process consists of the following six phases:

- Review and evaluation of the current situation
- Development of requirements
- Sensitivity and trend analysis
- Product definition
- Development and evaluation of alternatives
- Recommendation

Review and Evaluation of the Current Situation

To establish a framework for the current situation analysis, the strategic facilities planner should gain an understanding of the overall organizational goals by reviewing the organization's business plan or mission statement. The strategic planner should also gather all available information about past and current facilities, policies, attitudes, and trends. The objective of this review is to obtain as much insight into the organization as possible to assess what has or has not worked well in the past for meeting the organization's facilities requirements. This perspective on the organization's history and potential

future provides a context for interpreting data and making decisions throughout the planning process. It also serves as a basis for developing solutions
and evaluating their potential effectiveness against the organization's mission
statement.

The core of the current situation analysis is an examination of the following
information on the facilities that the organization owns and leases:

- Space inventory
- Planning standards and furniture inventory
- Real estate policies

Space Inventory

The objective of the space inventory is to ascertain the total amount of space
available to the organization for planning purposes and the characteristics of
that space. Each of the following space attributes should be included in the
current situation report.

- Location
- Size in gross and occupiable square feet
- Space efficiencies

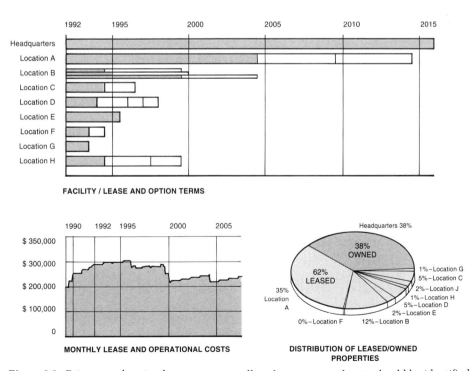

Figure 1.1. Primary and option lease terms as well as their associated costs should be identified
in the space inventory summary.

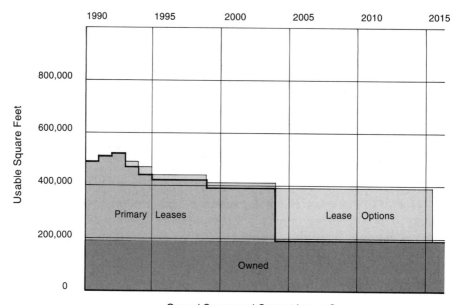

Figure 1.2. In the space inventory, owned space should be identified separately from leased space and lease options should be distinguished from primary terms.

- Type
- Users
- Ownership position, to determine how long the organization will have beneficial and economical use of the facility
- Cost, including leasing, depreciation, operating, maintenance, and repair
- Condition of the facility and its probable useful life, including support systems [heating, ventilation, and air conditioning (HVAC), power distribution]
- Other tangible and intangible qualities of the space (access to public transportation, convenience to retail, availability of parking)

The ownership position of the space should also identify lease expiration dates, to develop a long-term schedule for implementing the strategic plan. A summary space inventory is depicted graphically in Figures 1.1 and 1.2. Figure 1.1 illustrates the ownership position (leased or owned) for each of the organization's properties. Figure 1.2 represents the amount of space in inventory that is available to meet the organization's future needs.

Planning Standards and Furniture Inventory

The planning standards that the strategic facilities planner uses are square-footage allocations for workstations, support areas, circulation, and equipment (Figures 1.3, 1.4., and 1.5). These standards are the basis or planning unit for the development of total square-footage requirements for the organization.

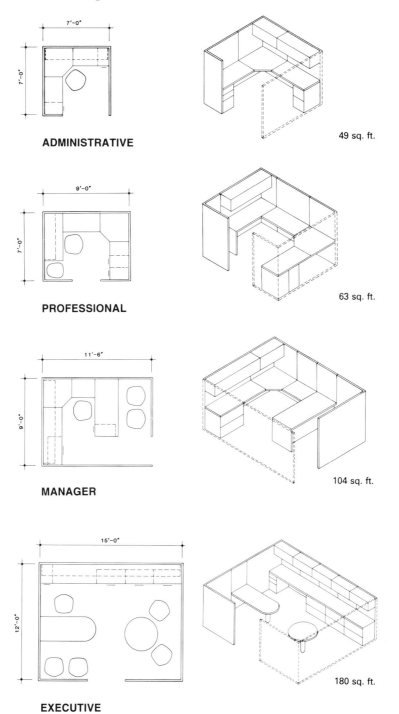

ADMINISTRATIVE

49 sq. ft.

PROFESSIONAL

63 sq. ft.

MANAGER

104 sq. ft.

EXECUTIVE

180 sq. ft.

Figure 1.3. Workstation planning standards illustrated here identify square footage and configuration for administrative through executive levels.

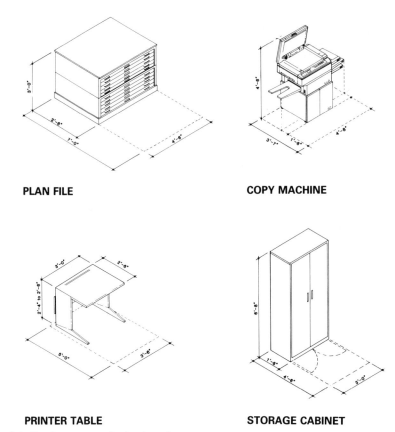

PLAN FILE   **COPY MACHINE**

PRINTER TABLE   **STORAGE CABINET**

Figure 1.4. Equipment standards identify space to accommodate equipment and stand space for operating the equipment.

During the current situation review, the strategic facilities planner evaluates existing planning standards to determine their adequacy for use in the study. At this time, if the analysis reveals any problems with the standards, they are modified accordingly.

An additional factor that the strategic facilities planner considers in modifying or creating planning standards is the organization's furniture inventory available for planning use. The objective in conducting the furniture inventory is to identify existing furniture that may be reused in the planning standards to determine how they might affect those standards. For example, if the organization has been using two different modular furniture systems with two distinct workstation standards, it might be useful to determine if one furniture system works better for the organization and, if so, eliminate the other workstation standard.

The level of detail required for the furniture inventory at this strategic facilities planning level is very general and should include:

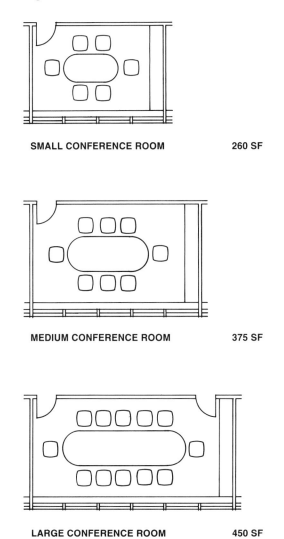

SMALL CONFERENCE ROOM   260 SF

MEDIUM CONFERENCE ROOM   375 SF

LARGE CONFERENCE ROOM   450 SF

Figure 1.5. Support area standards should be developed for all typical support requirements, such as conference, as depicted in this illustration.

- Type (freestanding or furniture system)
- Quantity
- Style (traditional, contemporary)
- General condition of each furniture type

Figure 1.6 illustrates a furniture inventory for a strategic planning effort.

| | | | DIMENSIONS | | | |
| PROJECT TITLE: | | | | DATE: | | |

PROJECT TITLE: **DATE:**

EXISTING SPACE INVENTORIED

ITEM CODE	INVEN- TORY #	ITEM DESCRIPTION	W	D	H	COND. CODE
D-STL	101	DESK / LEFT	60″	30″	29″	G
C-SP	102	CHAIR / TASK	24″	24″	36″	G
F-L3	103	LATERAL FILE / 3 DRW	36″	18″	39″	E
D-DP	104	DESK/DOUBLE PED.	72″	36″	30″	E
C-ES	105	CHAIR / EXEC. SWVL	30″	26″	32″	G
C-SA	106	CHAIR / SIDE	20″	18″	32″	F
C-SA	107	CHAIR / SIDE	20″	18″	32″	F
O	108	BOOKCASE	36″	12″	30″	G
O	109	CREDENZA	60″	18″	30″	G
O	110	STORAGE CABINET	36″	18″	60″	F
O	111	TERMINAL TABLE	36″	24″	29″	P
O	112	COAT RACK	18″	18″	60″	P
O	113	PLAN FILE	54″	42″	36″	G

CODES:

DESKS:
D-DP   DOUBLE PEDESTAL
D-SPL   SINGLE PEDESTAL (LEFT)
D-SPR   SINGLE PEDESTAL (RIGHT)

DESKS W/RETURNS:
D-STL   SECRETARY TYPING (LEFT)
D-STR   SECRETARY TYPING (RIGHT)
D-EXL   EXECUTIVE (LEFT)
D-EXR   EXECUTIVE (RIGHT)

CHAIRS:
C-ES   EXECUTIVE SWIVEL
C-SP   SECRETARY POSTURE
C-S   SIDE
C-SA   SIDE WITH ARMS

FILES:
F-VLT4   VERTICAL/LETTER (4 DRW)
F-VLG4   VERTICAL/LEGAL (4 DRW)
F-L3   LATERAL (3 DRW)
O   MISC/OTHER

CONDITION:
E –   EXCELLENT
G –   GOOD
F –   FAIR
P –   POOR

Figure 1.6. The information obtained from a furniture inventory contributes to developing future planning standards.

Real Estate Policies

The organization's current real estate policies affect the interpretation of the space inventory planning standards and furniture inventory data. They also affect the options available to meet future needs. For instance, a new real estate policy mandating a lease versus ownership position will determine the disposition of each facility in the organization's portfolio and, consequently, affect the strategic facilities plan in terms of quantity, type, and timing of space accessibility. Evaluating the organization's current situation provides a foundation for the subsequent step in the process: the development of requirements.

Development of Requirements

The objective in the development of requirements is to determine the total occupiable space required for the organization currently and in the future. To develop the organization's requirements, the strategic facilities planner collects both quantitative and qualitative needs through management and personnel interviews, questionnaires, and facility surveys.

Although programming during a design project details very specific design requirements, programming during strategic facilities planning is more general and identifies only space quantities and characteristics that would be affected by the building architecture or building support systems (mechanical and electrical systems). For example, programming during a design project would identify a specific number and type of file cabinets, the information necessary to plan and design the space. The strategic facilities program would identify a need for a central file room of a certain size with a specific requirement for floor (slab) reinforcement to carry the additional weight load. The information key to the strategic facilities plan is the square footage required for the room and the additional floor loading capacity that would be needed in the building.

The total square footage that the organization needs to meet current and future needs is considered a quantitative requirement. These requirements include all workstations (personnel), shared support, special support (auditoriums, cafeterias), and circulation area. Current numbers for the organization are obtained from actual personnel figures and a survey of the current space in use. Forecasts for personnel and support area requirements are typically three- to five-year annual projections. Projections beyond five years can be made but are less reliable. The source of the forecasts are questionnaires and personal interviews with key management and division or department representatives. Typically, the strategic facilities planner will distribute written questionnaires prior to meeting with each person (see Appendix 3 for a sample programming questionnaire). The strategic planner will then review the written response during the personal interview to clarify and augment the written responses.

The strategic facilities planner verifies these projections with the organization's senior management and compares the information against the organization's mission statement and current real estate policies. The validated current and forecasted quantities for workstation and support areas are then multiplied by the planning standards for total personnel and support area requirements. The personnel and support area total, plus a circulation factor of 40 to 50 percent, provides the total occupiable space required for the organization during the current and forecasted periods. Figure 1.7 illustrates a summary of program requirements and analysis of the requirements by space type and user. Figure 1.8 illustrates the projected growth as identified in the program compared with the available space inventory to meet that need. This comparison provides the strategic planner with insight into the discrepancy between *what the organization has* and *what the organization needs*.

The objective in identifying qualitative space requirements for the organization is to gather sufficient information to define building performance criteria

Useable Area Required
Division % of Total

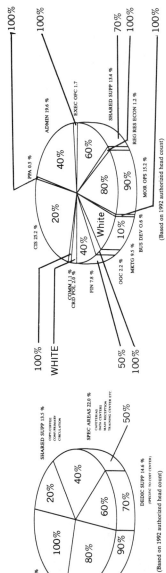

Space Types
By % of Total Useable Area Required

(Based on 1992 authorized head count)

SHARED SUPP 13.5 %
ENCL OFC 23.7 %
SPEC AREAS 22.0 %
CAFETERIAS
DATA CENTERS
MAIN RECEPTION
TRAINING CENTER ETC

100%
20%
40%
50%
80%
60%
70%
90%

OPEN WKSTA 26.2 %
DEDIC SUPP 14.6 %
(SPECIFIC TO COST CENTER)

PPA 0.5 %
ADMIN 19.6 %
EXEC OFC 1.7
SHARED SUPP 13.4 %
REG RES ECON 1.2 %
MOR OPS 15.2 %
BUS DEV 0.6 %
MKTG 9.5 %
OGC 2.2 %
FIN 7.8 %
CRD POL 2.0 %
COMM 1.1 %
CIS 25.2 %
White
WHITE

100%
100%
100%
100%
70%
100%
50%
100%
40%
20%
40%
10%
60%
80%
90%

(Based on 1992 authorized head count)

DIVISION	AUTH'D STAFF	AREA REQ'D	% OF REQ'D
EXECUTIVE OFFICE	15	10,900 SF	5.20 %
ADMINISTRATION	189	58,912 SF	28.30 %
BUSINESS DEVELOPMENT	25	3,762 SF	1.80 %
CORPORATE INFO SERVICES	217	48,919 SF	23.50 %
COMMUNICATIONS	34	6,873 SF	3.30 %
CREDIT POLICY	66	12,806 SF	6.20 %
FINANCE	32	7,316 SF	3.60 %
MARKETING	21	5,066 SF	2.40 %
OFFICE GENERAL COUNSEL	48	13,994 SF	6.70 %
POLICY & PUBLIC AFFAIRS	12	3,254 SF	1.60 %
REG, RESEARCH, ECON	31	7,927 SF	3.80 %
SHARED USER SUPPORT	N/A	28,180 SF	13.60 %
TOTAL REQUIRED	690	207,909 SF	100.00 %
USEABLE BUILDING SPACE		197,400 SF	
SPACE SURPLUS/(DEFICIT)		(10,509) SF	
(Includes 56 contract employees)			

DIVISION	AUTH'D STAFF '92	AREA REQ'D	% OF REQ'D
ADMINISTRATION	42	66,584 SF	16.20 %
CORPORATE INFO SERVICES	595	113,888 SF	27.60 %
FINANCE	176	43,315 SF	10.50 %
MARKETING	147	34,446 SF	8.30 %
MORTGAGE OPERATIONS	516	98,337 SF	23.80 %
SHARED USER SUPPORT	N/A	55,973 SF	13.60 %
TOTAL REQUIRED	1,476	412,515 SF	100.00 %
USEABLE BUILDING SPACE		366,800 SF	
SPACE SURPLUS/(DEFICIT)		(45,715) SF	
(Includes 150 contract employees)			

DIVISION	AUTH'D STAFF	AREA REQ'D	% OF REQ'D
ADMINISTRATION	4	800 SF	3.20 %
MARKETING (NRI)	107	21,632 SF	87.10 %
SHARED USER SUPPORT	N/A	2,400 SF	9.70 %
TOTAL REQUIRED	111	24,832 SF	100.00 %
USEABLE BUILDING SPACE		35,300 SF	
SPACE SURPLUS/(DEFICIT)		10,468 SF	

Program Assumptions

WORKSTATION STANDARDS			AVERAGE CIRC. FACTORS			
LEVEL	ORIG	PROG	BLDG	ORIG	PROG	CIRC
SR VICE PRESIDENT	(350 SF)	500 SF	4000	1.77	1.60	(37 %)
VICE PRESIDENT	(280 SF)	240 SF	3900	N/A	1.43	(30 %)
DIRECTOR	(200 SF)	220 SF	3939	N/A	1.40	(28 %)
MANAGER	(180 SF)	160 SF				
PROFESSIONAL	(80 SF)	80 SF				
TECHNICAL	(64 SF)	64 SF				
CLERICAL	(80 - 120 SF)	50 SF				

Figure 1.7. Pie charts are used in this illustration to summarize space requirements by space type and users.

Square Feet (Thousands)

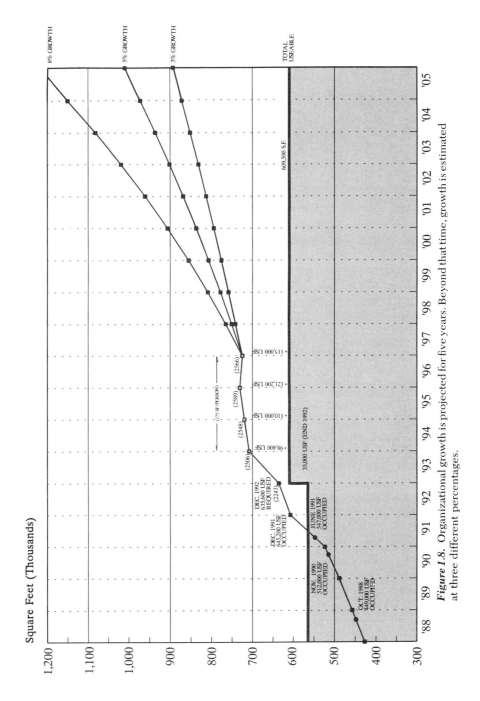

Figure 1.8. Organizational growth is projected for five years. Beyond that time, growth is estimated at three different percentages.

13

so that the facility closely meets user needs. The qualitative space requirements taken into consideration during the development of requirements are any characteristics of the space that influence base building architectural, support system, and other infrastructure design, such as:

- Floor loading capacity and sizing
- Core configuration
- Column spacing
- HVAC and power capacity
- Life safety, security, and code requirements

Sensitivity and Trend Analysis

Once the strategic facilities planner has compiled the quantitative and qualitative requirements for the organization, the data are analyzed in the context of trends, sensitivities, and potential risks. The purpose of conducting this analysis is to test the assumptions made during the study and the validity of the information developed, and to investigate the potential risk associated with each alternative solution. Ultimately, the sensitivity and trend analysis will assist the strategic facilities planner in designing an appropriate amount of flexibility into the plan to accommodate that potential risk.

The first step in the trend and sensitivity analysis is to review all organizational and industry trends to determine if the projected requirements for the organization are consistent with those trends. If any inconsistencies arise, the strategic facilities planner must identify the causes and their potential impact on future solutions.

The second step in conducting the trend and sensitivity analysis is to determine the sensitivity of the study's results. To accomplish this, the strategic facilities planner must identify all factors affecting the validity of information and decisions made during the course of the strategic plan. Factors can be internal or external to the organization. Internal factors include such changes as:

- Management directives
- Organization's mission statement
- Financial structure
- Technology use
- Corporate culture

External factors include:

- General economic conditions
- Market fluctuations
- Industry trends
- Legislation
- Geopolitical climate

The third step, after all the factors have been identified, is to assign potential risk to each factor. For instance, the strategic facility planner has assumed that the program information obtained during the development of requirements is accurate. What is the probability that the information is inaccurate, and if so, what is the potential risk associated with that misinformation? The risk attributed to the information, and the decisions based on that information, are considered in the next stage of the strategic facilities planning effort, the development of the product definition. It is also included in the development of alternatives and final recommendation. For example, if the final recommendation based on the programming information is that the organization should build a 500,000-square-foot headquarters facility, the strategic facilities planning effort must also identify the associated risk that the square footage is excessive, or inadequate.

Perhaps the organization has experienced no need for major changes in its facilities and has remained a largely closed-plan environment. Perhaps the organization has also been part of a static, low-tech industry for a significant period of time. Moderate growth, however, now necessitates that the organization consider expanding its facilities. Concurrently, the organization also anticipates major industry movement toward technology (a *trend*) that will completely revise the profile of the typical office and will change the sales/management/production ratios of employees (a *sensitivity*). With this information (the trend analysis and the study of the program's sensitivity) a completely different facility would be designed than if this trend and sensitivity analysis were not conducted and this information were not available.

Product Definition

The product definition phase of the strategic facilities plan defines those specific space characteristics that are necessary to meet the organization's long-term needs as quantified in the development of requirements. A complete product definition should include the following information:

- Amount of space required at each annual increment of the forecast period
- Type of space required, such as support areas, special areas, general office; the quantities of each type of space; and the general quality level of the space
- Configuration of space, defining the optimum floor sizing, number of stories, core configuration, floor loading, and column spacing for each facility
- Infrastructure requirements, such as vertical transportation (elevators), base building HVAC, and power and data distribution systems

The level of detail in the product definition should be sufficient to guide, yet not inhibit, the actual project design process resulting from the strategic facilities plan. In fact, the actual infrastructure specifications should be viewed not as design specifications that represent a particular product or system, but rather as performance specifications that identify only a level or character of performance. For example, Figure 1.9 illustrates a narrative and graphic description for an access floor that could be included in a product definition. This approach to the performance specifications allows the project architects, interior architects, and engineers on each specific project sufficient latitude

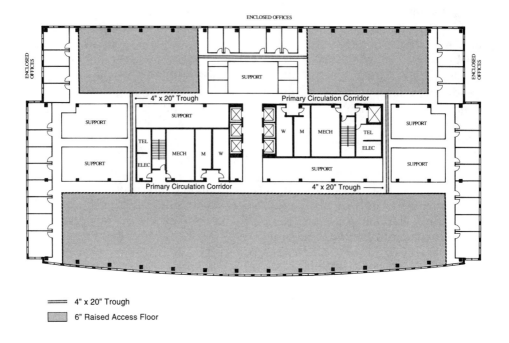

ACCESS FLOOR

All areas proposed for office use shall be constructed with a depressed slab and provided with a minimum six-inch-high raised access floor system. All service core areas including, but not limited to, elevator lobbies, restrooms, pantry/vending areas, mechanical and electrical equipment rooms, primary circulation paths and stair landings shall be a concrete floor slab assembly level with the top of the raised access floor system.

Access floor specifications shall meet test procedures in accordance with Ceiling and Interiors Systems Construction Association criteria. These specifications are as follows:

Office Areas: Raised 6" access floor system shall be a stringerless type and have a minimum load rating of 250 pounds per square foot for distributed loads and 1,000 pounds per square foot for concentrated loads. Floor panels shall be steel, concrete filled, or equivalent construction with positive attachment at the corners and/or sides. Attachment screws and/or other devices shall be captured in the panel. Floor panels shall be constructed in such a manner to afford an acceptable acoustical and rigid aesthetic quality. Finished surfaces shall accept carpet tile. Refer to the electrical section for cabling service requirements.

Computer Areas: Raised 2' - 0" access floor system shall be a bolted stringer type and have a minimum floor loading capacity of 1,250 pounds per square foot concentrated load. Floor panels shall be lay-in steel panels with high pressure laminate finish. Ten percent (10%) of the panels shall be perforated for return air capacities.

Underfloor surfaces must be smooth, level and sealed with an acceptable concrete sealer to prevent dusting and painted white Emergency water drains shall also be provided (refer to mechanical section).

Figure 1.9. Performance criteria for building systems such as access floor, as illustrated, are used to develop a product definition.

to create effective design solutions. Concurrently, the definition establishes the parameters for design and imposes a level of quality and cost control over the final product.

Flexibility is key to any successful strategic facilities plan and therefore must be inherent in the product definition. In addition to organizational and industry changes that necessitate an adaptive plan, the constantly evolving

Thousands

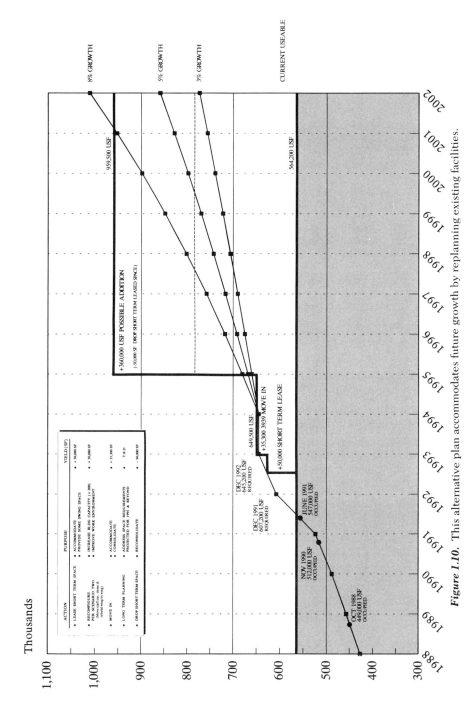

Figure 1.10. This alternative plan accommodates future growth by replanning existing facilities.

17

Square Feet (Thousands)

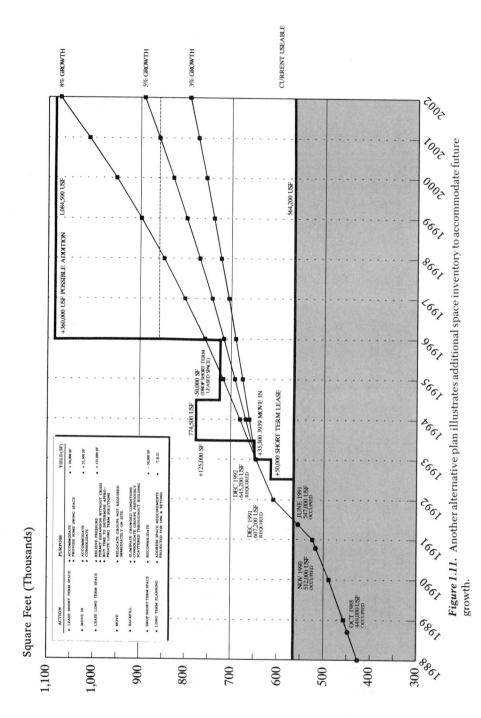

Figure I.11. Another alternative plan illustrates additional space inventory to accommodate future growth.

18

office and technological environments demand that each facility be capable of responding to new developments. Changing workstation standards and furniture systems, emerging computer technology, and telecommuting all suggest that the office environment of today will not resemble the office environment of the future. Flexibility is the best avenue for ensuring that these developments do not create premature obsolescence in facilities.

Development and Evaluation of Alternatives

Typically, many different options are valid for satisfying the product definition identified in the study. In this phase, the strategic facilities planner explores those options and evaluates the validity and relative value of each. To develop alternatives, the strategic facilities planner overlays the product definition with the organization's space inventory and real estate policies, integrating what the organization needs and when it is needed. The alternatives development phase provides options such as expansion, relocation, and consolidation to meet those needs. Each option includes associated schedule and cost data. Figures 1.10 and 1.11 suggest two alternative options for meeting a future space deficit. The alternative identified in Figure 1.10 reflects a decrease in future requirements through reduction in space standards and a reorganization of existing space. The alternative illustrated in Figure 1.11 reflects the option to increase future space inventory through leasing and new construction options.

A set of weighted criteria, each of which has a priority value, forms the basis for the evaluation of each alternative. The criteria should include:

- Cost (first and life cycle)
- How well the alternative meets the organization's mission statement
- How well the alternative meets the product definition

The weight assigned to each criterion is based on the importance of that issue to the organization. First cost may be an overriding priority to one organization, while the ability to meet product definition may constitute the priority to another.

Recommendation

Based on the selection of a specific alternative, the strategic facilities planner prepares a formal recommendation in the form of a written report to the organization's senior management. This recommendation, which defines a detailed strategy for meeting requirements through the recommended alternative, will be the foundation for short- and long-term objectives and solutions for the organization. The strategy identifies specific time frames and associated costs for implementing the plan.

If the plan must be presented to senior management for acceptance, it should be effectively packaged and documented to be persuasive. The plan should be comprehensive and substantiated, clearly communicating to the organization the anticipated benefits of the plan.

Once the plan is accepted and implemented, it should be reviewed regularly and modified to respond to the evolving needs of the organization. Ultimately, the plan should provide a context for decision making and a framework for organizing and executing individual design projects, the subjects addressed in the following chapters.

Chapter Two

Project Organization:
The Project Planning Process

A strategic facilities planning effort establishes a road map for meeting an organization's long-term facilities requirements and identifies as a part of the plan each project that must be implemented during the life of the plan. Although it provides general objectives and requirements for these individual projects and establishes when they are needed by the organization, the details of the project should be planned and organized during the step prior to executing the project, the project organization phase. This ensures that detailed project planning will respond more closely to the needs of the organization at the time of project implementation. If the organization does not have a strategic facilities plan in place, the project organization phase becomes even more critical to ensuring that the project ultimately executed will in fact be what the organization needs.

The significance of conducting a project organization phase prior to project execution is often overlooked by an organization, typically because a project is undertaken as a reactive rather than a proactive measure. Time is often short, and therefore the planning and organization phase is conducted in a cursory way or eliminated altogether. This initial planning period of assembling information, people, and procedures, however, is a wise investment, cultivating well-founded strategies, coordination, and communication.

The project organization phase (Figure 2.1) defines the project need and objective, identifies participants, their roles and responsibilities, and establishes a decision-making process. As a result, project participants can work toward common objectives under the same set of facts, assumptions, and

- Develop an in-house team
- Develop a decision-making process
- Define the project need and objectives
- Assemble pertinent organization and project-related information
- Select and organize the consultant team
- Develop a preliminary project schedule and budget

Figure 2.1. Organizing project-related information and team members facilitates the project execution process.

procedures for the duration of the project. The project organization phase comprises the following key tasks:

- Developing an in-house team
- Developing a decision-making process
- Defining the project need and objectives
- Assembling information pertinent to the organization and project
- Selecting and organizing the consultant team
- Developing a preliminary project schedule and budget

Throughout the project, certain objectives should remain constant: to maximize the productivity and value of each participant's time on the project, to minimize decision-making time, and to reduce or eliminate the need for changes in direction or strategy due to inaccurate information or indecisiveness. The key to achieving these objectives is to establish a framework for the project by organizing all resources and information within the organization by first identifying the in-house project team and the decision-making process. When this is complete, the project team, or team of project consultants, can be properly selected and effectively directed.

DEVELOPING AN IN-HOUSE TEAM

The in-house team should constitute a group of professionals capable of defining the project and managing the process through to a successful conclusion. The in-house team has two functions: internal and external. Internally, the in-house team is responsible for interfacing with the senior management, users, and special-interest groups. In this role, the in-house team manages all internal participants to gather and coordinate information and responses throughout the project. The in-house team defines the project need and objectives as well as works with user and special-interest groups in the development of requirements. As project consultants develop options, the in-house team reviews these alternatives, provides input, and makes recommendations for further action.

The in-house team's external function is to ensure that all consultants perform on the project by effectively managing them (not attempting to assume their roles on the project) and the project process.

The level of complexity of the project and the availability of in-house expertise dictates the size and composition of the in-house team, but at a minimum it should include the following participants:

- Facilities or administration representative(s)
- User groups
- Special-interest groups

The facilities or administrative representative acts as the in-house team project manager, directing the in-house team and project consultants. The project manager is also responsible for defining and monitoring the project scope, budget, and schedule as well as reporting to the organization's management on the project.

On a relatively simple project, a project manager and one representative from each of the user groups affected by the project is a sufficient in-house team. On a large or complex project, the in-house team should include a representative from the facilities or administrative department who is familiar with building operations. The in-house team should also include special-interest representation from such departments as management information systems, telecommunications, and human resources (Figure 2.2). The participation of user and special-interest group representatives will facilitate gathering accurate information and developing feasible solutions. Ultimately, it will also promote project acceptance by instilling in the users a sense of ownership in the final project.

DEVELOPING A DECISION-MAKING PROCESS

As important as the composition of the in-house team, the decision-making process can either expedite the project, or disable it through a maze of unnecessary procedures and indecisive participants. The primary objective, therefore, is to create a simple and effective decision-making process that identifies both the decision makers and the means for obtaining decisions on the project.

Depending on the level of expertise and seniority of the in-house team, it can also act as the decision-making group on a simple or small project. On a large, complex project the in-house team might make daily decisions and report to a senior management committee on all major decisions. In either case, all personnel with the authority to make and uphold project decisions must be included in the decision-making body. Additional involvement by anyone in the organization only complicates and impedes the process, whereas the omission of key management on certain issues makes if difficult to make or uphold decisions. Active senior management participation also ensures that the project team has clear direction and proper management support.

Decision-making procedures should also state the types of issues to be decided by each decision-making group and the points during the project at which their decisions will be required. Actual key milestone dates are built into the project schedule as it is developed later in the project organization phase to ensure that decision makers are accessible at those critical points in

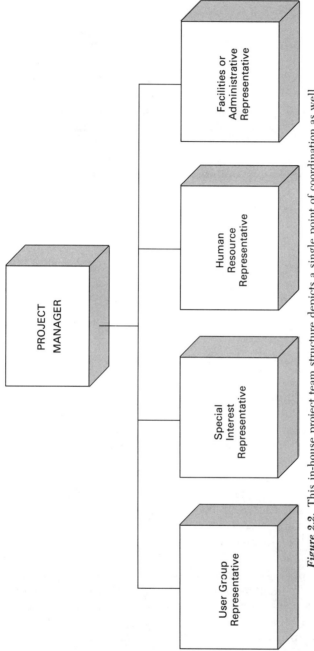

Figure 2.2. This in-house project team structure depicts a single point of coordination as well as representation from all key departments.

24

the project. The in-house team is responsible for delineating, documenting, and maintaining these procedures throughout the course of the project.

DEFINING THE PROJECT NEED AND OBJECTIVES

Once the decision-making process is in place, the in-house team can develop a project definition for use in assembling a project team of professional consultants and developing a strategy for resolution of the requirement. If the organization is operating under a long-term strategic facilities plan, the project and the project definition might already be incorporated into that plan. A comprehensive project definition addresses the following issues:

- Project need
- Reason for the need
- Goals for the project
- Parameters for a solution
- Predisposition to a solution

The *project need* defines the requirement for the project: for example, a need for additional office space to accommodate several divisions of the organization.

The *reason for the need* identifies what is causing the need. For example, the need for additional office space caused by staff growth, which, in turn, is caused by the organization's current diversification into new markets.

The *goal for the project* in this example is to create additional office space appropriately designed to meet the needs over the next 10 to 15 years for those divisions affected by the diversification.

The *parameters for a solution* are also an important part of the project definition. Budget and schedule parameters, for example, are central to developing a scope of work and associated fees for project consultants. These parameters and others, such as lease versus own for obtaining additional space, use of existing facilities to solve the requirement, or use of existing planning standards, form the foundation for any strategy to resolve the project need and must be identified, if only in general terms, at this point in the project.

Both in-house team members and project consultants must be aware of any *predispositions to solving* the requirement. This common understanding prevents wasted effort in pursuing solutions that are unacceptable to senior management. For instance, although renovation and expansion might be a worthwhile option to pursue in accommodating future growth, if the senior executive in the organization holds a strong preference for relocation, the project team should be aware of that predisposition so that their efforts can be directed accordingly.

ASSEMBLING INFORMATION PERTINENT TO THE
ORGANIZATION AND PROJECT

In addition to developing the project definition, the in-house team should assemble information on its organization and its project for use in selecting the consultant team. This information is also valuable for the subsequent orientation of consultants to the project. This information should include:

- Overview of the organization
- Products and/or services
- Mission/organizational goals
- Organizational structure and staff composition
- Plans of existing facilities potentially affected by the project
- Existing facilities planning standards
- Current or recent programming data
- Advantages and disadvantages of the existing facility
- Maintenance and/or repair information related to facilities affected by the project

With these resources in place, the in-house team is prepared to begin the selection process for the consultant team.

SELECTING AND ORGANIZING THE CONSULTANT TEAM

The consultant team comprises all of the management, technical, and creative expertise necessary to take the project from commencement through completion and is composed of professional consultants who augment the capabilities of the in-house team as necessary in the following principal areas:

- *Real Estate:* market research, analysis, purchase, sale, and leasing representation
- *Project Management:* owner representation in project team selection and coordination, cost and schedule control, project documentation, and construction quality assurance (project management consultants are typically used only on large, complex projects)
- *Design*
- *Interior Architecture:* program development, space planning, design, and documentation for construction and furniture procurement, construction monitoring
- *Engineering:* mechanical, electrical, plumbing, and structural analysis and design
- *Specialties:* audiovisual, lighting, acoustical, security, telecommunications, cost estimating, records management, art
- *Construction (General Contractor or Construction Manager):* management of the construction trades and construction of the space
- *Furniture and Furnishings:* procurement and installation of furniture, art, plants, and accessories
- *Equipment:* procurement and installation of computers, telecommunications, copiers, and other general office support equipment.

Although in the past, lines of distinction were clearly drawn among the consultants offering these services, many firms have now expanded their capabilities to include areas that overlap with others. For example, real estate consultants traditionally offer the leasing, purchase, and sales services required to procure or dispose of space. In an attempt to increase their competitive edge, some real estate consultants have diversified and now provide project management, strategic facility planning, program development, and space planning services as well. Project management firms have also moved into strategic facility planning and programming, services customarily provided by the interior architect. Some interior architects now offer project management services.

If the firm and personnel are well qualified in each area, it can make sense to retain one firm to provide multiple services. One of the primary advantages of a diversified firm is that by minimizing the number of participants, the team can be more easily directed, controlled, and coordinated. It can also be more cost-effective. The potential disadvantage, however, is that such a firm may be a generalist in many areas and a specialist in none. Also, in multidisciplinary firms, it is not uncommon for one discipline to become predominant over the other specialists. This can result in a project receiving unbalanced attention or insufficient expertise in some areas.

Although a more complex team (Figure 2.3) does require additional coordination and management, there are benefits to using a specialist in each area of service. Particularly significant is the system of checks and balances that can be established among the team members to monitor the caliber of the work each produces. Also, if directed properly, the creative tension that naturally develops among the disciplines can produce a superior solution for the project.

Paramount to a selection of these consultants and the assignment of their responsibilities, however, is the level of expertise and successful experience in each service area that the firm offers. The credentials of each consulting firm as well as the experience of the people who will be producing the work should be examined carefully in each area of proposed service.

Based on the composition of consultants as well as the scope of work each will perform, the team can be structured in several different ways. Ordinarily, the real estate consultant reports directly to the in-house team, with a secondary relationship to the interior architect and project management consultant (if used on the team). The project management consultant reports directly to the in-house team either with a dotted-line relationship to the other team members or a direct supervisory responsibility for the design members of the team. It is usual for the engineers and specialty consultants to report directly to the interior architect.

In structuring the project team, the overriding objectives are to:

- Allow each consultant the latitude for maximum performance
- Create a positive and cooperative working environment
- Establish clear lines of reporting and communication which foster responsiveness and effectiveness

In the past, the real estate consultant was typically the first consultant brought on to the project to identify alternatives and procure space. Then, after a specific space was secured, the project managment consultant and

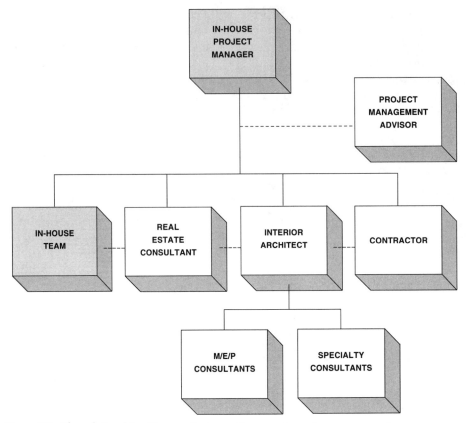

Figure 2.3. The relationship of key project consultants to the in-house team is illustrated by this team chart.

design team members were chosen. As a result, the organization's require-ments were not identified until after the office space was obtained. Often, the space did not meet the organization's requirements for the project. Organiza-tions are now finding that it is more productive first to determine their basic requirements and then to investigate options for meeting those needs. This method leads to the procurement of interior architectural assistance earlier in the process, often prior to or simultaneous with retaining a real estate advisor.

DEVELOPING A PRELIMINARY PROJECT SCHEDULE AND BUDGET

With the consultant team in place, the in-house project manager can employ these resources to develop a project schedule and budget. Both the schedule and the budget in particular should be fairly general at this point, reflecting the broad definition of the project. As the team develops the project concepts, the schedule and budget should become more specific.

Project Schedule

The project schedule establishes the sequence of events that must occur in order to execute the project successfully within its objectives. It provides each team member with the necessary information to plan and implement specific project tasks and responsibilities effectively. The schedule also serves as a tool for the in-house project manager and consultant team managers to measure project progress. The in-house team project manager should develop a preliminary project schedule that can be augmented and refined later with input from the interior architectural consultant selected for the project.

Ordinarily, one of two scheduling methods is used on an interiors project: Gantt or critical path method. A *Gantt chart* is a bar chart that identifies the linear sequence of events on the project. A Gantt schedule defines the project by phase, or if the project warrants a greater level of detail, each phase by task (Figure 2.4). A horizontal bar extending from the date the phase or task is initiated to the date it must be completed illustrates the duration of each phase or task. Significant milestones or approval dates are flagged on the schedule. The placement of the bars also indicates any work that is phased or overlapped.

Although the Gantt schedule can be developed in substantial detail, it does not illustrate the interrelationship of the tasks, a key consideration on a complex project or a project with a short time frame. A *critical path method* (CPM) schedule does illustrate those interrelationships and for that

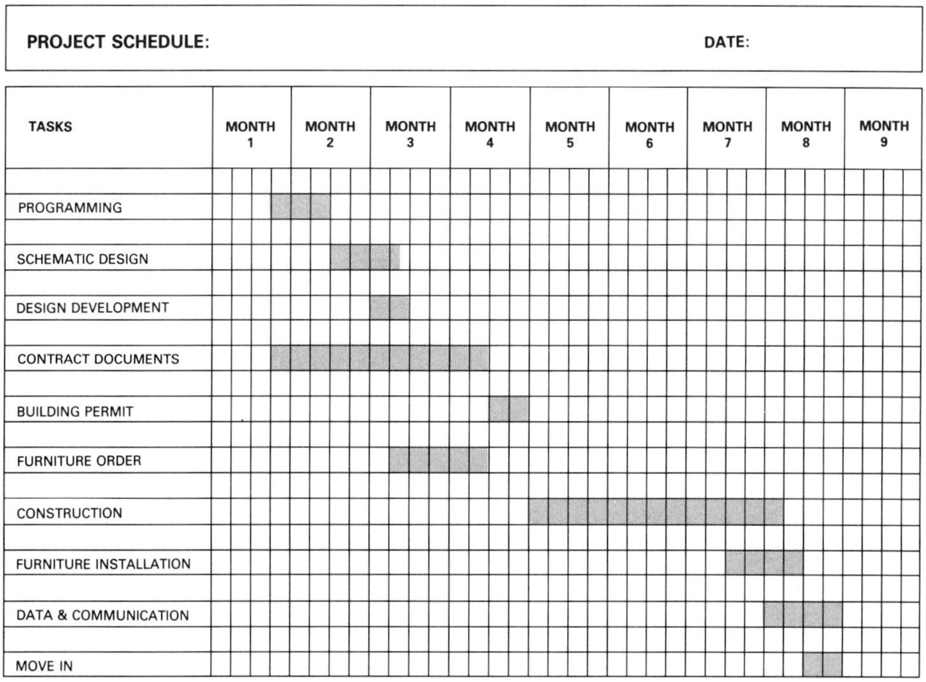

GANTT SCHEDULE

Figure 2.4. This simple Gantt schedule defines the project by phase.

PROJECT TITLE:	DATE:

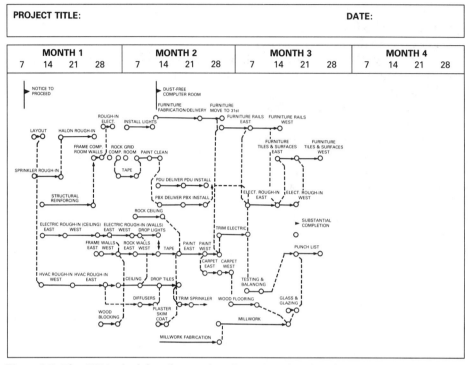

Figure 2.5. The CPM scheduling format identifies a critical path and interrelationships of tasks.

reason is frequently used for more sophisticated scheduling requirements (Figure 2.5). The CPM identifies each task, the specific time required to complete that task, its relationship to other tasks, and the overall impact on the project if that task is completed ahead of schedule or is behind schedule.

In either format the schedule should be developed as described below.

Identifying a Project Completion Date
The key to developing an effective project schedule is to begin with a proposed completion date that is both reasonable and achievable. All projects begin with a required or desired completion date in mind. Given that date, identify factors such as availability of the key decision makers, current market conditions, and the complexity of the project that may affect whether that date can be achieved, and make any necessary adjustments to the completion date. The in-house team project manager should compare the desired completion date with schedules from similar completed projects to ascertain the reasonableness of the date.

Identifying and Listing All Significant Project Activities
In many cases, a list of the project phases identifies major tasks in sufficient detail to manage the project. If more detail is needed for monitoring activities,

the list of project activities can be expanded to include individual tasks within each project phase (Figure 2.6).

Establishing Time Frames for Each Activity

Establish the specific time frames required to complete each project activity. Whenever possible, the in-house team member and consultant responsible

---

PHASE I: PROGRAMMING

- Orientation
- Project Schedule Development
- Questionnaire Development
- Questionnaire Orientation and Distribution
- Questionnaire Compilation
- Interviews
- Field Surveys
- Inventory Existing Furniture
- Space Standards
- Preliminary Project Budget Development
- Space Requirement Report Development
- Space Requirement Report Submittal
- Space Requirement Report Revisions
- Space Requirement Report Approval

PHASE II: ALTERNATIVES EVALUATIONS

- Test Fit Space Plans
- Building Systems Evaluation
- Workletter Evaluation
- Opinion of Probable Cost
- Comparative Analysis Development
- Comparative Analysis Report Submission
- Comparative Analysis Report Approval
- Building Selection

PHASE III: SCHEMATIC DESIGN

- Building Survey and Report
- ADA Survey
- Field Verification
- Base Building Plans Development
- Blocking/Stacking
- Schematic Space Plan
- Schematic Design Concepts
- Cost Update
- Schematic Design Presentation
- Schematic Design Revisions
- Schematic Design Approval
- Schematic Concepts to M/E/P Engineers and Specialty Consultants

---

PHASE IV: DESIGN DEVELOPMENT

- Final Space Plan
- Final Design Concepts
- Final Selection of Finishes, Materials and Furniture
- Equipment Specifications
- Cost Update
- Final Design Presentation
- Final Design Revisions
- Final Design Approval
- Final Design Concepts for M/E/P Engineers and Specialty Consultants

---

PHASE V: CONTRACT DOCUMENTS

- Interior Architectural Working Drawings and Specifications Development
- Furniture Drawings and Specifications Development
- M/E/P Engineering Document Development
- Issue Permit Drawings
- Issue Bid Package for Construction
- Pre-Bid Conference
- Issue Bid Clarifications/Addendums
- Issue Furniture Bid Package
- Bid/Negotiation
- Award Construction Contract
- Award Furniture Contract

PHASE VI: CONTRACT ADMINISTRATION

- Construction Progress Meetings
- Construction Site Visits
- Submittal Review
- Furniture Installation
- Punch List
- Punch List Implementation
- Punch List Verification
- As-Built Documentation
- Move-In
- Post Occupancy Evaluation

Figure 2.6. This illustration identifies the major tasks in each phase that are used to develop a project schedule.

for an activity should participate in establishing the start and completion dates for the activity to instill a sense of commitment to those dates. Participation by the consultant team members also helps to ensure that the time frames are accurate, reasonable, and achievable. As an additional check and balance, these dates should be compared with schedules on similar projects.

Establishing Key Decision Dates

Regardless of the level of detail in the schedule, it is important to establish key dates at appropriate points in the schedule. This will alert all team members to the dates by which approvals or decisions must be made for the project to proceed on schedule. The responsibilities for work or decisions related to those key dates should be assigned to the appropriate consultant or in-house team member. For example, the space requirements report is the responsibility of the interior architect. The final approval of the space requirements report is the responsibility of the in-house team project manager.

Publishing, Distributing, and Monitoring the Schedule

Once the schedule is published and distributed to all team members it becomes the responsibility of the in-house project manager and the consultant team project managers to monitor the progress of the project to make certain it is consistent with the intended schedule.

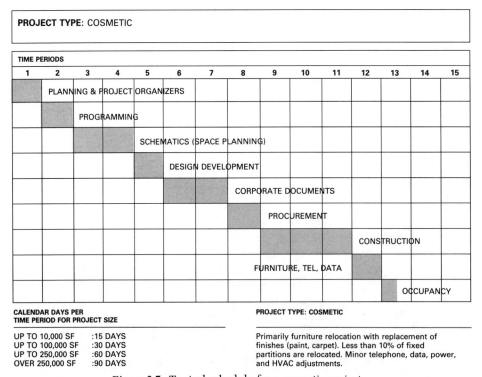

Figure 2.7. Typical schedule for a cosmetic project.

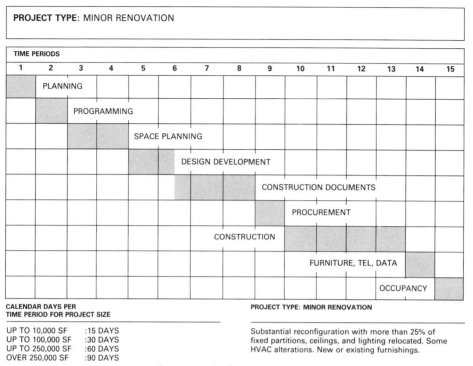

PROJECT TYPE: MINOR RENOVATION

TIME PERIODS

| 1 | 2 | 3 | 4 | 5 | 6 | 7 | 8 | 9 | 10 | 11 | 12 | 13 | 14 | 15 |

PLANNING

PROGRAMMING

SPACE PLANNING

DESIGN DEVELOPMENT

CONSTRUCTION DOCUMENTS

PROCUREMENT

CONSTRUCTION

FURNITURE, TEL, DATA

OCCUPANCY

CALENDAR DAYS PER
TIME PERIOD FOR PROJECT SIZE

UP TO 10,000 SF   :15 DAYS
UP TO 100,000 SF   :30 DAYS
UP TO 250,000 SF   :60 DAYS
OVER 250,000 SF   :90 DAYS

PROJECT TYPE: MINOR RENOVATION

Substantial reconfiguration with more than 25% of
fixed partitions, ceilings, and lighting relocated. Some
HVAC alterations. New or existing furnishings.

Figure 2.8. Typical project schedule for a minor renovation project.

Figures 2.7 through 2.10 illustrate typical project schedules for various degrees of project complexity. The scheduling period can be adjusted based on size. For example, in Figure 2.7 programming for a project size of 10,000 square feet would be 15 days, but for a 100,000-square-foot project, programming would extend over a 30-day period.

Project Budget

Creating a budget during project organization provides accurate and realistic financial parameters for the subsequent execution of the project. The budget, which should include design, construction, and furniture costs, will be based on the information established earlier in this phase: estimated project size, type of space and planning requirements, and preliminary schedule. As with the project schedule, as the design develops the project budget should be revised and refined accordingly. In fact, the budget should be updated at the conclusion of each phase of the project.

The following steps for budgeting are consistent throughout the process regardless of the level of budget detail. The most important consideration in establishing a preliminary budget is to include a substantial contingency (10 to 20 percent) to allow for variation in the definition of the final project. The contingency can always be decreased later if it is not required.

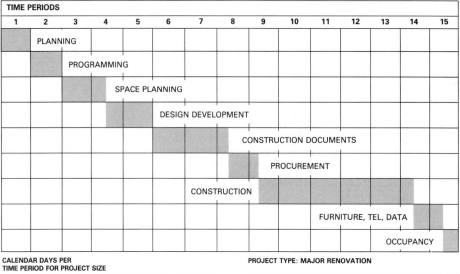

PROJECT TYPE: MAJOR RENOVATION

TIME PERIODS

1	2	3	4	5	6	7	8	9	10	11	12	13	14	15

PLANNING
PROGRAMMING
SPACE PLANNING
DESIGN DEVELOPMENT
CONSTRUCTION DOCUMENTS
PROCUREMENT
CONSTRUCTION
FURNITURE, TEL, DATA
OCCUPANCY

CALENDAR DAYS PER TIME PERIOD FOR PROJECT SIZE

UP TO 10,000 SF	:20 DAYS
UP TO 100,000 SF	:45 DAYS
UP TO 250,000 SF	:60 DAYS
OVER 250,000 SF	:75 DAYS

PROJECT TYPE: MAJOR RENOVATION

Complete interior renovation not including the replacement of base building support systems (HVAC, elevators). New construction throughout tenant space including lights, ceiling, finishes, HVAC, power distribution. New or existing furnishings.

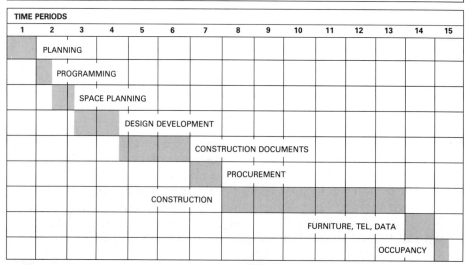

PROJECT TYPE: SHELL RENOVATION

TIME PERIODS

1	2	3	4	5	6	7	8	9	10	11	12	13	14	15

PLANNING
PROGRAMMING
SPACE PLANNING
DESIGN DEVELOPMENT
CONSTRUCTION DOCUMENTS
PROCUREMENT
CONSTRUCTION
FURNITURE, TEL, DATA
OCCUPANCY

CALENDAR DAYS PER TIME PERIOD FOR PROJECT SIZE

UP TO 10,000 SF	:45 DAYS
UP TO 100,000 SF	:60 DAYS
UP TO 250,000 SF	:80 DAYS
OVER 250,000 SF	:90 DAYS

PROJECT TYPE: SHELL RENOVATION

A "Major Renovation" with base building systems overhauled or replaced.

Figure 2.10. Typical project schedule for a shell renovation project.

34

SCOPE OF CONSTRUCTION	AREA (SF)	APPROX COST/SF	EXT COST
REFURBISH EXISTING Existing office space to remain. Modify Elec/Mech systems to meet requirements. Minor Arch changes: replace carpet, ceiling, paint. Cost ranges between $10 and $14/SF.	17,400 SF	$ 12	$208,800
NEW ENCLOSED AREAS Demo existing partitions, reconfigure as necessary. Modify Elec/Mech systems to meet requirements. Replace carpet, ceiling, paint, etc. Cost ranges between $28 and $32/SF.	4,350 SF	$ 30	$ 130,500
NEW OPEN AREAS Demo existing partition layouts. Modify Elec/Mech systems to meet requirements. Replace carpet, ceiling, paint, etc. Cost ranges between $18 and $22/SF.	21,750 SF	$ 20	$ 435,000
VENDING / FOOD SERVICE	2,500 SF	$ 75	$ 187,500
COMPUTER ROOM	2,000 SF	$150	$ 300,000
MAIN RECEPTION / SUPPORT / MAIL	1,500 SF	$ 45	$ 67,500
CONSTRUCTION TOTAL	**49,500 SF**		**$1,329,300**

Figure 2.11. This preliminary construction budget illustrates estimated costs for modifications to existing space and new construction.

Defining What Is Being Constructed

At this point in the project, the definition will be fairly broad: for example, "an estimated 60,000-square-foot project with 57,000 square feet of general office space and approximately 3000 square feet dedicated to a computer room."

Establishing a Construction Estimate

The best method of establishing a construction cost for a preliminary budget is to estimate the cost per square foot to construct each of the differnt types of space comprising the project. Using the project definition above as an example, the budget would allow for $25 per usable square foot for the general office areas and $200 per usable square foot for a state-of-the-art computer facility. Figure 2.11 illustrates a preliminary construction budget by estimating construction costs on a square-footage basis.

Determining the Furnishing Component

As with the construction component of the budget, a broad definition of the furnishing requirements with an associated quantity estimate should be used: for example, systems furniture workstations, cafeteria/dining furnishings.

The next step is to determine quantities for each required building or furnishing component. Figure 2.12, for example, illustrates quantity estimates and unit prices as a mean of developing a preliminary furniture budget.

SCOPE OF FURNITURE	QUANTITY	UNIT COST	EXT'D COST
OFFICE FURNITURE			
VP/Director - Private Office	9	$12,000	$108,000
Manager - Private Office	28	$ 7,100	$198,000
Professional - 9'x 9' Workstation	94	$ 4,700	$441,800
Technical/Consultant - 7'x 9' Workstation	57	$ 3,200	$182,400
Clerical - Freestanding Furniture	23	$ 5,000	$115,000
Files - 5 Drw Lateral / 3' Wide	150	$ 680	$102,000
CAFETERIA FURNITURE			
Chairs	70	$ 250	$ 17,500
Tables	18	$ 450	$ 8,100
RECEPTION AREA FURNITURE			
Sofas	2	$ 4,000	$ 8,000
Lounge Chairs	4	$ 1,200	$ 4,800
Occasional Tables	2	$ 800	$ 1,600
CONFERENCE ROOM FURNITURE			
Tables	6	$ 3,000	$ 18,000
Chairs	72	$ 400	$ 28,800
FURNITURE TOTAL			**$1,234,800**

Figure 2.12. A preliminary furniture budget can be developed by estimating quantities and unit pricing.

Applying Accurate Prices to Each Required Building or Furnishing Component

After the component and the quantity of each component have been determined, these quantities are multiplied by accurate prices that meet the component description to establish a total estimated cost for that item. These costs must be adjusted for any factors that may have an impact on the final cost of executing the work:

- Location (urban or suburban, first or tenth floor)
- Current market conditions
- Level of difficulty of execution
- Available labor pool
- Anticipated discounts for quantity orders

After costs have been estimated, a contingency of 10 to 20 percent of the total cost for all components should be added to the budget to compensate for unexpected costs. The total of all quantity costs plus the contingency establishes the total budget.

Establishing the preliminary project budget and schedule are the final tasks that should be completed by the in-house team during the project organization phase. The next step in the project process is project execution, the design of the project. Prior to proceeding with a explanation of the design process, however, one aspect of the project organization phase warrants additional elaboration because of its importance to the success of the project. The following chapter outlines a process recommended for evaluating and selecting the key consultant team member responsible for the design process—the interior architect.

Chapter Three

Selecting an Interior Architect

Ultimately, the capabilities of the interior architect and the caliber of the working relationship between the interior architect and the in-house team can affect the outcome of the project more than any other single factor. As one of the most important decisions the in-house team will make, the selection warrants a thorough process, the objective of which is to match the capabilities, experience, and attitude of the interior architect with the needs of the project. As the group responsible for the interior architect's performance, the in-house team should conduct the evaluation process and make the final selection of the consultant. The process should include the following basic stages, which can be abbreviated or augmented within the context of each project. The premise of this sequence of steps is to conduct an evaluation based on technical qualifications and predetermined priorities. Cost, is also taken into consideration but not until candidates have been prequalified based on technical merit. The evaluation progresses from the general to the specific, beginning with the prequalification of firms based on general credentials, proceeding to relevant qualifications to execute the project, the approach to the project, and finally, the negotiation of fee. As successful candidates continue through the evaluation and become more serious contenders, they are provided with increasingly more detailed information on the project and, in turn, are able to submit to the in-house team more accurately tailored in-depth responses specific to their approach to the project. The proper sequence of events is:

- Defining the evaluation criteria
- Prequalifying candidates
- Interviewing shortlisted candidates
- Requesting fee proposals

If this series of events is modified substantially, the process and outcome become less efficient and less effective. For example, if the in-house team eliminates the prequalification stage and proceeds to the next stage, candidates who have not yet met even basic criterion of size, geographic location, and experience level are asked to prepare detailed proposals. The result is that both the candidates and the in-house team waste valuable time preparing or reviewing potentially invalid responses from unqualified firms. At the same time, qualified contenders are asked to repeat stages of the evaluation that were structured or executed improperly by duplicating presentations or resubmitting proposals. The evaluation is delayed while information is regenerated or responses are clarified. By defining the scope of the work required, identifying evaluation factors at the beginning of the selection, and following a logical order that provides candidates with information they require to compile worthwhile responses, the process can move forward quickly and be modified to an appropriate level of complexity.

At this point in the evaluation, the in-house team should identify the general scope of work that will be required from the interior architect. The statement of work should be sufficiently detailed to serve as a framework for structuring the evaluation criteria and evaluating the candidates' capabilities to provide that scope of service. With a preliminary scope of work in mind, the in-house team should develop evaluation criteria that reflect the requirements and priorities for the project (Figure 3.1). The team should determine at what stage of the evaluation process the criterion will apply and the weight of each factor. The evaluation should always address technical qualifications. Cost can be considered as an evaluation criterion or can simply be negotiated with the successful candidate.

DEFINING THE EVALUATION CRITERIA

The technical evaluation criteria should include the following key issues:

- Qualifications of the firm
- Personnel assigned to the project
- The firm's proposed approach to the project

■ Services	■ Experience
■ Location	■ Design
■ Size	■ Chemistry
■ Structure	■ Project Approach
■ Staff composition	■ Proposed fees
■ Resources	■ Individuals assigned to the project

Figure 3.1. These evaluation factors reflect considerations related to the firm and individual team members.

In conducting the technical evaluation, the in-house team should strive to select a firm that is stable, properly sized, trained and experienced, and enthusiastic to undertake the work.

Qualifications of the Firm

Many interrelated components form a firm's qualifications and approach to its work. For the evaluation to result in the selection of the best interior architect for the job, the following factors should be evaluated in the context of each other and the specific needs of the project:

- Services
- Location
- Size
- Structure
- Staff composition
- Resources
- Experience
- Design

Services

Consider whether interior architecture is the primary source of the firm's business, and if it is not, what is. This will provide a sense of the importance that interiors commissions have to the firm and the priority they place on executing interiors projects. The amount of interior work the firm executes is also a reasonable indicator of the firm's level of experience in executing interiors projects.

Determine if the firm offers the complete range of services required on the project and if it does not, what additional expertise is needed to fulfill the fundamental scope of work on the project. Understand how the firm generates its revenues. Some interior architectural firms generate revenues solely from professional fees paid directly by its clients. Other firms derive revenues both through professional fees paid by clients and the sale of furniture. Knowing the nature of the firm's revenue base is valuable in comparing fees. Knowing if the firm sells furniture also reveals the firm's objectivity in specifying products.

Location

Proximity to the in-house team and decision makers is important on all projects and critical to those with tight schedules. The team should also be in close proximity to the project site, if possible. Proximity to the site is a particularly relevant factor while the project is actually under construction, when the team must monitor construction progress. If the firm is not located in the general geographic area of the project, the firm should have prior experience dealing with contractor, consultants, local codes, zoning issues, and government authorities in that jurisdiction.

Size

The firm or branch office executing the project should be of sufficient size to complete the work within the allotted time frame and to respond quickly to any unanticipated project changes requiring the assignment of additional staff to the project. The adequacy of the firm's size can be evaluated through a simple comparison of staff assigned to the project against the total production staff of the office.

Even more specific and valuable to determining adequacy of staff is an analysis of workload. In essence, the firm's workload capacity represents the total potential professional staff hours that could be expended in a month. Support staff is not included in this total. The adequacy of the capacity is then assessed by comparing the number of staff hours anticipated to execute each phase of the project plus staff hours committed to other contracts during that time frame against the firm's total capacity. If the project will be implemented over an extended period, the firm's record of employee retention is also relevant as an indicator of continuity of the project team members.

Structure

The firm's structure also has a substantial impact on how resources are directed toward project work. For instance, what level of participation do the owners have in the firm and in project work? What level of participation do senior members of the firm have in project work? How is work scheduled, and how is the staff managed?

Firms vary in the approach to staffing a project by either working within a departmental or team structure. With a departmental structure, a project manager stays with the project until it is complete. As the project progresses through different phases of work, however, the project is passed from one department to another. For example, a programming team develops the quantitative and qualitative requirements for the project, then turns the project over to another department for space planning and design development. Once the design is complete the project moves again, this time into the production department for the development of construction documents. With the exception of the project manager, a different group of people is working on the project at nearly every phase of the project. The potential disadvantages to this approach are inconsistencies in carrying forward the design and a lack of continuity in communication.

With a project team structure, the firm assigns a team to the project for its duration. That team comprises all of the skills necessary to execute all phases of the project. The team approach facilitates continuity of design and consistent communication throughout the project. The knowledge base of the organization and the project that the team develops early in the process is carried through the project. By remaining on the project, the team is also able to develop a rapport and strong working relationship with the in-house team.

Staff Composition

Firms offering interior architectural services employ staff members with a wide range of training and level of experience. Knowing the composition of the firm's staff and understanding the qualifications of that staff have never been as important as in today's increasingly complex office environment. It is essential to the success of a project that the skills of the professionals in the firm and, more specifically, those to be assigned to the project have the appropriate level of training to deal with the challenges that this complex environment presents.

With the proliferation of interiors practitioners possessing diverse backgrounds, standards are now in place to assist in understanding and comparing those differences. In 1984 the National Council for Interior Design Qualification (NCIDQ) was created to define to the public those persons who have met minimal standards for the professional practice through the administration of an examination. The test covers the following areas:

- Theory
- Programming
- Planning and predesign
- Contract documents
- Furniture, fixture, and equipment
- Building and interior systems
- Communication methods
- Codes and standards
- Business and professional practice
- Project coordination
- History

An interiors practitioner must pass this exam to use titles such as interior designer, certified interior designer, and registered interior designer as designated by some state legislatures. Membership in most of the professional organizations representing the interiors industry (Institute of Business Designers and International Society of Interior Designers, for example) also require that the practitioner be NCIDQ certified.

People with architectural training also practice in the interiors field. These professionals are either graduate architects or registered architects. A graduate architect holds a degree in architecture, a degree that represents training in:

- Architectural history
- Design
- Design philosophy
- Materials
- Professional practice
- Structural design

A registered architect has graduated with a degree in architecture, apprenticed for three years, and passed the architectural registration exam. A registered architect with a membership in the American Institute of Architects carries an AIA designation.

Resources

Resources that affect the ability of the interior architectural team to function effectively are the firm's facilities, support staff, and technology. These elements affect the team's attitude toward its work, its efficiency, and the quality of its product.

The firm's own space is a revealing reflection of its attitude toward its work and employees. Touring the firm's facilities provides the in-house team with an opportunity to investigate whether the firm implements the advice that it offers to its clients regarding the importance of a high-quality work environment. To function effectively on the project, the project team should have adequate workstation and support facilities, such as a resource library, copying, and conferencing.

The in-house team should consider the types of support staff the firm employs and how this support staff is structured to ensure that the design professionals in the firm are free to devote their attention to client and project responsibilities. This includes administrative, business development, and management support.

As with any other type of business, some interior architectural firms have been more successful in making office automation work for them than others. The effective use of technology should not be underestimated as a valuable resource in executing project work. Even standard office equipment such as the facsimile machine and telephone system can increase the accessibility and responsiveness of the team. For example, a voice mail feature on a telephone system allows members of the team to communicate if they are out of the office, avoiding delays resulting from missed telephone calls.

Of course, the most significant technological resource that firms employ to execute project work is the computer. The application of hardware and software as well as the training of the professionals operating them affect their value in achieving project objectives. Although the use of computers is not essential to successful completion of any project, nor is it always the best approach to a project, it is a mechanism for increasing the firm's ability to explore cost-effective alternatives and complete certain tasks quickly and accurately. For example, computer-assisted design and drafting (CADD) is often used for space planning, designing, and developing construction documentation. Use of the computer allows the design team to apply a planning concept to a large or repetitive project with exceptional expediency and to implement changes to that concept quickly and cost-effectively. These documents can then be updated and maintained easily for facility management purposes on CADD after completion of the project. CADD is also a useful tool for assisting designers in communicating complex design concepts to clients through the use of three-dimensional modeling.

Some firms also use computers for programming or forecasting quantitative space requirements, budgeting, scheduling, space, inventory, and presentation applications. If the organization utilizes computers for any of these tasks and anticipates a need for information after completion of the project, the in-house team should determine if its software and the interior architect's software are compatible.

Experience

One of the ways in which the firm can demonstrate its ability to undertake a project is through its previous experience executing similar work. The firm

should have at least one example, or ideally, three to five, which are comparable in the following ways:

- Type of facility (law office, computer facility, corporate headquarters)
- Project size
- Planning and design requirements
- Scope of work
- Budget
- Schedule

The greater the similarities, the greater the possibility that the firm clearly
understands the potential obstacles that might arise on the project as well as
their best solutions. These are, however, guidelines, not absolutes. It is just
as important to consider in a more general way the challenges that the firm
faced in performing the work and how well it was able to implement effective
solutions to achieve the client's objectives.

If the firm does not have previous experience with similar projects, it should
demonstrate expertise through related project work or through individual team
member experience. The in-house team can evaluate the expertise of the firm
and the individual team members in executing a similar scope of work by
reviewing actual work samples produced for the relevant projects. For example, if programming expertise is a critical factor on the project, the in-house
team can review program documents produced by the team previously. If
space planning of large open-plan areas is a significant portion of the scope
of work required, the in-house team can review plans developed for major
open-plan users.

References on relevant project work are invaluable. The in-house team
should always speak with previous or current clients to gain insight into the
attitude, responsiveness, creativity, and commitment of the firm and people
working on the project.

Design

By reviewing similar project work completed previously by the interior architectural firm and the project team members, the in-house team can assess
the creativity, quality, and responsiveness of the interior architect's solution.
Designers are trained to apply their technical skills to developing solutions
that are appropriate for each client and project. The in-house team should not
make the common mistake of looking for its design solution in the projects
implemented for other clients.

In reviewing the firm's design product, the in-house team's objective should
be to appraise the overall quality of the work in the following ways:

- Did it meet the client's functional and aesthetic requirements for the
  project within budget and schedule parameters?
- Is the solution well conceived, articulated, and consistently detailed
  throughout?
- Is the solution appropriate for the requirements?

- Is the design enduring?
- Is the design maintainable?

If design is a high priority and the in-house team wishes to evaluate the specific approach the candidates might take on its project, the in-house team can conduct a design competition for which the candidates are each paid a fee to develop preliminary concepts. For a design competition to have any relevance, however, the in-house team must provide each of the candidates with sufficient information on the project and allow the team sufficient time to develop worthwhile concepts. These concepts must then be judged in the context of the objectives and information provided to the candidates, with the understanding that design is evolutionary. It is doubtful that during the course of a brief design competition the candidates will have sufficient insight and time to prepare the best possible design solutions for the project.

Personnel Assigned to the Project

The capabilities of the people committed to the project are of even greater significance to the project than the qualifications of the firm in general. The expertise, talent, and commitment of the key staff members assigned to the project will have the greatest impact on the success of the project. In reviewing the credentials of the personnel assigned to the project, the in-house team should examine the following issues, at a minimum, within the framework of each person's assignment on the project:

- Number of years of experience
- Number of years of experience in a similar role
- Professional background and training
- Professional status (registered or licensed)
- Relevant project experience and expertise executing the scope of work required on the project
- Design, technical, or management record and capabilities
- Availability to work on the project

Additionally, the in-house team should attempt to gain insight into the way each person approaches problem solving and team work, looking for their level of motivation and enthusiasm in undertaking the project. The in-house team should determine the level of each key project team member's understanding of what will be required to complete the project successfully. In doing so, the in-house team should gauge how well the project team members will work together and the overall sense of creativity the project team members will apply to the project.

Every firm and project team has a unique personality that can either enhance or detract from its performance as a critical project participant. Both firms and specific project team members who are otherwise well qualified for a project can be inhibited in their ability to develop a strong working relationship with the organization's in-house team due to a lack of chemistry. The two groups must work closely together for extended periods, particularly on large projects. Without trust, strong communication, and the ability, or more important, the willingness to work through problems, the possibility of success on the project diminishes substantially. When all else is equal among the candidates, or even when it is not, the in-house team should take into account these less tangible considerations.

The Firm's Proposed Approach to the Project

The second portion of the technical evaluation is the firm's approach to the project. Based on the project objectives, budget and schedule parameters, and information on the organization and project such as growth forecasts, the firm can develop an approach to the project that reasonably can incorporate the following points:

- Staffing on the project
- Proposed services and phasing of those services
- Management of the project (schedule, cost, and quality control)

Staffing on the Project

The interior architectural firm should devise a strategy for staffing the project. The strategy should define the size, structure, and composition of the project. That strategy should provide for continuity of key staff, a final point of decision, clear allocation of responsibilities, as well as working, reporting, and communication procedures. If the firm is suggesting a team approach on the project in which a core team of professionals stay with the project throughout all of the phases, there are a myriad of options for structuring the team. In fact, the structure and composition of the project team is one of the ways in which a firm can distinguish itself during the selection process. In virtually any type of team structure, however, the following roles are key:

- *Project Principal:* The project principal is the ultimate point of responsibility on the project, with strategic, overview, and client liaison responsibilities. The project principal is usually an owner or senior manager of the firm. The principal should represent the senior management and technical expertise on the project and should possess excellent leadership and management capabilities.
- *Project Manager:* The project manager is the firm's daily point of contact with the in-house team and central point of coordination and direction for all project team members. The project manager staffs the project, monitors the budget and schedule, and ensures that the team is working toward common objectives. The project manager should demonstrate strength in leadership, management, and communication skills, an understanding of the entire project process, and the ability to manage cost, schedule, and quality control requirements on a project.
- *Designer:* The designer is responsible for programming (if no programming specialist is proposed on the team), space planning, and the develop-

ment of design concepts for furniture, finishes, furnishings, and interior architecture. Additionally, the designer is responsible for the selection and documentation of furniture and furnishings for procurement. A designer should possess the ability to elicit project requirements, a strong sense of design philosophy, and fluency with two- and three-dimensional design. The designer should demonstrate flexibility in the development of design concepts, be capable of designing to a budget (unless cost control is irrelevant), and understand basic construction methods, pricing procedures, and current costs.

- *Architect:* The project architect works in conjunction with the designer on the development of interior architectural concepts and is responsible for documenting those concepts through the development of the construction documents. The architect coordinates the architectural documentation with that of the engineering team and any other specialty consultants, such as audiovisual, lighting, and acoustical experts. The architect is responsible for monitoring fieldwork during construction. The architect should possess strong technical skills, demonstrating an understanding of how architectural elements must be designed to be constructable. The architect should be capable of developing a quality set of construction documents and must have a strong understanding of construction methods, pricing procedures, and current costs. Additionally, the architect must have knowledge of local approval processes, zoning, and code issues. A registered architect must seal the construction documents before a building permit can be obtained on the project.

The structure of the project team should always provide for a centralized point of coordination and responsibility on the project. The proposed project team members should clearly understand their roles and responsibilities on the project as well as all defined reporting procedures and lines of communication. The in-house team should be aware of any other project commitments that are of potential conflict to the project and should also obtain a commitment from the firm as to the basic percentage of time it can expect from each team member.

Proposed Services

In addition to the method of staffing the project, the interior architectural firm's approach should identify a scope of services to be provided and a preliminary schedule for implementing those services (Figure 3.2 lists the standard services offered by an interior architectural firm). The in-house team should evaluate whether the services offered are comprehensive and whether the interior architectural team is proposing a logical and reasonable approach to providing the services. The firm should identify who will execute each general phase of work and a time frame for accomplishing the tasks. If sufficient information is unavailable for use in developing a specific project schedule, the interior architectural firm can develop an ideal schedule for the project. That schedule can be refined as more information becomes available on the project.

- Alternatives evaluation
- Building evaluations
- Planning and furniture standards development
- Program development
- Budget and schedule development
- Space planning
- Schematic design
- Design development
- Selection and specification of furniture and furnishings
- Contract documentation
- Bid/negotiation assistance
- Construction site monitoring
- Furniture installation monitoring
- Coordination of mechanical/electrical engineer
- Coordination of specialty consultants (acoustical, food service)
- Move assistance
- Post occupancy evaluation

Figure 3.2. Standard interior architectural services.

Management of the Project

The critical project management issues on any project are cost, schedule, and quality control. The firm should identify the primary project team member (typically, the project manager) responsible for project management controls in these three areas and the mechanisms that are in place both on the project team and in the firm to ensure that all three areas are maintained effectively throughout the project. Reviewing the project manager's track record on the mangement of similar projects is useful for considering the team's ability to develop and document design concepts within cost and schedule parameters. The firm's record of cost and schedule control is also relevant.

   The in-house team should also review how the firm proposes that decisions be implemented on the project, and how the lines of communication and reporting procedures between the in-house team and the consultant project team should be established.

PREQUALIFYING CANDIDATES

Once the in-house team has defined the evaluation criteria and established the weight of each factor, the selection process can proceed. The next step is to prequalify firms to create a long list of candidates. In this preliminary stage of the selection, the in-house team should strive to develop a list of candidates who meet preliminary evaluation criteria as determined in the preceding phase of the process. The in-house team can obtain recommendations on firms to consider through the following sources:

- Professional contacts and references
- Real estate brokers

- Industry lists
- Local and national lists

The in-house team can initiate contact with these potential candidates through a brief telephone conversation with an appropriate firm representative or a letter of interest requesting a brief submission of standard firm credentials such as a firm brochure. At this time, the in-house team should not request materials that have been tailored to the requirements of the project, but should solicit the following types of prequalifyinig information:

- Firm overview
- Firm location(s)
- Firm size
- Services
- Representative similar clients
- Standard biographical information for senior staff

From this information, the in-house team should develop a long list of prequalified firms. A reasonable long list should comprise no more than 10 firms for large projects (over 100,000 square feet) and five firms for smaller projects. The in-house team should issue a request for qualifications (see Appendix 1) from the long-listed firms. That request should incorporate the following project information:

- Explanation of the requirement
- Description of the organization
- Description of the project: type of project, size, schedule, budget, and special requirements (computer facility, conferencing center)
- General scope of services required from the interior architect
- Selection process and evaluation criteria
- Required contents of the qualifications or technical proposal
- Due date and time for the submission

The in-house team should consider conducting brief meetings with each of the candidates separately or together to clarify and augment the information provided in the request. This step can also be conducted on the telephone.

The request for qualifications or technical proposals should address the following evaluation factors:

- Relevant firm experience
- Qualifications of proposed staff assigned to the project
- Firm resources
- Proposed approach to the project, including schedule and services

Based on this written submission, the in-house team can select a short list of three to five qualified candidates to continue on to the next phase of the evaluation, the interview process.

INTERVIEWING SHORTLISTED CANDIDATES

At this stage in the evaluation, the in-house team should be interviewing the three to five firms on the shortlist. Any more than that would be unnecessary and cumbersome. The purpose in conducting the interviews is to clarify information submitted in the written qualifications and to meet the proposed project team members personally. This is the best opportunity for the in-house team to gain a sense of chemistry with each of the proposed team members and to interact with them directly about their strengths, weaknesses, and approach to the project. The interview should cover the following key agenda items:

- Firm background
- Relevant experience
- Design examples for the firm and project team
- Proposed project team roles, responsibilities, and credentials
- Approach to providing the services required
- Project management approach

The in-house team should supply the candidates with the names and roles of the decision makers attending the presentation. The in-house team should also convey any priorities, agenda items, or concerns related to the qualifications submittal or technical proposal prior to the presentation.

The interviews can be conducted at the in-house team's offices or at the interior architect's offices. There are advantages to both; however, conducting interviews at the interior architect's offices provides the in-house team with an opportunity to assess the interior architect's offices.

With the complexity of the project and related issues as a guideline, the in-house team should allot approximately 1 to $1\frac{1}{2}$ hours for each interview. The minimum time that any firm should ever be allowed for a presentation is 30 minutes. Any less than that does not provide sufficient time for the firm to convey its credentials adequately. The in-house team should allow 15 to 30 minutes after the firm's portion of the interview for a question-and-answer session. The in-house team should schedule the presentations with approximately 30 minutes between interviews.

Depending on the number of candidates, the interviews should transpire based on a schedule of no more than two to three presentations in the morning and another two to three in the afternoon. If the interviews are not taking place at the candidates' offices, the presentation team should be provided with a conference room of sufficient size to accommodate the total number of presentation attendees and appropriate space for use of presentation boards or audiovisual support. If a slide projection system is unavailable, at least a room that can be darkened and an area for slide projection should be provided.

REQUESTING FEE PROPOSALS

Based on the results of the interviews, the in-house team should be able to select one or two firms with which it prefers to work. At this point, the in-house team can either award the project to one firm and proceed with fee negotiations or request fee proposals from the final candidates.

The information that the interior architect requires to prepare a reasonable response includes:

- Square footage for the project
- Project objectives
- Project schedule
- Project budget
- Decision-making process on the project
- Services required on the project
- Special design requirements or special areas such as computer rooms, special conferencing requirements, training facilities, cafeteria, and auditorium

The candidate(s) must understand any work that has been completed to date on the project and some specifics on how the project team will interact with the organization. For example, if programming services are required:

- Has any programming information been compiled?
- Approximately how many representatives would be interviewed during the programming process?
- Are there existing planning/workstation standards, and if so, are they valid or do they require review and modification?

A sample *request for fee proposal* (RFP) is provided in Appendix 2. A fee proposal should comprise a list of project assumptions and facts upon which the proposal has been developed, a detailed scope of work, and a corresponding fee. The scope of work is normally expressed as basic services and any additional services that the firm can provide that are not reflected in the proposed fee. Specialty consultant services, for example, are frequently considered an additional service.

Project fees are derived from a task analysis and historical fee data on similar projects. The task analysis is based on the following key project information:

- Services requested
- Complexity of the design as reflected, in part, by the project budget for construction
- Decision-making process
- Project schedule
- Special area components of the project

Fees are quoted in one of four ways: not-to-exceed maximum, lump sum, estimated, or hourly. A not-to-exceed maximum fee can be quoted in a total amount such as $100,000, or in a fee per square foot, such as $3 per square foot. The fee per square foot is normally quoted when the specific square footage for the project is unknown. Either translates into a cap for the fee. If the team completes the scope of work in fewer hours, the firm bills only for the hours actually expended on the project. If the team spends more time than anticipated in execution of the project, the interior architectural firm assumes that additional cost unless additional fees are negotiated.

A lump-sum fee is also based on a task analysis. Unlike the not-to-exceed maximum, however, the interior architectural firm bills based on percentage of completion of the work and bills the entire lump-sum amount regardless of how much or how little time was expended on the project.

These fees are quoted for basic services included in a proposal. Any work not included in the basic proposal is considered an additional service and is identified as such in the proposal. Additional services can be quoted on an estimated, not-to-exceed, lump-sum, or straight hourly basis.

Reimbursable expenses or the project team's out-of-pocket expenses related to the execution of the project should also be identified in the proposal. Under a not-to-exceed proposal, reimbursables are normally not included. With a lump-sum fee quotation, they might be included. That should be clarified in the proposal. The proposal should also state if the firm passes reimbursable expenses directly through or adds a percentage for handling to those expenses.

One of the most difficult things about evaluating proposed fees for design work is making an apples-to-apples comparison of the proposed scope of work and making an assessment of the level of service to be provided. A relatively effective method for assessing comparative levels of effort from one firm to another is for the in-house team to request that each proposal identify the anticipated personnel hours associated with each phase of work and the total personnel hours associated with the total fee.

No two firms are equal or totally similar. If the evaluation process has been executed effectively, the in-house team should be able to select a firm based upon the technical merits and chemistry rather than a low fee. Then fee proposals, if requested from more than one firm, can provide a basis for understanding what each firm proposes and for negotiating a fair and reasonable price for the work.

The process outlined above for the selection of an interior architect requires that the in-house team dedicate time and attention to this decision. The quality of the information that the in-house team provides to the candidates, the structure of the evaluation criteria, and the process itself directly affect the caliber of candidates' responses and, ultimately, the in-house team's selection.

With the interior architect and other key team members in place on the project, the in-house team can finalize the project budget and schedule and conclude the project organization phase. With a clear set of objectives and parameters to guide the team through the development of solutions, the foundation should be in place to proceed with project execution.

Chapter Four

Project Execution:
The Design Process

Design is evolutionary in nature, a process of expanding, modifying, and refining, each step building on the preceding one. In interior architecture, a design first takes shape as a written document, an analysis of needs. That analysis then evolves into a two-dimensional approach and finally, unfolds into a three-dimensional concept. This chapter outlines that evolutionary design process, marking the following distinct phases of the progression and identifying objectives, key points of decision, and the responsibilities of the in-house and consulting project team members at each step. The phases listed below are delineated in greater detail in Figure 4.1.

- Phase 1: Programming
- Phase 2: Alternatives Evaluation
- Phase 3: Schematic Design
- Phase 4: Design Development
- Phase 5: Contract Documentation
- Phase 6: Contract Administration

Throughout this progression, the foremost objective is to select an appropriate project site and to achieve a design solution for the project that responds to the needs of the organization.

PHASE 1: PROGRAMMING

Programming is a systematic approach to gathering, analyzing, and interpreting specific quantitative and qualitative project requirements. These re-

PHASE I	PROGRAMMING

- Programming
- Schedule and budget development
- Furniture inventory
- Cost estimate
- Presentation and approval

PHASE II	ALTERNATIVES EVALUATION

- Test fit analysis
- Building systems evaluation
- Workletter analysis
- Preliminary cost estimate

PHASE III	SCHEMATIC DESIGN

- Preliminary space plan
- Preliminary design concepts
- Cost estimate update
- Presentation and approval

PHASE IV	DESIGN DEVELOPMENT

- Final space plan
- Detailed design concepts
- Engineering and special consultants coordination
- Cost estimate
- Presentation and approval

PHASE V	CONTRACT DOCUMENTS

- Construction
- Furniture
- Furnishings
- Engineering and special consultant coordination
- Permits
- Bid/negotiation/award

PHASE VI	CONTRACT ADMINISTRATION

- Project consultation
- Site observation
- Submittal review
- Move assistance
- Punch list

Figure 4.1. Each major task is identified in this illustration of the six design phases.

quirements serve as the basis for selecting a project location as well as the planning and design of the project in that location. Throughout execution of the project, the program also serves as a benchmark for all decision making. Quantitatively, programming identifies the incremental amounts of space that will be needed to house the organization's operations throughout the occupancy of a selected space. Qualitatively, the program defines the type of space that will best meet the organization's needs.

This analysis requires a compilation of employee, technology, and organizational/cultural requirements. Because the programming effort must accurately define the organization's requirements at the time of occupancy as well as for the duration of the occupancy, the program must track both past and current organizational patterns and superimpose them on the organization's business plan as a method of projecting future trends in growth and operating procedures.

Even the most comprehensive planning and forecasting, however, cannot always accurately provide for the future, so one of the keys to ensuring the validity of a program over time is to build flexibility into the program: flexibility to respond to changing operational requirements, management approaches, workforce composition, and technology applications.

The product of programming is a written document called a *program, space analysis report,* or *space requirement report.* In its final form, the program should delineate the following information:

- Usable square-footage requirements
- Allocation of the square-footage requirements for each user group and type of support function
- Current and projected staffing requirements
- Adjacency requirements for individuals, user groups, and support functions
- Planning standards for housing individuals, support functions, and equipment
- Organizational structure
- Reporting and communication procedures
- Furniture and equipment requirements
- Requirements for the design of HVAC, power supply, and distribution to the space
- Aesthetic requirements for the space

Selected members of the interior architectural team should be called on to conduct the programming effort. Typically, these are the team members who will be responsible for translating the program into design solutions. In certain cases, a team of programming professionals separate from the design team is assigned to create the program. They, in turn, deliver the program to the design team. This approach varies depending on the philosophy of the interior architectural firm and the complexity of the project. Some firms believe that a division of responsibility yields the best analysis and design skills. Other firms believe that the continuity of using the same team through both phases of the project provides insight into the organization's needs that the team would not gain if responsibilities were divided. With either approach to staffing the programming effort, the programming team follows the same process:

- Data collection
- Standards development
- Furniture inventory
- Equipment Requirements
- Data analysis
- Cost estimate development
- Program report

Data Collection

The programming team gathers information on the organization through three primary methods of data collection:

- Review of existing documents
- Personnel surveys and interviews
- Observation of existing conditions

Review of Existing Documents
Organizational brochures, organizational charts, business and management plans, records of growth patterns, and human resource and technology policies all supply the team with a context for interpreting the organization's past, current, and future facilities needs. The team gains insight into the organization's operating procedures, organizational trends, culture, business objectives, and management style.

Personnel Surveys and Interviews
The primary source of input on the organization's current and future requirements is the organization's management and staff; one of the most effective methods for soliciting their input is through the combined use of written surveys and personal interviews. The effectiveness of this method of data collection depends on the appropriate selection of representatives and knowledgeable personnel to be surveyed and interviewed, the caliber of the questions, and the accuracy of the responses. To ensure the best possible quality of data, the programming team must tailor the process to the organization and to the size or complexity of the project.

For example, if the project is large (over 100,000 square feet), the programming team will typically structure a data-gathering effort through a written questionnaire to a cross section of approximately 10 percent of the organization's population. The objective is to obtain an accurate representation of the needs of each department and working group within the organization. The survey should include representation of any special use group, such as management information systems personnel who have detailed knowledge of special requirements for the project. To maximize the accuracy of the information obtained from the questionnaires, the programming team should also conduct training sessions with the respondents. The purpose of these sessions is to elaborate on the objectives of the survey effort and to clarify the questions contained in the form.

The survey comprises questions on the following current and future space requirements:

- Staffing numbers
- Support space requirements (conference, reception, shared filing, storage)
- Adjacency requirements for individuals and work groups to be located in close proximity to each other in order to perform job responsibilities efficiently
- Equipment needs (computers, copiers)

A sample questionnaire is provided in Appendix 3. The team also uses the questionnaire to assist in preparing those representatives of the organization who will be interviewed. By completing the questionnaire prior to the interview, the interviewees have the opportunity to prepare accurate responses in advance of the interview. This expedites the interview process, helps to ensure more accurate information, and enables the programmer to elicit more detailed responses from the interviewee. Normally, the programming team interviews only those people who can provide valid input on current and future planning or functional unit requirements, and qualitative direction on the space, such as organizational culture, image requirements, and preferred design direction for the project. Those interviewed will include executives, key managers, department heads, and special-interest representatives. In some cases, the programming team will conduct additional interviews of personnel to gain perspective on the organization's culture and employee attitudes. By exposing additional personnel to the project and allowing them to provide input, these interviews can also evoke greater user acceptance for the completed project.

Observation of Existing Conditions

The programming team should review any existing space plans or architectural and engineering documents and tour the existing space to supplement information gained during interviews or to identify any discrepancies in the information obtained from questionnaires and interviews. A tour of the site assists in defining existing conditions, operating procedures, support requirements, deficiencies, and what works well in the existing space.

Standards Development

During data collection, the programming team also addresses the development of planning standards. To apply a standard square-footage allocation to personnel and support areas for use in calculating the total square footage required for the project, the programming team generates planning standards for the following spaces:

- Workstations to accommodate personnel
- Support areas and equipment

The programming team can either develop preliminary standards comprising only square-footage allotments (Figures 4.2 and 4.3) for these spaces or detailed standards that include square-footage allocations as well as furniture and finish components. If the team develops only preliminary standards during the programming phase, those standards will be refined during the schematic design phase.

Workstation Standards

A workstation is the space allocated to house a person to execute a job or task on an ongoing basis. The term *workstation* refers both to a private office with full-height partitions and a door, and to an open-plan "cubicle" configured from systems furniture or low-height partitions. The term *standard* indicates that workstation size and configuration are assigned on a standard basis for all personnel performing a similar function or at a comparable organizational level or job classification. Ideally, the number of workstation standards is kept

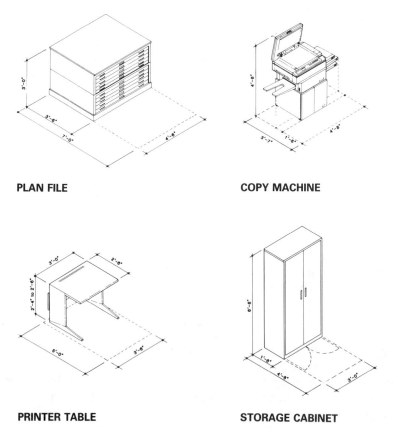

PLAN FILE   COPY MACHINE

PRINTER TABLE   STORAGE CABINET

Figure 4.2. Equipment standards identify space to accommodate equipment and stand space for operating the equipment.

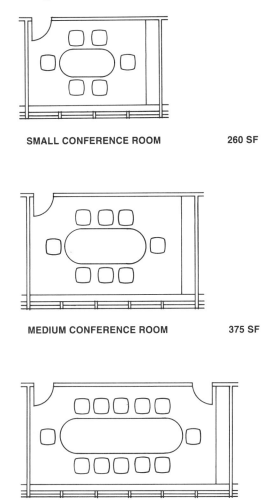

SMALL CONFERENCE ROOM   **260 SF**

MEDIUM CONFERENCE ROOM   **375 SF**

LARGE CONFERENCE ROOM   **450 SF**

Figure 4.3. Support area standards should be developed for all typical support requirements, such as conference, as depicted in this illustration.

to a minimum to simplify planning, future inventory, and facility maintenance. Workstation standards are generated based on:

- Functional requirements of each position
- Organizational culture
- Organizational status
- Industry or professional standards

To ensure that workstation standards are responsive to user needs, the programming team surveys and interviews representatives from each job classification or standards category to solicit detailed information that will affect workstation size, components, and configuration of those components. For example:

- Tasks performed
- Surface area requirements
- Technology/equipment requirements
- Storage requirements
- Conferencing/meeting requirements

The workstation standard size is the space necessary to accommodate these tasks. Figure 4.4 summarizes the considerations that the planner should use on the development of workstation standards. Workstation standards form the

▲ JOB CLASSIFICATION/
FUNCTION
—Workstation user and
job function.
  Executive
  Manager
  Supervisor
  Professional/Technical
  Clerical

▲ WORKSURFACE AREA
—Number and sizes of
worksurfaces.
  Primary
  Secondary
  Tertiary

▲ MACHINE USE
—Amount, types, and
sizes of electronic
equipment.
  VDT
  PC
  Printer
  Typewriter
  Other

▲ WORKSTATION AREA
—Amount of space to
be allocated for the
individual or task.

▲ WORKSTATION
DIMENSIONS
—Length and width
which will comprise the
area.

▲ CONFERENCE
REQUIREMENTS
—Number of guest
chairs.

▲ STORAGE
REQUIREMENTS
—Amount and type or
unit size of the material
to be stored and storage
locations (under counter
or overhead).
  Letter or Legal Files
  Computer Printout
  Binder
  Bulk

▲ CONFIGURATION
—Configuration of the
worksurfaces, primary
orientation, and opening
for the workstation.

▲ WIRE MANAGEMENT
—Type and location of
wire management
related components.
  Baseline Wireway
  Beltline Wireway
  Grommet Locations
  Wire Management
  clips or trays

▲ LIGHTING
—Quantity and location
of any task or ambient
lighting components.

▲ ACCESSORIES
—Type and number of
accessories.
  Tack Surfaces
  Pencil Drawers
  Other

Figure 4.4. Considerations for developing workstation standards.

basic planning units in the development of a program. During the data analysis portion of programming, these workstation standards are multiplied by the number of personnel required for each standard in a current period and forecasted for future incremental periods. This provides the design team with the total area required for personnel. Figures 4.5 through 4.8 illustrate typical workstation types for systems furniture. These standards represent options for administrator through executive levels.

Support Area and Equipment Standards

Support areas can be categorized as one of three types. Space located directly outside a workstation area used to house freestanding equipment such as copiers or files is considered *support space*. These support areas are used by personnel in those immediately adjacent workstations. A room or area such as shared reference, copy, or conference that provides common support to a group, department, or division is a *shared support space*. Space that houses a function (such as a cafeteria, conference room, or training center) that supports the entire organization or several organizations within a building or buildings is *special support space*.

The programming team establishes standards by assigning a square footage to each for similar and commonly required support areas. The team creates a prototypical plan for that standard which incorporates all of the items required in the support space. Equipment standards include not only the actual space required for the equipment itself, but also the circulation space required around the equipment to access and operate it (Figure 4.2).

Furniture Inventory

If existing furniture will be used on the project, that furniture should be identified during the development of workstation and support standards so that the furniture can be taken into consideration in determining square-footage requirements. Either the interior architect or a member of the in-house project team can inventory the existing furniture. The advantage of having a member of the design team conduct the inventory is that at the time the furniture is inventoried, it can also be evaluated for reuse. This evaluation should include recommendations for possible refinishing or reupholstering as well as evaluations to determine the best future location and use of the existing furniture as shown in Figure 4.9.

Equipment Requirements

To every extent possible, the in-house project team at this point should attempt to identify all office equipment that will be used in the project. The following information provides input for each piece of equipment for space planning as well as mechanical and electrical engineering.

- Size
- Built-in, freestanding, or work-surface
- Power requirements

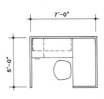

35 sq. ft.

30x60   Primary worksurface
24x54   Secondary worksurface
         pedestal
54 inch Overhead storage

WORKSTATION TYPE A

TASK PROFILE:
Wordprocessor as primary tool
Limited storage capacity
Partial visual privacy

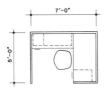

35 sq. ft.

30x60   Primary worksurface
18x54   Secondary worksurface
         pedestal
54 inch Overhead storage

WORKSTATION TYPE B

TASK PROFILE:
Nonautomated task
Limited storage capacity
Partial visual privacy

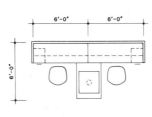

72 sq. ft.

24x72   Primary worksurface
30x45   Shared worksurface
         pedestal
72 inch Overhead storage

WORKSTATION TYPE C

TASK PROFILE:
Shared tasks
Limited storage capacity
Partial visual privacy

Figure 4.5.

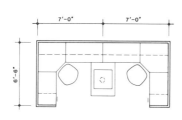 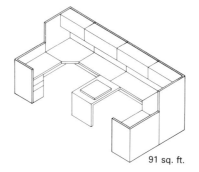

91 sq. ft.

25 sq. ft. Primary worksurface
30 x 45 Shared worksurface
1 Pedestal
84 L. inch Overhead storage

TASK PROFILE:
Individual EDP equipment
additional shared tasks
limited storage capacity
partial visual privacy

WORKSTATION TYPE D

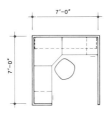

49 sq. ft.

24 sq. ft. Worksurface
2 Pedestal
84 L. inch Overhead storage

TASK PROFILE:
EDP equipment as primary tool
limited storage capacity
full visual privacy

WORKSTATION TYPE E

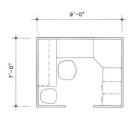

63 sq. ft.

1 Guest chair
24 x 60 Primary worksurface
24 sq. ft. Secondary worksurface
2 Pedestal
60 L.inch Overhead storage

TASK PROFILE:
Limited conference capability
ADP equipment as secondary tool
Limited storage capacity
Full visual privacy

WORKSTATION TYPE F

Figure 4.6.

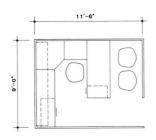

104 sq. ft.

2	Guest chair
30 x 72	Primary worksurface
25 sq. ft.	Secondary worksurface
1	Pedestal
2	Lateral drawer

WORKSTATION TYPE G

TASK PROFILE:

Extended conference capability
EDP equipment as secondary tool
Moderate storage capacity
Full visual privacy

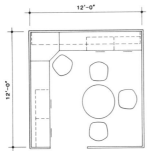

144 sq. ft.

3	Guest chair
42 dia.	Conference table
44 sq. ft.	Worksurface
8	Lateral drawer
144 L. inch	Overhead storage

WORKSTATION TYPE H

TASK PROFILE:

Extensive conference capability
DP equipment as secondary tool
Extensive storage capacity
full visual privacy

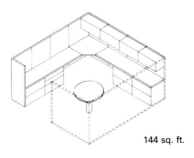

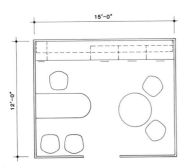

180 sq. ft.

4	Guest chair
42 dia.	Conference table
30 x 72	Primary worksurface
30 sq. ft.	Secondary worksurface
1	Pedestal
6	Lateral drawer
180 L. inch	Overhead storage

WORKSTATION TYPE I

TASK PROFILE:

Extensive conference capability
ADP equipment capability
extensive storage capacity
full visual privacy

Figure 4.7.

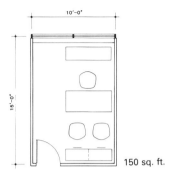

150 sq. ft.

30 x 66	Double pedestal desk
18 x 66	Credenza
2	Lateral file
1	Desk chair
2	Guest chair

WORKSTATION TYPE J

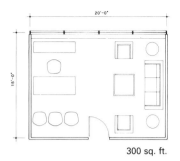

300 sq. ft.

30 x 72	Double pedestal desk
18 x 72	Credenza
1	Desk chair
3	Guest chair
1	3-Seat sofa
2	Lounge chair
36 x 36	Coffee table
2	End table

WORKSTATION TYPE L

225 sq. ft.

30 x 72	Double pedestal desk
18 x 72	Credenza
1	Desk chair
2	Guest chair
1	2-Seat sofa
1	Lounge chair
2	End table

WORKSTATION TYPE K

Figure 4.5–4.8. Typical systems furniture workstation standards for clerical, professional, and executive workstations include configurations and task profiles.

- Heat release
- Acoustic constraints
- Cabling requirements
- Special requirements such as special HVAC or plumbing

Data Analysis

When the standards are complete and the programming team has compiled all data on current and future space needs, the data can be manipulated to analyze requirements.

PROJECT TITLE: **DATE:**

EXISTING SPACE INVENTORIED

ITEM CODE	INVEN-TORY #	ITEM DESCRIPTION	DIMENSIONS W	D	H	FINISH/ COLOR	COND. CODE	LOCATION PRESENT	FUTURE
D-STL	101	DESK/LEFT	60"	30"	29"	WALNUT	G	SECRETARY	RM 306
C-SP	102	CHAIR/TASK	24"	24"	36"	BLUE FABRIC	G	"	"
F-L3	103	LATERAL FILE/3 DRW	36"	18"	39"	TAN METAL	E	"	"
D-DP	104	DESK/DOUBLE PED.	72"	36"	30"	WALNUT	E	PRESIDENT	RM 202
C-ES	105	CHAIR/EXEC. SWVL	30"	26"	32"	BLK LEATHER	G	"	"
C-SA	106	CHAIR/SIDE	20"	18"	32"	GRN FABRIC	P	"	RM 402
C-SA	107	CHAIR/SIDE	20"	18"	32"	GRN FABRIC	P	"	"
O	108	BOOKCASE	36"	12"	30"	WALNUT	G	"	"
O	109	CREDENZA	60"	18"	30"	WALNUT	G	"	"
O	110	STORAGE CABINET	36"	18"	60"	METAL/BLK	F	WORKROOM	RM 440
O	111	TERMINAL TABLE	36"	24"	29"	METAL/TAN	P	"	"
O	112	COAT RACK	18"	18"	60"	METAL/TAN	P	"	—
O	113	PLAN FILE	54"	42"	36"	METAL/TAN	G	"	RM 440

CODES:

DESKS:
D-DP DOUBLE PEDESTAL
D-SPL SINGLE PED. (Left)
D-SPR SINGLE PED. (Right)

DESKS W/RETURNS
D-STL SEC. TYPING (Left)
D-STR SEC. " (Right)
D-EXL EXEC. (Left)
D-EXR EXEC. (Right)

CHAIRS:
C-ES EXEC. SWIVEL
C-SP SEC. POSTURE
C-S SIDE
C-SA SIDE WITH ARMS

FILES:
F-VLT4 VERT.; LETTER (4 drw.)
F-VLG4 VERT.; LEGAL (4 drw.)
F-L3 LAT. (3 drw.)
MISC.: O OTHER

CONDITION:
E–EXCELLENT
G–GOOD
F–FAIR
P–POOR

Figure 4.9. This furniture inventory includes finish information and general condition of the item.

Total Square Footage

One overall objective for the programming effort is to determine the amount of square footage required for each department or operating division as well as the total square footage required for the project. Those totals are a compilation of all space needed to house personnel, support, and equipment. The amount of space required to house personnel and shared workstations is calculated by multiplying the total number of workstations needed by the appropriate standard. The number of support and equipment areas is also multiplied by the appropriate support standard.

This total alone, however, does not provide an accurate total of the square-footage requirement. In addition to the space allocated for standards, a percentage of that total space must be added to accommodate the percentage of the space required to accommodate inter- and intradepartmental (primary and secondary) circulation. As a percent of the total square footage required for the project, circulation ranges from 15 to 60 percent based on the type of space, the efficiency of layout, type of furniture, and the ability of the building to meet the space requirements of the project. For example, a closed-plan layout using private offices typically requires only 20 to 30 percent circulation. Open-plan concepts using systems furniture, however, require as much as 50 percent circulation as a result of the need for more intradepartmental, secondary, circulation.

Not only is it critical to understand the significant amount of space required to accommodate circulation, it is also critical to understand how that circulation is expressed. Circulation is expressed as a factor that represents the percentage of the project's total area that is allotted to circulation space. During the programming process, a circulation factor (percentage) is often confused with a circulation multiplier. This is a frequent and critical mistake that can result in a significant error in the calculation of the circulation area requirement. For example, for a project of 100 square feet with an anticipated circulation requirement of approximately 40%, the common error is to use a 0.4 multiplier to arrive at the total required area. That calculation would yield a total usable area of 140 square feet (ft^2), or a total circulation of less than 30 percent (40 ft^2/140 ft^2 = 28.6 percent). The correct approach to defining the total usable area is to use a circulation multiple, not an anticipated circulation factor. For example, on a project of 100 square feet the correct multiplier to achieve a 40 percent circulation factor is 0.67. The correct formula for calculating the circulation multiplier is (percent circulation/1.0 − percent circulation), or in this example,

$$\frac{40\%}{100\% - 40\%} = \frac{0.40}{1.0 - 0.60} = \frac{0.40}{0.60} = 0.67$$

The requirement is developed in the following way:

$$100 \text{ ft}^2 \text{ of office} \times 0.67 \text{ multiplier} = 167 \text{ ft}^2$$

Therefore,

$$\frac{67 \text{ ft}^2}{167 \text{ ft}^2} = 40 \text{ percent}$$

The space required for workstations, support, and circulation is totaled for the current and forecasted periods to give the total space required for the project (Figure 4.10). All projected requirements are made for incremental periods so that additional space or growth within the space can be planned and brought on line as needed.

INDUSTRY RELATIONS OFFICE

PRELIMINARY SPACE REQUIREMENTS – STATISTICAL SUMMARY

Item	Space Type	Size (SF)	Qty	Staff	Area (SF)	Size (SF)	Qty	Staff	Area (SF)
		CURRENT SPACE REQUIRED				FUTURE SPACE REQUIRED			
OFFICE									
President	Ofc	400	1	0	400	400	1	0	400
Vice President	Ofc	300	1	1	300	300	2	2	600
Director	Ofc	168	6	6	1,008	168	7	7	1,176
Manager	WKST	80	5	5	400	80	7	7	560
Professional	WKST	80	7	7	560	80	5	5	400
Administrative	WKST	80	3	3	240	80	5	5	400
Subtotal: OFFICE SPACE & STAFF				22	2,908			26	3,536
SUPPORT									
Reception (seat 2-3)		400	1	1	400	400	1	1	400
Small Conference (seat 8)		510	2	0	1,020	510	2	0	1,020
Large Conference (seat 20)		1,500	1	0	1,500	1,500	1	0	1,500
A/V Rear Screen Projection Room		400	1	0	400	400	1	0	400
Service Pantry		100	1	0	100	100	1	0	100
Coat Closets		30	1	0	30	30	1	0	30
Library		250	1	0	250	250	1	0	250
Employee Lounge/Pantry		250	1	0	250	250	1	0	250
Copy/Work Room		250	1	0	250	250	1	0	250
Equipment Room		200	1	0	200	200	1	0	200
Printers – Shared		30	3	0	90	30	3	0	90
Supply Storage		60	1	0	60	60	1	0	60
Mail Room w/clerk		250	1	1	250	250	1	1	250
Bulk Storage Room		100	1	0	100	100	1	0	100
File Room – Centralized		300	1	0	300	300	1	0	300
File Cabinets		14	10	0	140	14	10	0	140
Subtotal: SUPPORT				2	5,340			2	5,340
Subtotal OFFICE & SUPPORT NET Square Feet				24	8,248			28	8,876
Corridors & Building Layout Factor – Estimated					3,299				3,550
Total Usable Area Required in Square					11,547				12,426
Rentable Area Range:									
1. Core Factor @ 10%					1,155				1,243
Grand Total Rentable Area in Square Feet					12,702				13,669
2. Core Factor estimated @ 15%					1,732				1,864
Grand Total Rentable Area in Square Feet					13,279				14,290

Figure 4.10. Statistical summary of program requirements.

Adjacency Requirements

At this point, the programming team should have identified all of the elements required for the project and accommodated those needs in the total square footage for the project. The next focus of the program analysis is to establish spatial relationships, or adjacency requirements, between each element to determine placement in the space. The programming team establishes adjacencies through an analysis of the organizational structure and the adjacency requirements that were identified during the data collection effort. These adjacencies, reflecting fundamental and communication requirements, are identified and assigned a priority. The adjacencies can be graphically illustrated using either an *adjacency matrix* (Figure 4.11) or a *bubble diagram* (Figure 4.12). An adjacency matrix is normally more effective in depicting the relationships among many entities, such as several departments in a large or complex organization when the communication of the relationships would be confusing with a bubble diagram. The bubble diagram, conversely, is usually more effective in communicating adjacencies among a limited number of entities, such as individuals or small working groups.

Special Requirements

During data analysis, the programming team is also looking for any atypical architectural or engineering requirements such as supplemental or 24-hour heating or cooling, augmented floor loading capacity, a high ratio of perimeter offices to internal support areas, or extraordinary power requirements. Any of these special requirements affect the selection of a location, the negotiations for that location, or the total cost of constructing the project.

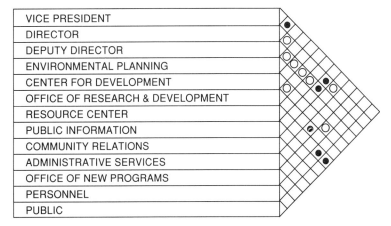

● IMMEDIATE PROXIMITY   ○ CONVENIENT PROXIMITY

Figure 4.11. This adjacency matrix identifies requirements for proximity.

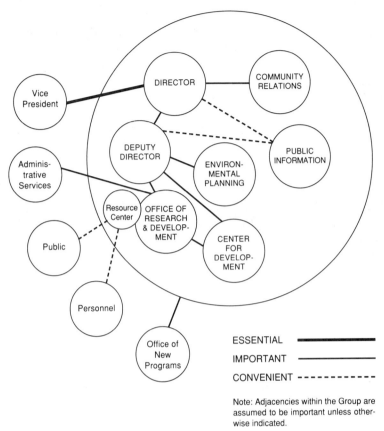

Note: Adjacencies within the Group are assumed to be important unless otherwise indicated.

Figure 4.12. This bubble diagram indicates with weighted lines the relative importance of locating different individuals and departments.

Cost Estimate Development

The programming team should establish a preliminary estimate of the cost of constructing the project based on the needs identified during programming (Figure 4.13). A preliminary cost estimate during programming assists the in-house team in measuring how realistic the program is in relation to the preliminary budget for the project. At this stage, the in-house team can still make adjustments in the project requirements with very little impact on the project.

Program Report

The programming team organizes the data collected during the programming phase and compiles them into a written program report. The written program document can take several different forms, depending primarily on the complexity of the project requirements. An abbreviated program that is primarily quantitative in nature often suffices for a small project with limited design

CSI #	CATEGORY	UNIT COST	QTY	ESTIMATE	QTY	ALLOWANCE	QTY	DIFF	BUDGET	FORECAST	DIFF
10	General Conditions										
	Allowance	500,000	1	500,000	0	0	1	500,000	500,000	500,000	0
10	Subtotal			500,000		0		500,000	500,000	500,000	0
20	Sitework										
	N/A	0	0	0	0	0	0	0	0	0	0
20	Subtotal			0		0		0	0	0	0
30	Concrete										
	Allowance	100,000	1	100,000	0	0	1	100,000	100,000	100,000	0
30	Subtotal			100,000		0		100,000	100,000	100,000	0
40	Masonry										
	Allowance	100,000	1	100,000	0	0	1	100,000	100,000	100,000	0
40	Subtotal			100,000		0		100,000	100,000	100,000	0
50	Metals										
	Allowance	100,000	1	100,000	0	0	1	100,000	100,000	100,000	0
50	Subtotal			100,000		0		100,000	100,000	100,000	0
60	Wood & Plastics										
	Allowance	500,000	1	500,000	0	0	1	500,000	500,000	500,000	0
60	Subtotal			500,000		0		500,000	500,000	500,000	0
70	Moist Thermal Control										
	Allowance	250,000	1	250,000	0	0	1	250,000	250,000	250,000	0
70	Subtotal			250,000		0		250,000	250,000	250,000	0
80	Doors/Windows/Glass			1,165,000		1,845,000		(680,000)	(605,000)	(605,000)	0
90	Finishes			6,378,445		4,190,725		2,187,720	2,550,000	2,550,000	0
100	Specialties			4,349,875		0		4,349,875	4,730,000	4,730,000	0
120	Furnishings			370,000		90,000		280,000	287,500	287,500	0
130	Special Construction			250,000		0		250,000	250,000	250,000	0
140	Conveying Systems			250,000		0		250,000	250,000	250,000	0
150	Mechanical			2,425,000		1,800,000		625,000	650,000	650,000	0
160	Electrical			4,892,250		1,472,500		3,419,750	3,622,500	3,622,500	0
170	Special Areas			13,276,900		0		13,276,900	13,925,000	13,925,000	0
FIT UP TOTAL				34,907,470		9,398,225		25,509,245	27,210,000	27,210,000	0
	Furniture			18,127,500				18,127,500	19,652,500	19,652,500	0
	Equipment			7,050,000				7,050,000	7,640,000	7,640,000	0
FURN/EQUIP TOTAL				25,177,500		0		25,177,500	27,292,500	27,292,500	0
	Arch/Eng Services			3,450,000		0		3,450,000	3,450,000	3,450,000	0
	Contingency			5,774,300				5,774,300	6,264,500	6,264,500	0

Figure 4.13. The estimated relocation budget pictured here is based on program requirements.

objectives. Larger projects with multifaceted requirements involve more extensive organizational and operational analysis. This type of programming report includes the following information:

- Programming methodology
- Statistical analysis for current and projected personnel and support requirements

- Planning standards
- Adjacencies requirements
- Special requirements
- Image and aesthetic requirements
- Preliminary cost estimate
- Recommendation

The in-house team should review a draft of the report prior to final modification. Although the program should be a living document for the organization, it is critical that the in-house team and decision makers for the project concur on the conclusions and recommendations presented in this report because once the program is approved, all subsequent space planning and design development work is based on the evaluations, opinions, facts, and recommendations stated in the program. The more accurate and thorough the information, the better resource the report will be in serving as a foundation for subsequent design work.

Ultimately, the report should define the most appropriate planning approach to maximize efficiency and effective organization of personnel, support space and equipment, provide flexibility for future growth or reorganization, and accommodate changing technology. The program defines for the organizations its space needs and when those space needs must be met. The next step in the project process is to investigate and evaluate real estate options for meeting those needs. This occurs in phase 2.

PHASE 2: ALTERNATIVES EVALUATION

The objective of an alternatives evaluation is to assist the organization in evaluating real estate options to meet its requirements as identified in the programming document. The value to the organization in conducting an alternatives evaluation prior to selecting a location and negotiating a contract is substantial. Quantified, a successful evaluation effort can save a moderate space user hundreds of thousands of dollars and a larger space user millions of dollars over the course of the life of the space. For instance, if an organization is anticipating a space requirement of approximately 100,000 rentable square feet and, as a result of an alternatives evaluation, found that it could meet its space needs effectively in only 90,000 rentable square feet, the organization could realize potential savings of over \$3,000,000 (10,000 rentable square feet × \$30/rentable square foot × 10 years = \$3,000,000) in lease cost alone.

With a completed program in place, the interior architectural team should begin working with the in-house team and its real estate consultant when the selection of locations has been narrowed down to three to five alternatives based on considerations such as location, price, and amenities. Normally, if a building is under serious consideration, the building owner or representative will agree to pay for the cost of the evaluation. The price is normally quoted as a cost per rentable square foot.

In essence, during the alternatives evaluation, the interior architectural team conducts an architectural and mechanical/electrical engineering evaluation of the locations. The interior architectural team evaluates each site for comparison against the organization's program and then conducts a comparative analysis among the sites under consideration. As a part of this phase of work, the interior architectural team should also provide assistance to the real estate team regarding facilities and construction-related issues that will affect the lease or purchase negotiations.

The interior architectural team conducts a *test fit space plan* for the floor or floors under consideration at each building. A test fit space plan is a quick, rough, and preliminary space plan, not a recommended or final plan. If the project will be located on one floor, the test fit includes the entire floor. If the project will be located on several floors, it is unnecessary to test fit all the floors. It is typically sufficient to plan a prototypical floor and, perhaps, an atypical floor. The interior architectural team uses the test fit to ascertain the amount of square footage needed to meet the program, dramatically reducing the risk of acquiring inadequate or excess space. The square footage needed to meet the same program requirements can vary by as much as 10 percent from building to building as a result of different floor sizes and configuration, and column and core locations. The test fit also illustrates planning advantages or disadvantages of the building, exposing space constraints or building inefficiencies such as core placement and configuration, column spacing and bay sizing, or window mullion spacing. These issues affect how well the building can be used for the organization and whether or not it is compatible with the organization's planning standards. The alternatives evaluation should also include a review of the base building systems. For example, a cursory mechanical/electrical evaluation measures the adequacy of the base building HVAC and power distribution systems.

The interior architectural team also contributes to the lease or purchase negotiations by assessing the workletter value to the organization. A *workletter* is a written document defining for the potential tenant the types and quantities of construction materials that the landlord will provide for the construction of the tenant space. A typical workletter identifies such items as type of lighting fixtures and number provided per square foot, number of electrical outlets, and amount of drywall partitioning. The tenant is responsible for the cost of materials required to construct the space in excess of the workletter. The materials and quantities defined in the workletter are also referred to as the *building standard.* The interior architect can estimate the dollar value of a workletter, such as $18 per square foot, but each workletter varies in its specific value to the potential tenant, depending on the design requirements for the space. As a result, it is becoming increasingly common for the tenant to request monetary credits for unused portions of the workletter or a cash allowance in place of the entire workletter. The interior architect should also review the landlord's specified procedures for interior construction and proposed construction schedule. These factors alone can add as much as $10 per square foot to the cost of the space.

The product of the alternatives evaluation is a report containing for each location:

- Test fit space plans
- Mechanical/electrical evaluation

- Facilities input on lease or purchase agreement
- Cost estimate for interior construction

The report should summarize the advantages and disadvantages of each location as well as a recommendation as to which space best meets the organization's needs from a facilities perspective. Ultimately, the in-house team might make the final decision on a location based on factors other than the alternatives evaluation; however, the in-house team will be making an informed decision.

PHASE 3: SCHEMATIC DESIGN

With a site selection complete, the progression from programming to schematic design and design development represents a transition from the gathering and analysis of data to the development of a conceptual design in a two- and three-dimensional format. Schematic design is the preliminary stage in that conceptual work. The project develops in schematic design along two parallel paths: space planning, and preliminary concepts for furniture, finishes, and interior architectural elements.

Schematic Space Planning

During schematic design, the design team's first task is to develop a space plan that responds effectively to the program. The design team locates all of the functional program elements in the space efficiently with the desired adjacencies to each other. This involves the placement of individuals, working groups, support areas, and circulation in the space.

If the project is large and involves several departments located on multiple floors, the design team begins schematic space planning with a blocking and stacking plan. The blocking and stacking plan illustrates the placement elements of the program, normally departments, within the space. Blocking represents the horizontal placement of those elements on a floor (Figure 4.14) and stacking represents the location of the departments vertically on each of the floors of the building (Figure 4.15). The goal is to allow the required square footage for each major element of the space plan while achieving the preferred adjacencies. Blocking/stacking plans do not detail specific information about layout of the space within the departmental areas. That effort occurs once the blocking and stacking plan has been refined and approved by the in-house team.

The preliminary or schematic space plan takes the blocking and stacking plan to the next level of detail by defining the layout of areas within each department. The design team works with the planning standards created during programming, and the current and projected space requirements, to develop schematic planning concepts. Frequently, the design team uses the insight gained from the test fit space plan as a basis for proceeding with schematics. The schematic space plan locates workstations, support spaces, and circulation. To illustrate these concepts, the plan graphically depicts partitions (walls), doors, and generic furniture (Figure 4.16).

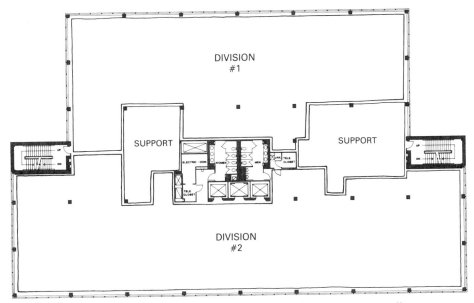

Figure 4.14. This blocking plan locates support areas in close proximity to allow maximum flexibility for space planning the divisions.

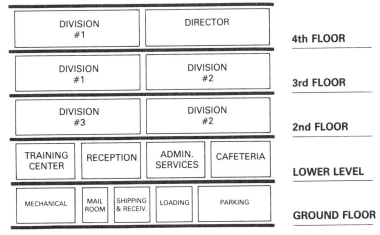

Figure 4.15. This stacking plan locates all service areas on the ground level for access and structural capacity on grade.

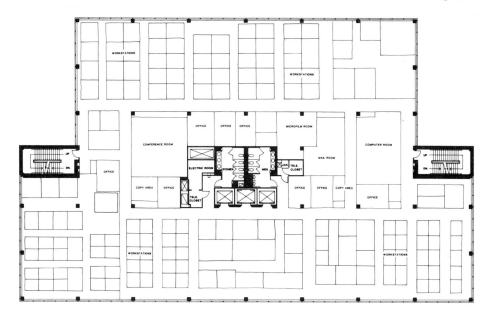

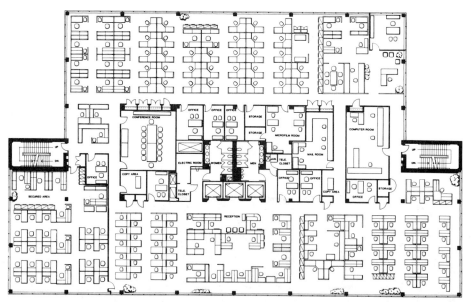

Figure 4.16. The progression in detail from the schematic or preliminary space planning concept (top) to the final plan is depicted in these two plans.

In addition to locating all of the elements within the space plan with adequate square footage and the appropriate adjacencies, the design team must address other key planning issues, such as:

- Flexibility to accommodate growth
- Efficiency
- Economy and spatial order
- Life safety
- Americans with Disabilities Act (ADA) compliance
- General quality of the environment (natural light, vistas)

Flexibility to accommodate growth should be approached either by centralizing, or providing space for growth in one area, or decentralizing space for growth among existing departmental parameters. Regardless of the approach, the design team should consider planned flexibility and anticipate requirements for space to accommodate the growth.

To ensure efficiency and economy of space use, the design team should configure elements of the plan in a way that maximizes the potential of the space while still meeting user requirements for support and adjacency. The plan should suggest spatial order, a sense of rhythm, and organization. It should display a logical progression and arrangement of elements, balance, and symmetry as well as consistency of design intent.

Schematic Design

Concurrent with schematic space planning, the design team begins to work with preliminary design concepts for interior architecture, finishes, and furniture. The concepts that the design team explores should be integrated with the two-dimensional concepts and their extension into three dimensions. The team considers issues such as the general feel and image of the space and how that will be articulated through the use of architectural components and materials.

In formulating these ideas, the design team should be cognizant of costs to ensure that concepts are achievable within the project budget. For example, the design team must consider the level of detailing in the space, and the application of materials such as wood, stone, glass, carpet, and paint. Each type of material and the way it is used in the space has cost ramifications. The design should consider how and where those materials are applied to best meet the program needs for the organization.

At this point in the development of the design concepts, the design team is working with general concepts and general types of materials. The team does not select and recommend specific materials and furnishings until the next phase of the project, design development.

Consultant Coordination

As early as the schematic design phase, the design team should begin coordinating with key specialty consultants on the project to ensure effective coordination among the disciplines. On an office project, these specialty consultants often include lighting, acoustical, telecommunications, communications, food service, security, and engineering.

Of particular importance is early interaction with the mechanical/electrical engineer. As soon as the design team has established preliminary space planning concepts, the design team should meet with the mechanical/electrical engineer to ensure that the space plan presents no obstacles for the design of the engineering systems as is necessary to meet the program requirements and to achieve the design of effective mechanical and electrical systems on the project. By coordinating with the engineer during schematic design, the design team can ensure close coordination and avoid conflicts or miscommunication when changes are costly to the project.

Cost Estimate Update

Based on the concepts developed during schematic design, the design team should update the project construction cost estimate to confirm that the concepts developed are within the budget established for the project. If any costs are out of line, it will be more cost-effective to make the necessary modifications at this time rather than waiting until the design concepts are complete.

The design team should present all schematic design concepts to the in-house project team in conjunction with the associated cost estimate update prior to moving on to phase 4.

PHASE 4: DESIGN DEVELOPMENT

The purpose of the design development phase is to create a further definition of the concepts agreed upon in the schematic design phase. As in schematic design, the progression of the concepts continues in tandem with a space planning effort and the refinement of concepts for interior architecture, furniture, and finishes.

Final Space Plan

After receiving approval from the in-house team on the space plan, the design team finalizes the space plan. At this time, the team is only making minor revisions to the plan—in essence, polishing it. The differences between schematic and final space plans is illustrated in Figure 4.16.

Design Development

At this stage, the design team also progresses to the selection of specific finish materials and furniture for the project. For example, if during schematic design the design team recommended the use of stone as a floor covering for the reception area, during design development the design team would actually select a specific marble and design a pattern for its application to the floor. If during schematic design the team proposed the use of millwork (built-in cabinetry) in the conference rooms, during design development the design team would design that millwork. As another example, during schematic design, the design team might recommend the use of soft seating, perhaps four upholstered chairs in the reception area. In design development, the design team selects specific chairs and fabric for the chairs.

Consultant Coordination

During this phase of work, the design team continues to coordinate with specialty consultants. The communication and effective integration of the efforts of all of the team members become increasingly critical as the design progresses and becomes more complex. Each of the team members is working from information provided by the others. If that information is not current and comprehensive, the work will be inaccurate and nonresponsive to the rest of the project.

Cost Estimate Update

Again, the design team should update the cost estimate to incorporate the specific selections and details developed during this phase of the project. The cost estimate should reflect the work of all of the specialty consultants.

Presentation and Approval

At the conclusion of the design development, the design team presents to the in-house team a final space plan and a recommended design solution graphically illustrated through the use of color presentation boards, renderings, and plans. The design team might also use a computer-generated model or manually constructed model to convey these three-dimensional concepts.

The in-house team should carefully review every project detail at this point to be completely satisfied prior to providing the team with approval to proceed. At this point, the design is complete and the design team moves on to document the design for construction and procurement. Subsequent changes are costly and can affect the project schedule substantially.

PHASE 5: CONTRACT DOCUMENTATION

At this point, with all of the design decisions complete, the in-house team's involvement diminishes and the design team turns its efforts toward documenting those concepts. Its primary task in this phase is to produce drawings and specifications that convey to the contractor how to construct the project and define for the vendors those products that they must supply. This phase of the work is the most time-intensive portion of the project for the design team.

Contract Documents

The contract documents include all of the construction drawings and specifications (construction documents) as well as furniture, furnishings drawings, and specifications. These are the documents that by contract the interior architect must deliver to the in-house team. The number of drawings and level of detail of the contract document package is in direct proportion to the size of the project and the complexity of the design—the more detail, the more drawings. The design team produces these documents manually or through the use of a CADD software program. The decision to use the computer for the production effort is based on the following factors:

- Project size
- Amount of repetitive design on the project
- Anticipated frequency of changes to the design concepts
- Use of the documents after completion of the project for facilities management purposes

The design team uses a base building architectural plan that is drawn to scale and illustrates the base building structure, including stairways and core elements (elevators, toilets, mechanical room) as a foundation for creating the following contract documents package (Figure 4.17):

- *Cover Sheet:* identifies the project by name and location and lists the major project team members.
- *Construction Specifications:* the first document to appear in the construction documentation package, construction specifications outline general conditions of performance for all contractors and specific conditions of performance for subcontractors.

DRAWING NUMBER	DRAWING TITLE
–	Cover Sheet
A - 0	Construction Specifications
A - 1	Partition Plan
A - 2	Reflected Ceiling Plan
A - 3	Telephone, Electric and Data Plan
A - 4	Elevations
A - 5	Sections
A - 6	Furniture Plan
A - 7	Finish Plan
A - 8	Floor Finish Plan
A - 9	Plant and Signage Plan
M - 1	Mechanical Plan
E - 1	Electrical Plan
P - 1	Plumbing Plan
FP - 1	Fire Protection Plan

Figure 4.17. The contents of the standard construction documents package are shown here with a fairly typical drawing numbering system.

- *Partition Plan:* describes the partition (wall) and door locations and types, critical partition dimensions, and reference codes to other drawings, elevations, and sections (Figure 4.18)
- *Reflected Ceiling Plan:* delineates the placement and type of all lighting fixtures, ceiling air diffusers and air return grills, and fire exit signs that appear in the ceiling (Figure 4.19)
- *Telephone, Electric, and Data Plan:* provides locations for telephone, electric, and data cabling outlets and switches, and identifies their types. The plan also identifies critical dimensions
- *Elevation:* gives a vertical image of a partition or other element viewed to scale with dimensions. The elevation does not illustrate perspective
- *Section:* illustrates a cut through a wall or other element viewed to scale, identifying critical dimensions
- *Furniture Plan:* indicates the location of all furniture throughout the space. The furniture plan is coded to specifications detailing all information necessary for procurement of each item. Systems furniture plans require both panel and component plans. Panel plans show locations and dimensions of panels or other structural parts of the system. Component plans illustrate component locations and are coded to specifications, listing all information necessary for procurement
- *Finish Plan:* provides the finish placement coded to finish specifications
- *Floor Finish Plan:* shows the placement and type of floor finishes. A complicated combination of materials and floor changes necessitates a floor finish plan
- *Plants and Signage Plan:* identifies the plant and signage locations keyed to specifications

The design team is responsible for coordinating its drawings with those of specialty consultants, including the mechanical/electrical engineers who are responsible for developing the following documents:

- *Mechanical Plan:* heating, ventilating, and air-conditioning systems (Figure 4.20)
- *Electrical Plan:* electrical distribution to lighting and electric outlets and switches (Figure 4.21)
- *Plumbing Plan:* plumbing fixtures and lines as well as sprinkler locations

Permits

During the documentation process, the design team often issues a preliminary set of contract documents for the purpose of reviewing those documents with local officials who are responsible for issuing construction permits. These review sessions can expedite the permitting process and uncover code issues before they become problems. Although the responsibility of obtaining the permit rests with the interior architect and the contractor, it is advantageous for the owner (a member of the in-house team) to be involved in the process.

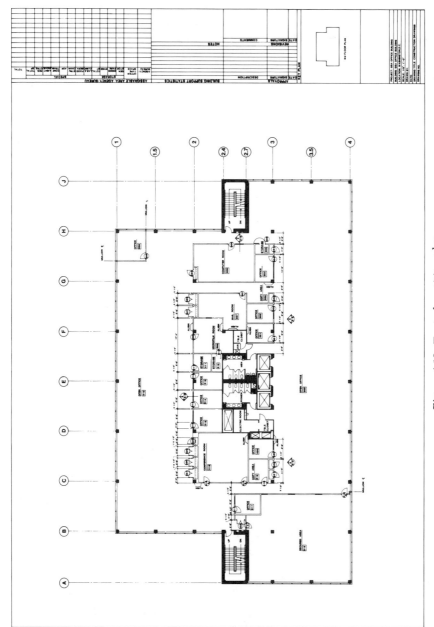

Figure 4.18. Typical partition plan.

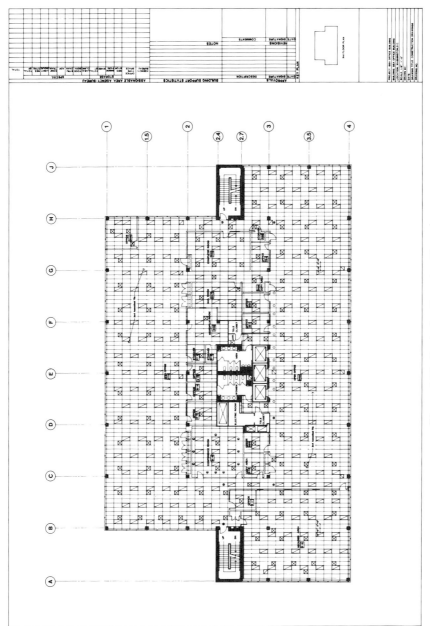

Figure 4.19. Typical reflected ceiling plan.

83

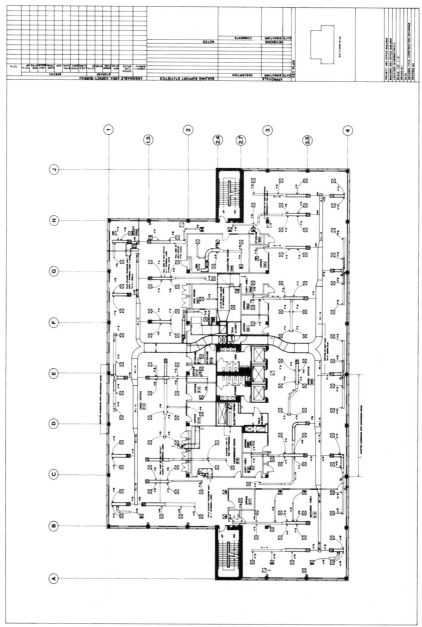

Figure 4.20. Typical mechanical plan.

84

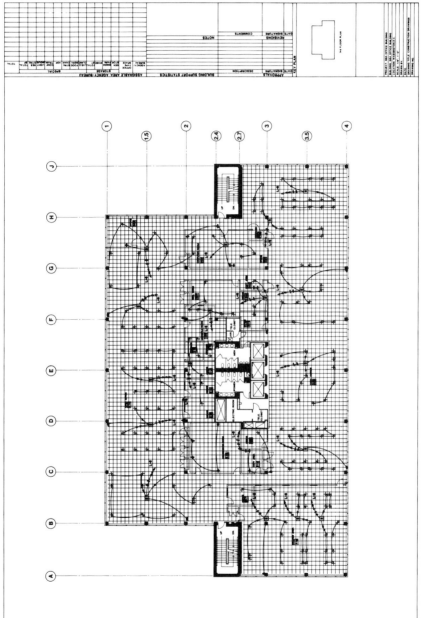

Figure 4.21. Typical electrical plan.

Bid/Negotiation/Award

Once the contract documents are complete, the design team prepares a bid package that is distributed either to one contractor for price negotiations or several qualified contractors for bidding. The bid package contains the construction drawings, specifications, general conditions, owner/contractor agreement, and any other special project provisions.

The most common type of construction contract is a lump-sum contract. Another common contracting method is the cost-plus or construction management contract. The benefits and risks associated with both types of contracts vary based on the needs of the project. A lump-sum contract is simpler and generally beneficial to all parties when the documents are complete, the schedule reasonable, and no special conditions exist that might complicate the process. A cost-plus or construction management approach allows the owner more flexibility in terms of selecting contracting teams, modifying procurement and standard installation methods, while maintaining a cost-competitive environment. (Sources of information on contracting procedures are listed in the Resources section following Chapter 7.) The design team reviews the pricing with the in-house team, selects a qualified contractor, and negotiates a final price for the work.

PHASE 6: CONTRACT ADMINISTRATION

Contract administration encompasses services that the design team provides to the in-house team throughout the course of the contract as well as certain services that the team provides during the construction and installation period. Two services that the interior architect provides on an ongoing basis which are essential to the project are project consultation and contract administration.

Project Consultation

Project consultation is integral to the design process. It represents the ongoing advice that the interior architect provides to the in-house team regarding all aspects of the project throughout the course of the project. The interior architect is available to respond to questions, clarify information, and provide counsel.

Contract Administration

Contract administration includes a number of different services, some of which are provided throughout the course of the project and others only during the construction period. Those that occur over the course of the project are administrative services to the in-house team, including project documentation and review of consultant contracts. The design team also monitors and updates the budget and schedule as required throughout the project.

Contract administration services that are specific to the construction and installation period of the project include:

- *Construction/Installation Monitoring.* The interior architect visits the site periodically during construction and installation of the furniture to ensure that construction and installation are proceeding generally in accordance with the contract documents.

- *Shop Drawing and Materials Review.* As the project proceeds through construction, subcontractors who are responsible for constructing millwork or other non-general construction items on the project submit to the interior architect specific plans and drawings for constructing the design concept. The shop drawings are the documents from which the subcontractor actually builds, so it is essential that those drawings correctly interpret the design concepts. The interior architect reviews these drawings to ensure consistency with the design concept.

- *Change Order Processing.* During construction, any work that deviates from the construction documents and for which the contractor is requesting additional monies is a change order. A change order results either from a client-driven decision, an error in executing construction in accordance with the construction documents, or a problem with the construction documents. With a client-driven change order or an inaccuracy with the documents, the interior architect reviews the contractor's pricing for fairness and reasonableness. In the case of a problem in the field, the interior architect, during regular construction monitoring visits to the site, identifies the problem so that it may be corrected in accordance with the construction documents.

- *Punch List.* Once the contractor submits for final payment based upon substantial completion (the space is sufficiently complete to allow occupancy), the interior architect tours the project to identify any outstanding construction and installation items or any work that is incorrect or inferior. This is referred to as a *punch list.* The interior architect presents this list to the contractor for resolution. After the contractor has completed the punch list, the interior architect verifies that the punch list has been implemented.

The final step in the approval process is obtaining the *certificate of occupancy,* which is the final governmental approval that must be issued prior to occupancy. The certification represents that an inspection by the government concludes that the space has been built out in accordance with the construction documents and that construction is in compliance with all codes. The contractor is responsible for obtaining the certificate of occupancy; however, the interior architect and the owner (a member of the in-house team) typically participate in the process.

For the sequence of events identified in the chapter to proceed productively toward a successful culmination, all team members should strive to develop and maintain open communication throughout the process, recognizing that problems will arise and that mistakes will occur. It is how those problems are handled that will determine the project's success.

During the course of the project, the project team must consider innumerable decisions related to aesthetics, functionality, comfort, safety, and environmental factors. To achieve success, they must also integrate a myriad of design elements at the right time. The following chapters outline those considerations.

Part Two

Design

Chapter Five

Planning Components of
the Office Environment

From a written program, the design team's first step in developing a design concept is to address the planning requirements of the project. These requirements relate to the organization of the space components of the program into a functional, efficient space plan.

In approaching a solution, the design team works with the three primary space components of the office environment: general office areas, circulation, and support areas. This chapter describes the planning objectives, considerations, and approaches to planning these components, and summarizes the impact of the Americans with Disabilities Act (ADA) on these planning considerations.

Each of the three primary space components is both an individual space element as well as a building block or integral part of the whole. Each area should function successfully as a unit within the whole and in tandem with the other components to support the organization's program requirements. From a planning perspective, the interior architect works to achieve a number of different objectives in creating a space that fosters a high-quality work environment.

The space planning concept first should provide the appropriate square footage for each component. It should also provide a feasible mechanism for accommodating future growth. The space plan should organize the space in an efficient and orderly way, delineating a logical progression while achieving the desired adjacencies among individuals, working groups, and departments.

Flexibility is also a key consideration in the contemporary office environment. As businesses must be capable of changing rapidly to capture market opportunities, so must the office environment be capable of responding easily and rapidly to those changes. Therefore, a successful plan should establish spaces that are flexible and interchangeable to the greatest extent possible.

The space plan should also reflect the priorities and culture of the organization. The organization's attitude toward its clients and employees is reflected in how its spaces are planned and designed. For example, does the space have a sense of openness, light, and warmth? How are public spaces or employee support areas treated? The planning concept has a tremendous impact on the image and the atmosphere of the space. A strong space planning concept can contribute as much to the overall image of a space as can the finishes, furniture, and accessories. The plan should project the appropriate image and support a stimulating work environment that is motivating to employees.

Finally, the interior architect must achieve all of these objectives while maintaining compliance with all applicable codes—all fire, life safety codes, and the Americans with Disabilities Act for handicapped access.

The following sections describes each of these space components and discusses the planning considerations and options related to each of the areas.

GENERAL OFFICE AREAS

General office areas are the spaces that accommodate workstations. There are three basic approaches to planning general office areas: closed plan, open plan, and modified open plan.

Planning Approaches

The primary considerations in identifying the most appropriate approach to planning general office areas are:

- The amount of planning flexibility required
- The amount of visual and acoustical privacy required for personnel
- Initial and life-cycle construction and furniture costs

In a closed plan (Figure 5.1), full-height walls or partitions divide the space into offices and support space by floor-to-ceiling partitions (walls) with doors. Private offices typically are located along the window wall. Administrative support is housed in workstations along corridors or in shared rooms.

An open-plan concept (Figure 5.2) locates all workstations in open space with no division by floor-to-ceiling partitions with doors. Support spaces are located in floor-to-ceiling partitioned rooms with doors.

Modified open plan (Figure 5.3) combines elements of both open plan and closed plan by locating certain workstations in open plan with systems furniture and others in private offices. In a modified plan, support spaces are also located in enclosed rooms.

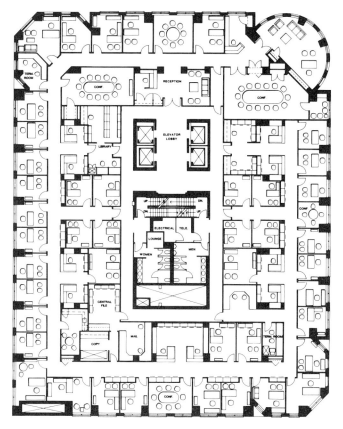

ADVANTAGES

- Controlled environment
- Security
- Visual privacy
- Physical separation
- Traditional and systems
  furniture applications

DISADVANTAGES

- Less efficient than open plan
- Lack of flexibility
- Cost of relocation
- Restricted individual and
  group interaction
- Views
- More extensive mechanical
  systems required

Figure 5.1. Closed plan is an appropriate planning approach for organizations with strong privacy requirements and for which planning flexibility is not a priority.

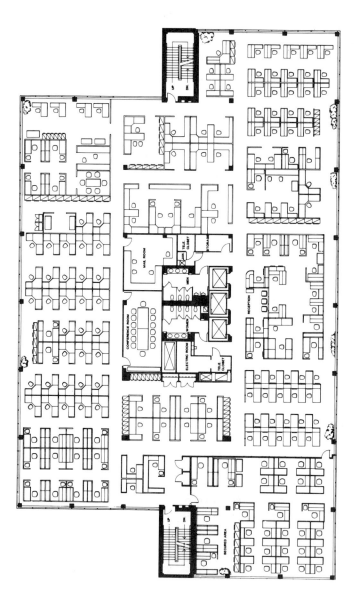

ADVANTAGES

- Efficient space utilization
- Greater planning flexibility
- Views
- Ease of communication
- Life cycle cost lower

DISADVANTAGES

- Higher *initial* cost
- Visual privacy
- Less environmental control

Figure 5.2. Open plan provides significant planning flexibility

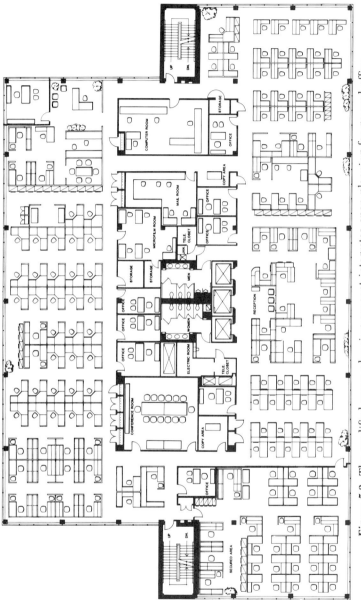

Figure 5.3. The modified space planning concept integrates open planning for general office areas with closed planning for conferencing and other support areas.

Evaluating Open Versus Closed Plan

Through the years, at one time or another the interior architectural profession
has been a proponent of each of these planning concepts, working almost
exclusively with a total closed-plan concept and then gradually evolving to
the other extreme, the total open plan. The changes have always reflected
the trends in organizational management investigating variations on culture,
openness of communication, and reporting structure within the organization.
Basically, the changes have resulted from continuing attempts to find the best
office environment formula for providing flexibility, efficiency, and a better,
more productive work environment.

Some organizations still implement a total closed-plan or total open-plan
environment. Most organizations today, however, implement a more balanced
approach with a modified plan. The issue of open versus closed plan is not a
question of right or wrong but a matter of two distinct approaches to office
planning. Each approach has both advantages and disadvantages. Ultimately,
an organization's decision should be based on the approach that best meets
the organization's culture and mission statement. Typically, organizations that
require substantial planning flexibility use open plan. Open plan can increase
potential planning efficiencies, reduce the life-cycle cost of providing general
office space, and allow for quick and cost-efficient response to increasingly
frequent changes in office organization and function. Organizations with little
requirement for flexibility and a significant need for privacy typically implement a closed plan. The following criteria provide the foundation for evaluating the two planning approaches:

- Space utilization
- Planning flexibility
- Cost
- Communication among personnel
- Office technology flexibility
- Visual expansiveness
- Visual privacy
- Acoustical privacy
- Security

Space Utilization. Space utilization refers to the efficiency and density of
the planning concept. Essentially, it reflects the quantity of people that can
be accommodated in the space. In most cases, closed plan is less efficient
than open plan for three reasons. First, the enclosed rooms of a closed-plan
concept are rectilinear, creating rigid modules that cannot be manipulated to
maximize the density of a specific building floor plate. Second, if the location
of offices or enclosed rooms is along the building perimeter, office partitions
should align with window mullions and column locations. The mullions and
column locations, therefore, create a rigid office size that may result in less
efficiency than an open-plan concept. Third, additional space is required to
accommodate the door swing and stand space associated with the private
offices. The way in which the circulation space relates to or accesses the door
locations can also create inefficiencies in the layout of the circulation pattern.

Open plan provides greater opportunity to maximize the utilization of space than does closed plan and minimizes the circulation space required because workstations can be modified slightly to fit available space. This is particularly true if the open space is large and regular in configuration. The use of systems furniture in open plan can also improve space utilization because a job function can normally be accommodated in less space in a systems furniture workstation than in a closed-plan office.

Planning Flexibility. Closed-plan concepts provide less planning flexibility than open-plan concepts. The modification of constructed areas is much more difficult and disruptive than the reconfiguration of systems furniture. In modified closed-plan areas, floor-to-ceiling partitions must be demolished and reconstructed.Additionally, all of the related support systems, lighting, engineering, and acoustics as well as floor finishes must be modified to meet the requirements of the new configuration.

In a closed plan, carpet is installed around partitions (as opposed to under them) and lighting fixtures are located in the ceiling grid within the context of the private offices. All mechanical systems and electrical distribution are designed to provide the required airflow, temperature control, and electrical distribution to each room. If modifications are made in the closed plan, relocating drywall partitions, changes must also be made to the mechanical, electrical, and lighting systems, and carpeting must also be modified to maintain the quality of the environment. The demolition and construction of new space is costly, time consuming, and causes disruption to employees during the entire construction period.

With the use of open plan in conjunction with systems furniture, furniture can be reconfigured with relative ease. Mechanical, electrical, lighting, and floor finishes are designed to accommodate a large open area. As a result, changes require only furniture reconfiguration and possible minor modification to lighting, HVAC, or electrical distribution. Cost and employee disruption are minimized.

Cost. An evaluation of cost with either planning approach must be considered in the context of the life of the project and the number and extent of modifications to the space. Closed plan is the less expensive plan to implement initially. This initial cost difference is due to the lower cost of constructing drywall partitions required for closed plan versus the higher cost of purchasing systems or modular furniture. However, if significant planning changes requiring modification to the construction are made to the facility, closed plan becomes more expensive to demolish and reconstruct than the cost of reconfiguring furniture. Consequently, with frequent changes, the life-cycle cost of closed plan can become more expensive than open plan.

Communication Among Personnel. Closed plan is less conducive to intraoffice communication among personnel than is open plan. The presence of physical barriers in closed plan makes personnel less accessible. This can be an advantage or disadvantage, depending on the level of interaction that is necessary for people to perform their job functions. Open plan, on the other hand, limits privacy and the mechanisms available to personnel to isolate themselves from general office activity. In open plan, communication can be affected by varying the systems furniture panel heights.

Office Technology Flexibility. Closed plan provides more limited flexibility in responding to changes in office technology, primarily because of the difficulty in changing wire distribution for electrical and data cabling and outlets. Again, the use of full-height partitions is limiting to flexibility. Open plan removes those barriers, allowing greater ease in reconfiguration, particularly if systems furniture is used in conjunction with an access floor, a raised floor that allows for the distribution of power and data cabling between the building slab and the raised floor.

Visual Expansiveness. The feeling of visual expansiveness is limited in closed plan, again due to the partitions. In addition, the location of private offices along windows blocks views from other office areas. Open plan can provide a visually more expansive office space than closed plan. This is particularly true if systems or modular furniture workstation panel heights are close to or below standing vision height an workstations are grouped by panel height. With this planning approach, windows are open to the interior spaces rather than only to private offices. Vistas to the perimeter are preserved and visual space is borrowed from surrounding areas, making the area appear larger than it is and lending an overall expansive feel to the entire space.

Sensitivity to visual expansiveness as well as sensitivity to well-organized and clearly defined circulation patterns help to eliminate the impression of maze or rabbit warren in both closed- and open-plan space.

Visual Privacy. Visual privacy may be desired or required for specific job functions or to reflect organizational culture. Of the two planning approaches, closed plan offers the greater potential for visual privacy. In fact, visual privacy can be almost total. This is true for all personnel except those who remain in open space, such as clerical support personnel who must deal with the public.

In open plan, visual privacy is provided to a workstation only as is necessary to perform a job function. In those cases, visual privacy is achieved with floor-standing panels that screen in the workstation from other people in the space. Therefore, in open plan, the screen heights are selected to provide partial seated-height privacy (36 to 42 inches), seated-height privacy (48 to 54 inches), and standing-height privacy (66 to 80 inches).

In addition to the use of panels, visual privacy is achieved in open plan through the placement of workstations in relation to the others, location of openings to workstations to inhibit views into the workstation and orientation of the person within the workstations. The placement of file banks and plants can also contribute to additional visual privacy in the open-plan space.

Acoustical Privacy. Acoustical privacy is achievable in both open- and closed-plan environments if the spaces are designed correctly. In closed plan, different degrees of acoustical privacy are achieved by insulating walls, extending partitions from slab to slab, and caulking at the point where the partition and slab meet. Sound-absorbing surfaces are placed on ceilings, walls, and floors. Solid-core gasketed doors are installed in the rooms and the mechanical systems are designed appropriately for noise control and acoustical privacy. Acoustical privacy is achieved in open plan through the use of acoustical panels, sound-absorbing finishes, and the use of a sound-masking system that makes normal speech unintelligible.

Security. If material and information handled by employees are confidential or classified, closed plan provides the opportunity to secure materials more easily than does open plan. This is achieved by limiting access to specific areas in the space. The private office also provides an environment in which a person can work on confidential materials without interruption by other employees.

Planning Considerations for General Office Areas
The following are general considerations that should be addressed in planning general office areas:

- Building configuration and systems
- Private office placement and sizing
- Location and clustering of workstations
- Systems creep

Building Configuration and Systems. As buildings differ in their external appearances, they also vary, often substantially, in the characteristics that comprise their infrastructures: floor sizes, building shape, and architectural elements such as column and mullion spacing, and core (mechanical rooms, toilets, elevators) size and location. All of these considerations affect how well a building can accommodate a specific space program by affecting space efficiencies and the potential to create the necessary functional and aesthetic requirements of a project. It is important, therefore, for the interior architect to assist the in-house team in evaluating a potential building for compatibility with the organization's programs.

- *Column Spacing:* Typically, the greater the distance between columns, or the larger the column bays (that is, the area within four columns), the better the planning conditions. Carried to an extreme, the optimum planning situation would be a building without columns.
- *Window Mullion Spacing:* A mullion is the vertical bar separating two windows panes. Window mullion spacing should be consistent. Irregular mullion spacing leads to difficulty in achieving consistent office sizes and providing a perpendicular interface between the partition and the perimeter without awkward conditions.
- *Core and Fire-Stair Location:* The optimum conditions are planning areas with minimal interruption from core elements of fire stairs. The core space should be small in relation to the floor size, centrally located, and regular

in configuration. Also, the depth of the building from the core to the perimeter should be as great as possible.

- *Core Massing:* In an open-plan approach, in which core corridors are not present and the floor is totally open, the configuration of the core becomes an important planning consideration because it affects the circulation pattern and becomes an aesthetic element in the space. Consequently, to the greatest extent possible, it is desirable to create a regular massing to the core. This is achieved by placing the support and service rooms against the core, enlarging the core, and creating a regular shape from an irregular building core (Figure 5.4). In certain circumstances it is possible to reshape the core to be more responsive to the overall plan and desired circulation pattern. This should be done in such a way that, if possible, the previously existing doors leading to core spaces are still accessible from the primary circulation path. Access to fire stairs as well as clear and direct access to the secondary circulation pattern must be maintained.
- *Slab-to-Slab Dimension:* In general, the greater the distance from slab to slab, the higher the ceiling and, consequently, the more comfortable and pleasant the office environment. The greater slab-to-slab dimension will reduce clearance problems with mechanical systems and recessed lighting fixtures. The finished ceiling height should be a minimum of 8 feet.
- *Perimeter Mechanical Systems:* Mechanical system elements such as heat pumps and fan coil units which are floor-standing and occur at the perimeter create planning constraints. These elements take floor space in the plan and have the effect of creating an area of approximately 2 feet on the perimeter that is not plannable.
- *Building Shape:* A regular-shaped building can result in a more efficient space plan than that of an irregularly shaped building. Although irregular shapes can provide an opportunity for creativity in planning configurations, they also often result in some areas that are awkward and inefficient to plan.

Private Office Placement and Sizing. In a closed-plan concept, private offices are located along the building perimeter. Additional private offices are placed on the interior when perimeter space is no longer available. In a modified plan, private offices typically are located at the interior of the space to allow for maximum light and visual expansiveness throughout the office space. If any private offices are located on the perimeter, they are grouped together to maintain open areas elsewhere along the perimeter.

Partitions for private offices or support areas should be aligned with interior columns and perimeter pilasters (columns) within the walls. To achieve, this, the office size must be related to the column spacing, such as one-half or one-third of the column-to-column dimension. Figure 5.5 illustrates that, optimally, the location of private office partitions should coincide with window mullion spacing to create a regular and efficient plan.

The size of private offices and support rooms should also relate to the window mullion spacing. The mullion spacing establishes the width of the planning module, so the room sizes are varied in multiples of the mullion module. If mullion spacing is irregular, it is difficult to establish consistent

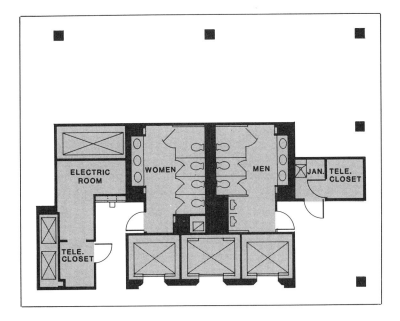

ORIGINAL CORE

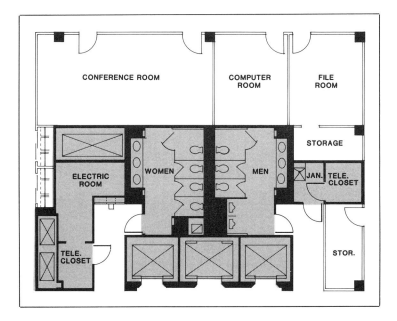

PLAN MODIFIED CORE

Figure 5.4. This core massing diagram illustrates support areas located immediately around the building core to create a regular planning and circulation areas.

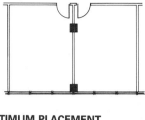

OPTIMUM PLACEMENT

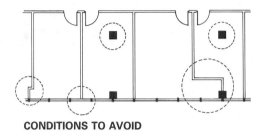

CONDITIONS TO AVOID

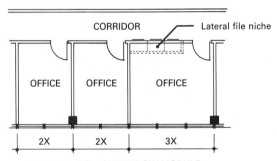

X = DIMENSION OF WINDOW MODULE

Figure 5.5. Private office partitions should be located at regular intervals to coincide with window modules.

office sizes. It is also possible if the office wall is not in line with the mullion to *jog* a wall so that it hits the mullion. However, this usually creates an awkward detail at the perimeter and is not as aesthetically pleasing as a straight, perpendicular wall meeting the mullion on line.

It is also important in sizing private offices or support rooms to maintain a consistent depth or distance from the perimeter to the core in order to maintain a uniform circulation width along the private office corridor. If it is necessary to vary the office depth, planning devices such as file niches should be used to create uniformity in the corridor path.

Location and Clustering of Workstations. Workstations in open plan and, to a lesser degree, offices in closed or open plan should be clustered, or grouped, in a consistent rhythm throughout the space to prevent an appearance of disorganization in the space. Workstation clusters can be only two workstations deep (wide) to provide accessibility to each workstation. In the other direction, the length of the workstation run, the workstation grouping or cluster, can potentially extend the length of the space. Although a longer cluster is more efficient, it should be penetrated by cross corridors at regular intervals to allow circulation (Figure 5.6).

Openings to workstations within the clusters should be placed as far apart as possible to provide maximum privacy within each workstation and for traffic control around the workstations. For the same reasons, the workstation opening should also be located consistently along the cluster rather than side by side.

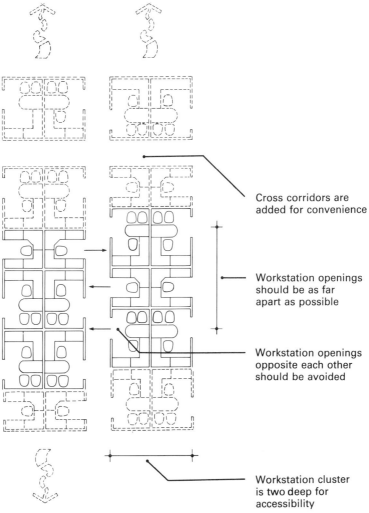

Cross corridors are added for convenience

Workstation openings should be as far apart as possible

Workstation openings opposite each other should be avoided

Workstation cluster is two deep for accessibility

Figure 5.6. This diagram illustrates the planning considerations for furniture system workstations clusters.

The placement of workstations should relate to the column spacing and eliminate the placement of columns in the workstations. Column placement in the workstation results either in the loss of that workstation entirely for occupancy or substantial loss of usable space within the workstation.

Systems Creep. A phenomenon called *systems creep* occurs in planning general office open-plan areas with systems furniture. Systems creep occurs when an inaccurate dimension is used to represent the systems furniture module for space planning purposes. The inaccuracy stems from the use of a dimension for the furniture system that is less than it should be because it does not include the panel connection hardware dimension. This error results in a systems furniture cluster which, when installed, would actually be larger than anticipated in plan. Figure 5.7 illustrates the difference in panel connector dimensions that results in systems creep. A serious planning issue in large open areas, failure to adjust for systems creep may result in insufficient density to meet program requirements because the number of workstations needed will not fit in the space. Space plans that are based on the accurate dimensioning of the specific systems furniture to be used on the project will eliminate the planning risk of systems creep.

CIRCULATION

Circulation is the area required to connect functional spaces in the office. In closed plan, circulation comprises the corridors through the space; in open plan, it is the paths through the workstations. The three basic types of circulation are primary, secondary, and tertiary (Figure 5.8).

- *Primary circulation* is the circulation area around the building core used to access and interconnect the core spaces and the general office areas. It is the main corridor looping the core. This circulation path is required by fire safety and local codes for access to and egress from the space. In most circumstances, this corridor should be enclosed with slab-to-slab fire-rated partitions.
- The main circulation through general office areas of the organization is considered *secondary circulation.*
- *Tertiary circulation* is the additional circulation in general office areas required to access open-plan workstations that are not located directly on secondary circulation.

Circulation constitutes a significant portion of the total space. Specific circulation planning factors should be developed for each planning situation. In all situations, however, developing clearly defined circulation patterns and eliminating circulation path duplication (two paths between two points that are in close proximity) minimizes the amount of circulation and increases the aesthetic appeal of the space. The following are key planning considerations in the design of effective circulation concepts.

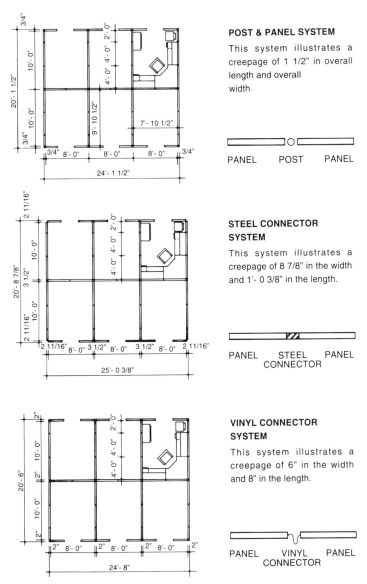

POST & PANEL SYSTEM

This system illustrates a creepage of 1 1/2" in overall length and overall width.

PANEL   POST   PANEL

STEEL CONNECTOR SYSTEM

This system illustrates a creepage of 8 7/8" in the width and 1'- 0 3/8" in the length.

PANEL   STEEL   PANEL
             CONNECTOR

VINYL CONNECTOR SYSTEM

This system illustrates a creepage of 6" in the width and 8" in the length.

PANEL   VINYL   PANEL
             CONNECTOR

Figure 5.7. The difference in panel connectors that causes systems creep is represented in this illustration.

Circulation Path Width

Circulation path widths should be considered carefully to create totally clear and unobstructed space. Generally, the wider the circulation path, the more spacious and comfortable the plan will appear and feel. Conversely, overly wide circulation paths unnecessarily consume space and decrease planning

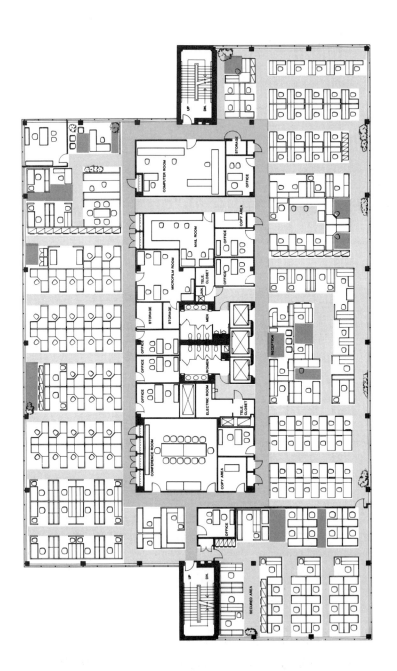

KEY

■ Primary
□ Secondary
■ Tertiary

CIRCULATION

Figure 5.8. This plan depicts primary, secondary, and tertiary circulation patterns in an open-plan configuration.

efficiency. Ideally, the main circulation paths should be at least 5 feet and should never be narrower than 4 feet.

Circulation Path Length

Long, straight circulation paths provide maximum efficiency and optimum organization; however, they can also appear tunnel-like. This is particularly true if the paths are narrow. To provide maximum efficiency and at the same time create an interesting and aesthetically appealing space, the path should be slightly modified to create irregularities. This can be done by opening the circulation with cross corridors at regular intervals, opening the corridor to low partition open areas, or creating an offset in the corridor (Figure 5.9).

Fire Safety

Fire safety is a primary consideration in planning any circulation pattern. If fire safety regulations are taken into consideration at the beginning of the space planning process, extensive replanning can be avoided later in the

Figure 5.9. This perspective illustrates the use of a cross corridor to create interest in a long primary circulation path.

project. The main fire safety considerations are related to minimum width, maximum travel distances, choice of two distinct exit paths, and avoidance of dead-end corridors. The plan must comply with the local code's safety requirements.

The minimum width required for public corridors by fire safety code is 44 inches. This code applies to traditional partitioned corridors and all circulation spaces in open plan. Prior to the life safety review, it is advisable to plan for the worst conditions.

The circulation space must be free and clear of any obstructions. Chairs should not be located in a position which requires that they are pushed into the circulation space to be used. If file cabinets are located in corridors, the corridor must be sized with the cabinets taken into consideration to meet ADA and fire safety codes. Doors cannot swing into the circulation path. Generally, any drawer pull and stand space (the space required to stand in front of the file cabinet and operate the drawers) should be avoided in circulation space, if possible.

The circulation pattern must be laid out in such a way that the maximum travel distance from the most remote office to the point of decision, that is, the point where the alternative means of egress can be elected, does not exceed 50 feet. The distance is measured as travel distance, that is, the distance that must be traveled on the circulation path without passing through intervening doors or rooms, unless absolutely necessary. Circulation must provide for two separate and distinct means of egress from any point in the space. That is, from any point there must be a choice of two distinctly different routes to two different fire stairs or exits. These two exits from the space should be as far from each other as possible. The exception to this is referred to as a dead-end corridor. A dead-end corridor cannot exceed 20 feet in length from the dead end to the point of decision.

Handicapped Accessibility

Circulation must be designed in compliance with all ADA requirements. The primary ADA considerations related to circulation are readily accessible accommodations to persons with disabilities. This includes the width of circulation, the appropriate wheelchair turnaround clearance at appropriate intervals within the space, and the ramping or grade slope of any circulation areas and door-swing clearance space.

The minimum width for single wheelchair passage in corridors is 36 inches. Wheelchairs passing in corridors must be allowed 60 inches, and wheelchair turns of 180 degrees require clear space of 60 inches in diameter or a T-shaped space (Figure 5.10).

A change in floor level of less than $\frac{1}{2}$ inch is acceptable. If the change in floor level exceeds $\frac{1}{2}$ inch, a ramp or elevator must be provided (Figure 5.11). The least possible slope must be used for any ramp. The maximum slope of a ramp in new construction must be 1 inch of rise to 12 inches of run. The maximum height of a ramp is 30 inches. If the change in floor level exceeds 30 inches, a 60-inch by 60-inch landing must be provided. If a ramp has a rise

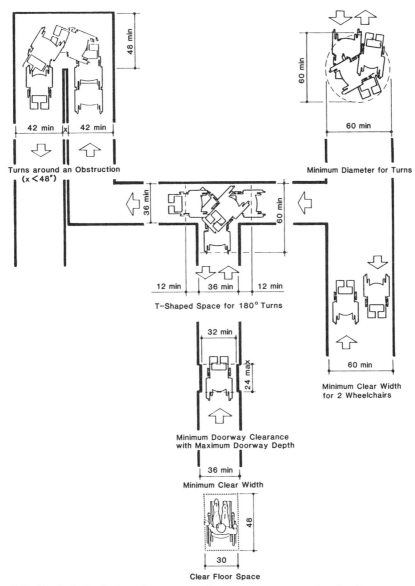

Figure 5.10. Typical circulation planning considerations to accommodate handicapped access.

greater than 6 inches or a horizontal projection greater than 72 inches, the ramp must have handrails on both sides.

Objects protruding from a wall 27 to 80 inches above the floor can protrude no more than 4 inches into passageways. Objects mounted with their leading edges at or below 27 inches above the finished floor may protrude any amount. Protruding objects, however, cannot reduce the clear width of an accessible route. A minimum clear headroom of 80 inches must be provided.

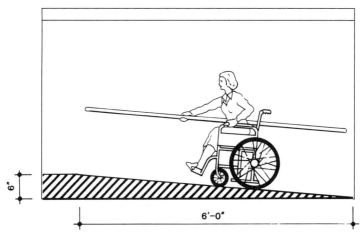

Figure 5.11. Ramping to provide handicapped access in areas with floor-level changes.

SUPPORT AREAS

Support areas are spaces that are used by a group within the organization or the entire organization to accommodate shared needs. Common support areas include:

- Reception
- Conference rooms, workrooms, and training rooms
- Computer rooms
- Equipment rooms
- File rooms
- Copy rooms
- Supply rooms
- Mail rooms
- Libraries
- Pantries
- Special support

The sizing and location of these support areas are based on the number of people who use the space, the frequency of that use, and the adjacency requirements to internal groups or visitors to the space. Support areas such as conference rooms, pantries, or copy rooms that support a specific group or groups within the organization should be sized accordingly. Figure 5.12 lists the typical square-foot ranges for support areas for projects of various sizes. For ease of access, they should be located within close proximity to those groups. A support space that functions for the entire organization or even the public, such as conference centers, auditoriums, or cafeterias, should be centrally located. The level of design in these support areas is often based on

SUPPORT SPACE	SQ. FOOTAGE RANGE (30,000 SF Office or less)	SQ. FOOTAGE RANGE (30,000 - 100,000 SF Office)	SQ. FOOTAGE RANGE (100,000 SF Office or more)
Reception	250 SF / 300 SF	300 SF / 400 SF	1,000 SF
Conference Room	250 SF / 300 SF	300 SF / 500 SF	750 SF
Workroom	250 SF	250 SF	300 SF
Training Room		750 SF	1,500 SF
Computer Room	400 SF	1,000 SF	2,500 SF
Equipment Rooms	120 SF	250 SF	250 SF
File Room	120 SF / 200 SF	200 SF / 400 SF	1,200 SF
Copy Room	200 SF	300 SF / 400 SF	1,000 SF
Mail Room	200 SF	300 SF / 400 SF	1,000 SF
Library	200 SF / 300 SF	400 SF / 600 SF	1,200 SF
Pantry	200 SF	300 SF	300 SF
Day Care Center			8,000 SF
Fitness Center			4,000 SF / 6,000 SF
Cafeteria			10,000 SF / 12,000 SF
Conference Center			12,000 SF
Auditorium			5,000 SF

Figure 5.12. Square-foot ranges for typical support areas.

whether the support area is used as an interface with the public and, therefore, a space that is important in conveying the organization's desired image. The following section identifies each of these common support areas and the general planning and design considerations for each. The illustrations associated with each support area suggest a typical layout as well as a reflected ceiling plan. The reflected ceiling plan is represented as an integral planning consideration.

Reception

Reception areas, the initial point of interface between the office and the public, are fundamental to establishing the organization's public image. As a public space, the reception area's level of design and finish is frequently higher than in general office areas in order to gain the greatest impact for the dollars spent.

The basic elements that compose the reception area are reception desk, visitor seating and coat closets, and guest telephone or adjacent telephone room (Figure 5.13). Frequently, a multifloor user will locate a monumental stair to connect two or more floors within the reception area. The location of the stair in the reception area makes it visible to all guests and therefore can be used to reinforce the image element. Conference or training areas should be located immediately adjacent to reception areas to allow accessibility by visitors to the space. The breakout areas, areas that are immediately adjacent to meeting rooms and are used for informal discussions or relaxation during meeting breaks, can be incorporated into the reception area. The size of the reception area and amount of seating are based on the number of visitors that must be accommodated at any one time and the desired image for the space.

The location and design of the receptionist desk is another primary consideration in the design of the reception area. Since the desk functions not only as a point of reception and security but also as a workstation for administrative

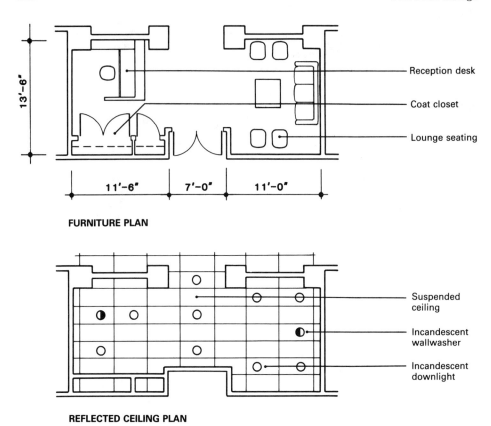

FURNITURE PLAN

REFLECTED CEILING PLAN

Figure 5.13. Typical reception area plan.

support, it should be designed to accommodate a telephone console and word processing equipment. The desk should be functional for the user, while keeping necessary equipment and tools out of public sight (Figure 5.14).

Satellite reception areas are necessary in a large organization in which outside visitors are received in general office areas removed from the main reception area. These satellite areas can vary from an informal holding space for two people to a small formal area with a receptionist. The number, size, and type of satellite reception areas are dependent on the number of visitors, the size of the organization, and the frequency of visits.

Conference Rooms, Workrooms, and Training Rooms

Conference Rooms

Conference rooms provide a space designed specifically as a meeting place that is separate from the general office areas to avoid disturbances to or from other personnel. The size and number of conference rooms needed for any project are related to the size and frequency of groups using meeting space.

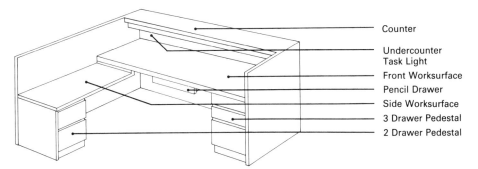

Counter

Undercounter
Task Light

Front Worksurface

Pencil Drawer

Side Worksurface

3 Drawer Pedestal

2 Drawer Pedestal

Figure 5.14. A reception desk should be designed to hide workstation equipment from view.

Conference rooms should accommodate small, medium, and large meetings. A small conference room typically seats 6 to 8 persons, a medium room 10 to 12, and a large room 16 or more. Typically, more conference/meeting spaces should be provided in open plan than in closed plan to compensate for a lack of private offices to accommodate small meetings.

Most conference rooms (Figure 5.15) are furnished with a pedestal leg table and swivel caster chairs for ease of movement to and from the table. Counter space for coffee and food service, collating, and equipment is usually accommodated by a built-in wall unit with under-counter storage. Audiovisual support is also a consideration in conference/meeting rooms. At a minimum, conference rooms should be equipped with a rail board for presentation materials, a marker board, and a projection screen.

A conference center (Figure 5.16) supports the entire organization and should be located centrally in the facility for internal convenience and accessibility to visitors. The conference center includes separate reception and a diversity of room sizes to provide maximum flexibility.

Workrooms

Workrooms are conference rooms that are used primarily as team work areas rather than meeting rooms. Again, the number of rooms required depends on the number of people using the rooms and the frequency of use. Workrooms should contain a table and chairs with counter and storage space (Figure 5.17). Workrooms are usually smaller, less formal, and have fewer audiovisual elements than do conference rooms.

Training Rooms

The function of a training room dictates that it be larger than a conference room. These facilities are used primarily as lecture or instruction areas. They offer a classroom-style environment with auditorium or theater-style tables and chairs (Figure 5.18). Stackable chairs and small, folding training tables make reconfiguration easy.

The frequent need for extensive audiovisual and acoustical elements in

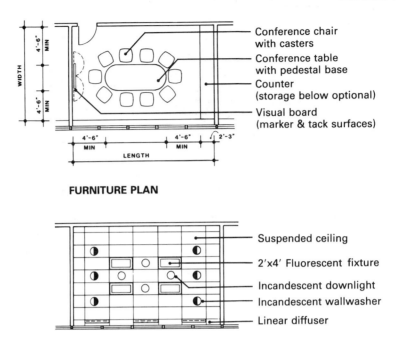

FURNITURE PLAN

REFLECTED CEILING PLAN

Figure 5.15. Typical conference room plan.

training rooms often necessitates that they be located in the interior rather than along the perimeter of the space. This allows for better control of light and noise conditions. Layout of the space, lines of sight, and column locations are much more critical here than with conference rooms and workrooms.

Sizing of the training room is based on the desired seating capacity of the room, beginning with the number and size of the table(s) and the number of chairs. Generally, the table should be the same length in feet as the number of chairs to be accommodated at the table. A 10-foot table, for example, would seat 10 people. This guide becomes less accurate, however, as the table length increases. A sizing alterative is to allow 30 to 36 inches of perimeter frontage at the table for each person. The rooms can also be sized by planning approximately 20 square feet per person to be accommodated in the room.

At a minimum, a dimension of 14 to 16 inches should be allowed on all sides of the table to provide sufficient space to move chairs to and from the table. Usually, 6 feet is provided adjacent to the door and the lecture areas, or the table is centered and 5 feet is allowed on each side. Lecterns, counter space, and gallery seating should also be considered in planning the room size.

Training rooms that are used in auditorium style can be sized by determining the number of chairs to be accommodated in the room and allowing approximately 3 feet between rows from the back of one chair to the front of the next.

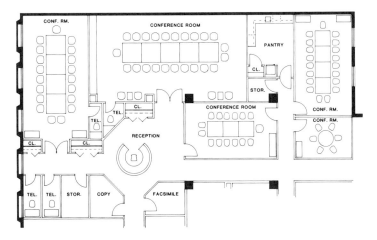

FURNITURE PLAN

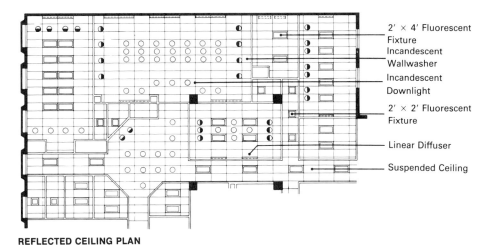

2′ × 4′ Fluorescent Fixture

Incandescent Wallwasher

Incandescent Downlight

2′ × 2′ Fluorescent Fixture

Linear Diffuser

Suspended Ceiling

REFLECTED CEILING PLAN

Figure 5.16. This plan illustrates the funtional requirements of a typical conference center.

The longer the row, the greater the space that should be provided between the rows. Aisle space between sections should allow 4 to 5 feet for two people to pass. A classroom-style training room should provide approximately 40 square feet per person. A training room in auditorium style should provide approximately 10 square feet per person.

Room sizing is also related to the specific function for which the room is intended. Formal, image rooms are usually larger than general conference rooms or workrooms. If the meeting room houses a large number of people, a breakout area provides space for people to congregate before and after meetings and during breaks.

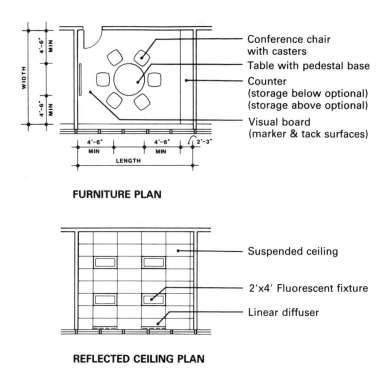

FURNITURE PLAN

REFLECTED CEILING PLAN
Figure 5.17. Typical workroom plan.

Facsimile machines are often required support for meetings or teleconferencing. The machine may be located in an adjacent separate room for noise control. Counter space should be planned adjacent to the machine for materials, storage, and telephone.

Computer Rooms

Although certain computer equipment such as personal computers, workstations, file servers, and some minicomputers can be housed in typical office space with slight supplemental support (such as additional cooling), computer rooms that house densely packed, high-capacity central systems or mainframes require significant infrastructure support. Extreme care should be taken in locating, designing, or modifying these computer areas because of the enormous costs involved.

Critical issues related to locating a mainframe computer room are proximity to:

- Users whom the room supports
- Necessary support systems such as HVAC, power, fire protection

At the same time, potential hazards such as water lines, interference from

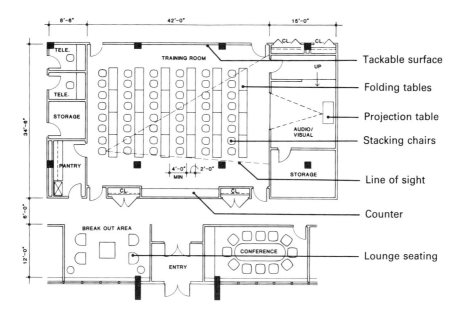

FURNITURE PLAN

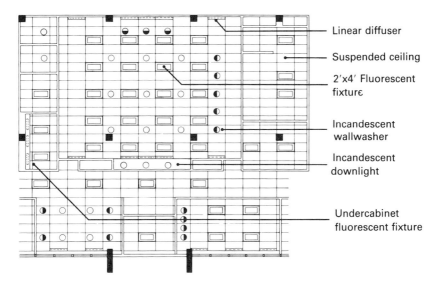

REFLECTED CEILING PLAN

Figure 5.18. This plan illustrates the functional requirements of a typical training center.

electrical/radio power sources, gas mains, and chemical storage should be avoided. One other additional consideration is potential expansion opportunities. The computer operations representative or equipment vendor normally supplies the sizing, equipment layout, and support system requirements (Figure 5.19).

Once the facility has been located in the building and properly sized, the primary design considerations become:

- HVAC system design for proper climate control, including humidification to maintain proper operating conditions for the equiment
- Lighting
- Power capacity and wire management
- Structural capacity
- Security
- Fire detection and suppression

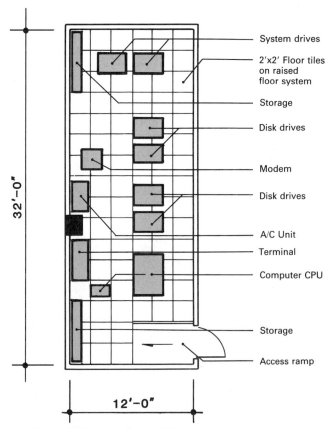

Figure 5.19. Typical mainframe computer room plan.

HVAC systems are typically designed with redundancy and are self-contained within the computer room. Air should be supplied by highly reliable chilled water or condenser water sources. Power should be provided through independent clean (isolated from other power requirements and protected from power surges) redundant (completely duplicated for reliability) power sources. These power sources include battery systems that clean the power and provide uninterrupted power and short-term emergency power. Emergency power generators provide continuous power for critical loads.

The intense wire management requirements of a large computer room normally require the installation of a raised access floor. In addition to wire management capabilities, an access floor allows for under-floor air distribution, which is critical to some mainframe systems.

In the past, fire suppression for computer equipment was provided by nonwater sources (Halon). Today, suppression is handled with dry pipe systems, Halon substitutes, or a combination of both systems.

Structural requirements are always a primary consideration in the planning and design of computer rooms. The computer rooms themselves require approximately twice the live-load capacity of normal office space. Live load is the capacity of the building to support interior construction, furnishings, and occupants. Live load does not include the weight of the structure itself. Power battery rooms can require as much as three to four times the normal office live load.

Equipment Rooms

Equipment areas house copy, facsimile machines, printers, and other support equipment. For aesthetic and acoustical reasons, it is important to isolate the equipment from the general office environment in a separate room, yet in a location convenient to the office function. Most equipment rooms should accommodate the equipment as well as counter space for collating and storage.

File Rooms

Active files that staff members regularly access and maintain should be located in file banks thoughout general office areas. File rooms should house central filing systems or provide areas for secured file storage (Figure 5.20). File rooms are sized according to the amount of filing to be accommodated and the appropriate amount of aisle, stand, and drawer pull space. Adequate aisle space assumes that a person must bend to reach into lower drawers. If this access space is reduced in the interest of conserving space, the files become difficult to access.

In planning a file room, it is important to evaluate the floor loads and the capacity of the slab to meet these weight loads. The slab capacity in typical office buildings rarely support load levels created when filing is banked and grouped in a small area. This is a particularly important consideration in the case of movable or high-density filing where the systems concentrate

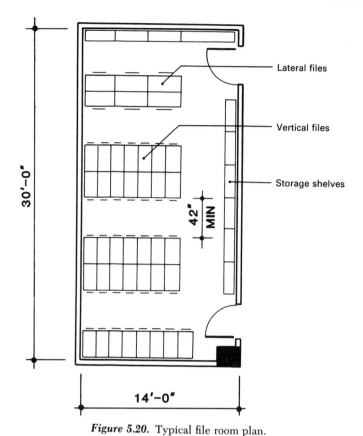

Figure 5.20. Typical file room plan.

significant weight load over a relatively small floor area. (See Chapter 7 for information on movable and high-density filing systems.) For this reason, file rooms are often located in core areas to take advantage of the core area structural floor loading capacity.

Copy Rooms

Satellite copy rooms should be planned throughout a large office space in locations convenient to the users. Central copy rooms should be located in or in close proximity to core areas adjacent to supply and mail rooms. The primary planning considerations for copy rooms are the number, sizes, and type of copying equipment to be located in the room (floor-standing or tabletop) and providing sufficient user and servicing access space for the equipment (Figure 5.21). The room should include over- and under-counter storage for copy supplies and sufficient counter space for collating activities. Space should be provided for trash and recycling receptacles. If the copy room is a central support facility, consideration should be given to providing a controlled point of interface to allow for drop-off and pickup of materials.

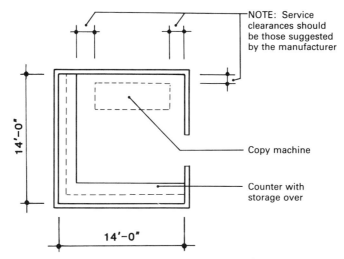

NOTE: Service clearances should be those suggested by the manufacturer

Copy machine

Counter with storage over

14'-0"

14'-0"

Figure 5.21. Typical copy room plan.

Supply Rooms

Supply rooms store general office supplies. Small supply rooms should be located throughout a large office space where smaller quantities can be stored at convenient locations. One large, central supply room should be designed and located for receiving and distributing supplies throughout the space. A central supply room should also be combined with or located adjacent to copy and mail functions.

Mail Rooms

The basic consideration in locating, sizing, and planning a mail room is whether the room is a central or satellite facility. In a large building, the central mail room should be located in close proximity to the loading dock. Satellite mail rooms should be disbursed at convenient locations throughout the facility. If, however, the mail room operates with an automated system, all satellite mail rooms should be located on each floor directly above or below the central mail facility for vertical distribution and collection. The types of materials that the mail room processes (large palette items, for example) affect floor loading considerations, which, in turn, affect the location of the facility.

The functional areas of the mail room are:

- Incoming and outgoing
- Sorting
- Storage
- Internal distribution

The facility should be sized based on the components, how the mail is processed, the size of the mail room staff, and the quantity and type of mail processed. The mail facility can also be sized to accommodate copy and supply storage functions.

Incoming mail should be totally segregated from processed or stored mail items. Access to the loading dock and security at that point of access is a planning consideration. If security related to the actual incoming mail items is a concern, x-ray or other security equipment should be located at the point of entry to the facility. The entrance from the loading dock should be equipped with double doors that have vision panels and kick plates.

If the mail room also accommodates messengers and deliveries, access and control of that point of access are also factors. Telephones should be provided for the messengers' use at this location. Trash and recycling receptacles should also be provided.

The mail sorting function is either manual or automated. If the sorting function is manual, the mail room should be planned to provide adequate counter space with storage above and below as well as an adequate divider or pigeonhole system for organizing the mail prior to distribution. If the sorting function is automated, the sorting area should be sized and designed to accommodate the equipment.

The mail room should provide sufficient hold space for carts, hand trucks, and bulk mail carts, and a portion of the mail room should have cage storage set aside if security for stored items is a consideration.

The primary planning consideration related to distribution is whether the mail will be picked up by employees or delivered to them. With a mail pickup procedure, the mail sorting dividers or pigeonhole system can function as a pickup location. If the mail is picked up and access to the mail room is controlled, the room should include a counter with direct access to the corridor to accommodate mail pickup. The counter should be securable.

All circulation corridors leading to the mail room should be finished with wall guards to protect the walls and finishes from cart damage. Finishes in the mail room should be selected for their durability and ease of maintenance. Figures 5.22 and 5.23 illustrate typical plans for small and large mail rooms.

Libraries

The location, sizing, components, and level of design of the library are based on the following primary considerations:

- Is the library considered an image element—that is, a space which is important in communicating the desired image of the organization—or a *back-of-house* function?
- Is the library a self-service or a supervised research facility?
- Is the location of the library convenient to the majority of its users?

If the library is considered an image element of the space, it should be located on the plan in close proximity to the reception area, a stairway internal to the organization's space which connects contiguous floors, or conference facilities in a location that is visible by visitors to the space. If the

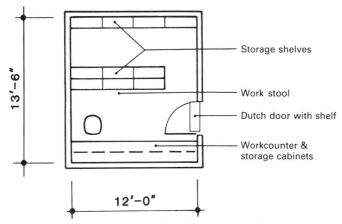

13'-6"

12'-0"

Storage shelves

Work stool

Dutch door with shelf

Workcounter &
storage cabinets

Figure 5.22. Typical small mail room plan.

library is only a functional element of the space, it should be located in a back-of-house area in close proximity to those staff members who use it most frequently. In great part, this decision should be based on the type of materials stored in the library and the type of work that the organization executes.

The size of the library should be based on the components that it must accommodate:

- Stacks (shelving) for materials storage
- Staff
- Circulation desk
- Staff work areas for mail, cataloging, and copying
- Carrels, worktables, or research rooms

These components, illustrated in Figure 5.24, are described in detail in the following section.

Stacks, shelving for books and periodicals, is the primary space component of any library. The amount of stacking required is assessed through a survey of historical data for prior growth records and uses, current shelving needs, and an estimate of growth. The projection for growth should take into consideration the increasing use of technology in the form of on-line research services as well as CD ROM storage systems.

The second consideration is the staffing of the library. The size of the staff depends on the amount of control and supervision the library will require. This can range from a self-service facility to a fully supervised library. A librarian, for example, would require a private office or a circulation desk as a work space. If additional clerks are employed, they would typically cover the circulation desk and also require individual work spaces or a shared workroom. Some libraries may have researchers who require private, quiet individual work spaces. The circulation desk is sized based on the number of people

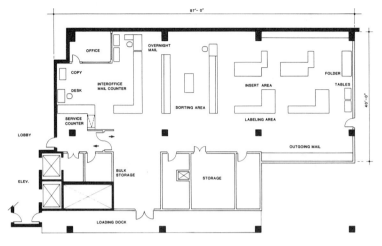

FURNITURE PLAN

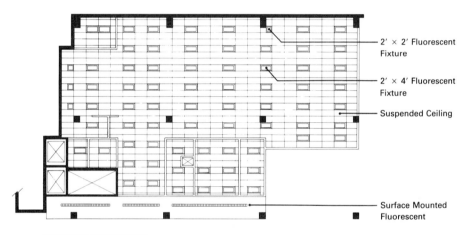

REFLECTED CEILING PLAN

Figure 5.23. This plan illustrates the functional requirements of a large mail room.

who will be staffing it at one time, the checkout procedures for materials, and whether the circulation desk also handles book return.

Work areas in the library provide space for stalls for receiving and sorting mail, cataloging functions, and copying equipment. If these work areas are not accessible to the library users, copy equipment should be located elsewhere so that it can be accessible to all. Research areas consist of individual carrels, work tables, or even work (or research) rooms, depending on the type of research to be done and the preference of the users. The total amount of research space will depend on the average number of users expected at any one time.

Other space requirements in the library include space for a card catalog or computer terminals, a private telephone closet to accommodate telephone use

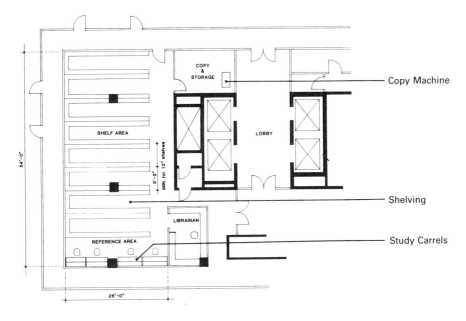

FURNITURE PLAN

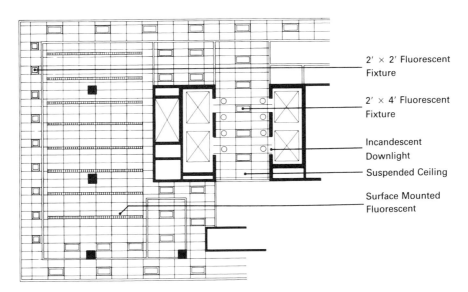

REFLECTED CEILING PLAN

Figure 5.24. Typical library plan.

without disturbing others, an informal reading area with current periodicals on display, and space for any file cabinets that may be required.

The organization of all of these components into a functioning library depends on the required amount of control over the access to materials. The circulation desk normally provides that control point. The location of the librarian's office is determined by the desired amount of access by library users and supervision of clerks. The workroom should be located to provide easy access from the circulation desk so that clerks can easily supervise both areas. Appropriate segregation of noisy functions (circulation desk, workroom) from quiet functions (research areas) is a primary consideration (Figure 5.24).

Finishes in the library vary, depending on the budget and the importance of the image of the space. Shelving can range in quality from painted wood, painted steel, or hardwood to a combination of these items. The circulation desk is often used as a design element. When image is important, glass is often used to allow guests to see into the library without disturbing library users.

The nature of the materials housed in some libraries often requires special planning considerations, such as humidity and temperature control and sprinklers. As with any other high-density storage areas, library stacks should be evaluated for special floor loading requirements.

Pantries

Pantries are small kitchen facilities frequently with an adjacent employee lunch area. Employee pantries should be convenient to general office and conference areas. Pantries are not cooking kitchens and do not contain cook surfaces (burners) or conventional ovens and are therefore only convenience facilities used for the preparation of coffee and light meals. The size and contents of the pantry are based on the number of personnel served. A typical pantry, however, contains a refrigerator, coffee maker, sink, microwave, and vending machines as well as counter and storage space. Sufficient space should be provided for trash and recycling receptacles (Figure 5.25).

Special Support

Special support refers to areas or rooms that support an entire organization or several organizations within a building or complex. These areas include:

- Day-care centers
- Fitness Facilities
- Cafeterias

Day-Care Centers

Many organizations now provide day-care centers to assist employees with child-care responsibilities. These facilities are normally licensed and regulated by state or local jurisdiction. These regulations dictate the planning and design of child-care facilities as well as the management and operation of the

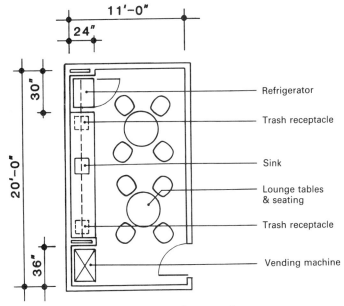

Figure 5.25. Typical pantry plan.

facility. All of the normal considerations for an interior environment become increasingly important here: fire and life safety, comfort, air quality and temperature, accessibility, security, and cleanability. The regulatory requirements for day-care facilities vary based on the type of operation and the age group(s) of the children. For example, some day-care facilities are emergency or occasional-use facilities, while others are full-care centers.

Typically, licensing requires an in-depth review process of the proposed program and facility, including:

- Staffing requirements/qualifications (adult–child ratios vary among different age groups)
- Program/curriculum (specific activities, amount of rest time, physical activities, play materials)
- Food preparation and snacks (national requirement)
- Health requirements (daily care and care of sick children)
- Record keeping
- Physical facilities

A day-care center should be located on grade in the building to provide for drop-off and pickup of the children and access for emergency vehicles. The center should also be convenient to a secure, fenced outdoor playground with play equipment.

The facility should comprise open-plan areas that are sized in accordance with regulations specifying square-footage allocations for children based on age group. The regulations also govern the design and location of the following types of support spaces:

- Sick room for isolation
- Toilet facilities and adjacent diapering areas with water-resistant, nonabsorbent floors, hard-finish walls, and adequate ventilation
- Storage space that is accessible to the children for toys and supplies
- Secure storage for administrative support equipment, supplies, and any substances or materials that might be harmful to the children
- Food service area and equipment
- Administrative staff support offices

Age groups are typically segregated within the day-care center. The specific planning and requirements of the open areas and support rooms vary based on those age groups. Figure 5.26 illustrates the segregation of functional areas based on age group.

Infants (2 to 12 months)
- Changing areas
- Low-height walls within space for visibility
- Food-preparation area with refrigerator
- Sink, storage, and microwave for heating formula
- Separate changing area with sink and storage
- Storage for each child's personal items

Infant areas must be located adjacent to exit for crib removal in case of fire.

Toddler (12 to 24, and 24 to 36 months)
- Classrooms
- Toilet area
- Staff work area
- Child-height sinks
- Changing table
- Storage for each child's personal items

Preschool (36 to 60, and 60 to 72 months)
- Classroom
- Central toilet facilities for both age groups
- Child-height sinks
- Staff work area

In addition to the state or local day-care regulatory requirements, the design of the space must adhere to all local building, fire and life safety codes. Obviously, the quality of the environment is an important consideration. The following are key design considerations:

- *Safety and Health:* The space must be completely free of lead or lead-containing finishes and all other toxic materials. In addition, all finishes

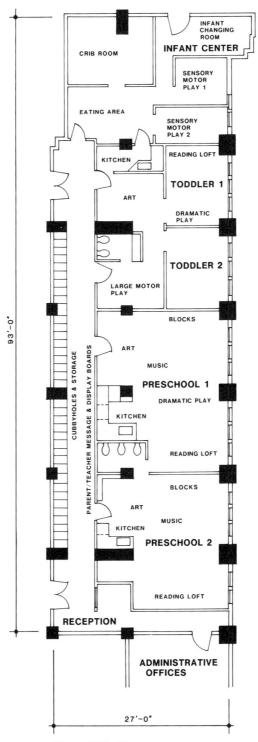

Figure 5.26. Day-care center.

should be durable, easy to maintain, and splinter free. Any sharp corners, protruding objects, or items hung from walls at a low height should be avoided. Accessible electrical outlets should be minimized. All accessible outlets should be childproofed. Internal hardware should be selected and placed for children's use. All exit doors must be installed with panic-released hardware that is not lockable from the outside. Carpet should be fire rated and of woven or cut pile. The floor should be heated in play areas. The space should have access to natural light and should be properly ventilated.

- *Scale and Accessibility:* The scale of all items to be reached and used by the children is a consideration in constructing, furnishing, and decorating the space. Sinks, toilets, and cabinets should all be at an appropriate height.
- *Visual Access for Staff:* The space should be designed to provide the facility's staff critical visual access to the children. These measures include the use of glass and low-height partitions.

Overall, the space should be designed as a stimulating, safe, and comfortable environment for the children.

Fitness Facilities

A growing awareness of the benefits of employee fitness has led to the increased use of office physical fitness facilities. These facilities vary dramatically in program and therefore in their planning and design requirements. Some facilities are simply small exercise rooms with weight equipment. Others include cardiovascular fitness programs as well as weight-training facilities (Figure 5.27). Often, the fitness center is designed with the intent to become a wellness facility with nutritional and health-related programs.

Decisions such as these related to the type of facility and the program direction for the facility must be resolved in order to determine the location and sizing of the fitness facility. The second consideration in planning the facility is the required capacity. Capacity is based on the hours of operation and the anticipated percentage of employee participation. A 20 to 25 percent participation rate is typical.

The facility should be located away from office areas to ensure that noise generated in the fitness facility does not intrude into office areas. The additional traffic to and from the facility can also affect general office areas if the fitness center is not removed from office areas. If the facility is open to users other than occupants of the building, the facility should be accessible to the public. Floor loading, plumbing and ceiling height requirements to accommodate equipment, and wet areas such as whirlpools or pools also affect the location of the facility. Components of a fitness center are described below.

Reception/Administrative Support. A typical physical fitness facility includes a desk/counter work area for a professional assigned to conduct exercise programs and monitor health safety practices. This area serves as a point of control for access to the facility.

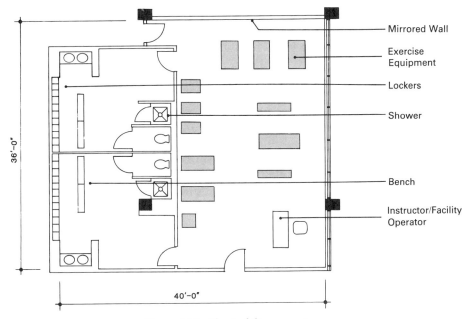

Figure 5.27. Physical fitness center.

Aerobic Rooms. Aerobic rooms should be sized in accordance with the typical class size and the anticipated activities during those classes. The floor is a primary design consideration in an aerobics room. The floor should be a wood aerobic floor with a cushioned back. If cost is a consideration, carpet is an alternative solution. Carpet should be level-loop nylon and antimicrobial. (See Chapter 7 for additional information on carpet). Walls in the room should be equipped with built-in mirrors of safety glass and a sound system for music.

Free-Weight Areas. Free-weight areas should be sized based on the number of weights and the required capacity. Again, the floor is a key consideration in the design of the room. The floor should be constructed with plywood subflooring. The flooring should be finished with a workout surface of thick, high-density, interlocking rubber squares designed for free-weight facilities.

Cardiovascular Training and Open Exercise Areas. These areas house cardiovascular equipment and provide open areas for individual exercise as well as warm-up and cool-down. These rooms should be carpeted with level-loop nylon antimicrobial carpet and equipped with mirrors, again constructed of safety glass.

Women's and Men's Dressing Rooms. These rooms should consist of a shower area, separate vanity area, and locker area with benches. Lockers should be provided in appropriate quantity to provide one locker per person for the maximum capacity of the center. The finishes in these areas should be antimicrobial, nonskid, durable, and easily maintainable.

Cafeterias

The first consideration in cafeteria planning is to determine the size of the area. The size is based primarily on the number of people to be served, and secondarily, on the menu to be served (a single-entrée menu requires less space than does a multiple-entrée menu.)

The number of people to be served should be determined based on an employee survey. Factors affecting attendance are proximity to other food establishments, relative cost of the food offered at the cafeteria, quality of the food served, and employee dining habits, such as whether employees typically bring their own meals.

After the number of people to be served is established, the number of shifts should be determined. Typically, two or three shifts are planned based on the hours of operation and level of service to be provided. The total number of people to be served divided by the number of shifts provides the dining area requirement. This dining area requirement multiplied by 10 to 15 square feet per person establishes the dining room seating area. Generally, the kitchen and serving area are the same size as the dining area.

The location of the cafeteria is the next consideration. The cafeteria should be centrally located to the people it serves; however, fire and life safety egress (exit) considerations are critical due to the large number of people who will be located in the area at the same time. For this reason, cafeterias normally are located on or near ground level.

Adjacencies to loading docks, refuse disposal, and service elevators are also critical. For acoustical reasons, a cafeteria that generates substantial noise levels should not be located directly adjacent to any general office or support areas. The extensive mechanical requirements for plumbing and drains below the cafeteria as well as exhaust shafts above the cafeteria should also be taken into consideration in locating the facility.

Most cafeterias consist of three primary areas: food preparation or kitchen, serving (which may be single line or scatter), and dining (Figure 5.28). The cafeteria space plan is dictated by achieving an orderly flow of people and food through the space. A successfully designed cafeteria prevents any conflict of circulation among people entering, obtaining food, eating, and disposing of the trays, and exiting. This circulation must be accomplished in such a way that it also supports the kitchen requirements.

The basic requirement of the kitchen is to move the food from the loading dock through the preparation area to the serving area. The soiled china, hardware, and trays must then be moved back from the dining area for cleaning and reuse.

Finishes in all three areas should be considered for durability and cleanability factors. Both wall and floor surfaces in dining and serving areas should be nonabsorbent, hard, and cleanable. Materials should be selected to meet health code requirements. The dining area carpet and upholstering should be of 100 percent nylon fabric and should be made of colors that resist soiling.

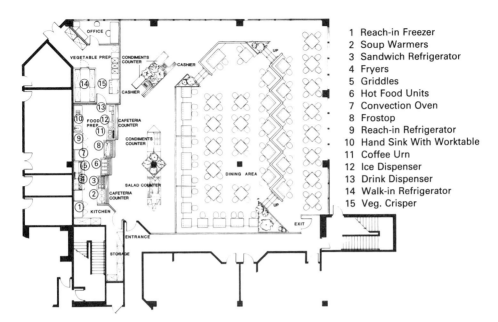

1 Reach-in Freezer
2 Soup Warmers
3 Sandwich Refrigerator
4 Fryers
5 Griddles
6 Hot Food Units
7 Convection Oven
8 Frostop
9 Reach-in Refrigerator
10 Hand Sink With Worktable
11 Coffee Urn
12 Ice Dispenser
13 Drink Dispenser
14 Walk-in Refrigerator
15 Veg. Crisper

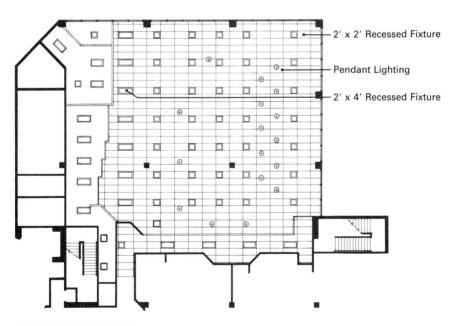

2' x 2' Recessed Fixture

Pendant Lighting

2' x 4' Recessed Fixture

REFLECTED CEILING PLAN

Figure 5.28. Cafeteria.

Tables and chairs should also be selected for cleanability and durability. Dining trays should be sized appropriately for the dining tables.

These considerations are general and will vary based on the specific facility. A food service consultant should be brought into the project to assist in sizing, locating, and designing the cafeteria.

THE AMERICANS WITH DISABILITIES ACT

The Americans with Disabilities Act (ADA) of 1990 makes it unlawful to discriminate against a qualified person with a disability in the areas of employment, state and local government services, public accommodations, transportation, and telecommunications. Title III of the six-title act specifically addresses public accommodations. This title affects the standards for the design and construction of public accommodations and commercial facilities.

The ADA defines as public accommodation any private entity that owns, leases, or operates a place of public accommodation and lists 12 categories, such as hotels, restaurants, public transportation station, sales or service establishment, place of recreation, or place of education.

The ADA defines *commercial facilities* as facilities intended for nonresidential use by a private entity and whose operation affect commerce. Examples of a commercial facility are office buildings, factories, and other buildings of employment.

Public accommodations must meet the requirements for removal of architectural and communications barriers, whereas commercial facilities must do so to the extent that the facility must be accessible to employees, clients, or customers with disabilities.

As a civil rights law, the ADA cannot actually be enforced by code or permit unless the requirements are adopted by local or state jurisdictions. If they are not adopted by jurisdictions, action may be taken by a person or persons thought to be discriminated against or about to be discriminated against. This person or persons can pursue remedies through civil rights action.

Impact on Office Design

The ADA calls for the removal of architectural and communication barriers. An architectural barrier is a physical object that impedes a disabled person's access to or use of a facility. These types of barriers would include stairs (if they are the only means of access), or corridors that prevent passage in a wheelchair. Communication barriers that are architectural or structural in nature include fire annunciation systems, signage programs, or telephone locations.

The ADA requires that the removal of these barriers be done in compliance with the act's specification, unless not readily achievable. In that case, it is acceptable to make other alterations as necessary to make the facility accessible.

The act provides technical specifications for building parking, accessibility for exterior, and accessibility for interior. The following is a summary of key items covered by ADA. More detailed information on ADA can be obtained from the resources listed in the reference section.

- *Accessible Routes:* entrance requirements, elevator requirements, widths, passing space, headroom, slope, changes in level, ground and floor surfaces, carpet, protruding objects, clear floor space, reach ranges, controls and operating mechanisms, means of egress, areas of rescue assistance
- *Ramps:* slope, clear width, landings, handrails, surfaces, cross slope, edge protection, outdoor conditions
- *Stairs:* treads and riser, nosings, handrails, outdoor conditions
- *Elevators:* where elevators are required, automatic operation, hall call buttons, hall lanterns, characters on hoistway entrances, door protective and reopening devices, door and signal timing for hall calls, door delay for car calls, floor plan of elevator cars, floor surfaces, illumination levels, car control buttons and indicators, car control height and location, car position indicators, emergency communications
- *Doors:* number of accessible doors, double-leaf doors, clear width, maneuvering clearances, two doors in series, thresholds, hardware, closures, opening force, automatic doors
- *Drinking Fountains:* location and number, spout height and location, controls, operation, clearances
- *Toilet Rooms and Bathrooms:* number and location of accessible rooms, doors, clear floor space, signage, controls and dispensers, accessible elements as well as specification for water closets, toilet stalls, urinals, lavatories and mirrors, sinks, bathtubs, shower stalls
- *Assembly Areas:* wheelchair locations, assistive lighting systems, access to performing areas, placement of wheelchair locations, size of wheelchair locations, surfaces, placement and types of listening systems
- *Storage:* location, clear floor space, height, hardware
- *Alarms:* location and number of audible and visual alarms, auxiliary alarms
- *Signage:* location, type, character proportion and height, raised and brailled characters and pictograms, finish and contrast, mounting location and height, symbols of accessibility
- *Telephones:* location and number of accessible telephones, clear floor space, mounting height, protruding objects, hearing-aid compatible and volume control, controls, books, cord length, text telephones
- *Seating and Tables:* seating, knee clearances, table and counter height

This chapter has highlighted the planning considerations associated with the three primary space components of the office environment: general office areas, circulation, and support areas. In addition to the accurate location and sizing of these spaces, the building support systems, specifically, HVAC, power, and fire safety, must be appropriately designed for the spaces to ensure that all user requirements are met. The following chapter describes these basic systems, the objectives associated with them, and their applications.

Chapter Six

Support Systems

Any description of design considerations for the office environment would be incomplete without a discussion of the primary engineering systems that support the function, comfort, and safety of the office user:

- HVAC systems
- Power distribution systems
- Fire protection systems

Although these systems are, for the most part, in evidence only above the ceiling, below the floors, and behind the walls, we have become reliant on their effectiveness and dependability.

As our needs have become more sophisticated and as technology has improved, the design and operation of the systems have become increasingly complex. The purpose of this chapter is to convey in simple terms the design of the basic systems and their applications in the office environment.

HVAC SYSTEMS

Heating, ventilating, and air conditioning (HVAC) systems condition outdoor and indoor air to create a desired indoor environment. In the office, the desired environment is one that provides a safe, healthy, comfortable climate and supports the productivity of employees. These systems work by taking in outdoor air, conditioning that air, and combining it with indoor air. The mixed air is then delivered to indoor spaces through a distribution system of ducts. Effective conditioning of the air requires the manipulation of several variables:

- Heating and cooling

- Air motion and distribution
- Humidification and dehumidification
- Ventilation
- Indoor air quality

The design of HVAC systems warrants serious consideration in the context of the office environment, for several reasons. First, the effectiveness with which the indoor environment is controlled has a significant impact on employee performance by affecting both their comfort and health. Second, the health implications of poor indoor air quality are becoming increasingly clear, as are the associated responsibilities of employers and building managers to provide a safe work environment for workers. Third, the conditioning of outside air for use in the indoor environment constitutes approximately 10 percent of the energy consumed in the United States. The need for conservation in the face of dwindling energy supplies demands energy-efficient design of HVAC systems.

Heating and Cooling

The primary purpose for heating and cooling the indoor environment is to create a temperature range comfortable for the occupants of the space. Generally, that range is between 68 and 78 degrees Fahrenheit. Temperature control is also a consideration for the proper operation of office equipment, particularly sensitive computer systems. To achieve this control, the HVAC system must provide heating and cooling to compensate for external and internal heat loads created in the space. External heat loads are created by the sun and vary based on geographic location, season, and time of day. Internal heat loads are created by lights, people, and equipment and vary from area to area within the office, depending on the use of the space. An effective HVAC system design must provide the flexibility to accommodate these changing loads.

Air Motion and Distribution

As conditioned air is delivered to a space, it is delivered at a specific velocity. That velocity affects the level of comfort in the space by altering the temperature as perceived by the occupant. Generally, more air motion is more comfortable in higher temperatures with more humidity, and less air motion is more comfortable at lower temperatures and humidity. Also, the greater the air velocity, the greater the potential for drafts, an unwanted and uncomfortable cooling of the body.

The distribution of air throughout a space is also a consideration. If improperly distributed, the conditioned air is stratified and creates uneven temperatures throughout the space. Both the air velocity and distribution must be controlled to prevent unnecessary noise in the space. The objective, therefore, is to deliver air efficiently at the desired temperature and humidity while minimizing temperature stratification, draft, and noise.

Humidification and Dehumidification

The acceptable humidification in the office environment is 20 to 50 percent, a range that is considered comfortable for human beings. Higher or lower humidification levels not only are less comfortable but contribute to poor air quality by promoting microbial growth in the space.

Ventilation

Ventilation is outdoor air or fresh air delivered to the indoor environment. Ventilation was provided in even the earliest HVAC system designs by bringing outdoor air into the system, heating or cooling the air, and delivering the conditioned air to the occupied office space. That air was then exhausted as additional ventilation was conditioned and introduced into the space. A substantial amount of ventilation was also achieved through infiltration: the air that "leaked" into the space around doors and windows, or through walls and roofs.

This approach to ventilation changed dramatically, however, during the energy crisis of the 1970s, because of the significant amount of energy required to condition then-accepted levels of ventilation. To reduce the amount of energy expended on conditioning ventilation, the building industry responded by reducing the amount of ventilation brought into the indoor environment. This was achieved by taking in less ventilation through the HVAC system and by implementing tighter construction methods to decrease natural infiltration. This modified approach to building design did realize greater energy efficiency, but unfortunately did so at the expense of air quality.

Indoor Air Quality

The quality of indoor air in the office environment has become a major consideration because poor air quality has been identified as a threat to worker health and productivity.

Health problems related to indoor air quality were first attributed to the modified construction practices of the 1970s and 1980s when workers occupying energy-efficient buildings began to suffer from fatigue, headaches, and irritation to mucous membranes. These symptoms were named *tight building syndrome* in reference to the perceived cause: reduced building ventilation.

Tight building syndrome is now called *Sick Building Syndrome* in recognition of the fact that reduced ventilation is only one factor affecting air quality–related illnesses. Sick building syndrome refers to a condition in which building occupants experience such discomfort as fatigue, headaches, and irritation to eyes and nose. These symptoms are associated with the building and usually subside within 1 or 2 hours after workers leave the building. The building occupants have no actual clinical illness. In contrast, building-related illness refers to a specific disease that is attributed to air quality and is accompanied by physical signs and clinical abnormalities, such as Legionnaire's disease.

Hundreds of chemical, gas, and particle contaminants found in indoor air are the cause of these symptoms and illnesses. These contaminants are introduced into the indoor environment from a number of sources, including people, office equipment, furnishings, cleaning solvents, and the building construction materials (Figure 6.1).

Building materials and furnishings contribute to indoor pollution in two ways. The first is by microbial growth or colonization by fungi and bacteria on interior services such as fabrics, carpet, wall covering, rubber, and electrical conduit. The second is through *volatile organic compounds* (VOCs). VOCs are synthetic materials found in office furnishings and building materials. These materials emit harmful vapors or gases such as formaldehyde, acetone, benzene, propane, and butane. The impact of VOCs in the office environment is exacerbated by tight construction schedules. Previously, construction schedules allowed most of this emission to occur during the manufacturing process or while the materials remained warehoused as inventory. Early occupancies now drive shorter and shorter construction schedules. Shorter construction schedules result in abbreviated manufacturing processes and shipment of materials directly to the construction site, which results in the off-gassing of these harmful chemicals in occupied offices.

HVAC systems can also be a significant contributor to poor air quality. In fact, two-thirds of building-related illnesses are due to mechanical systems, and one-third to two-thirds of building-related sicknesses result specifically from humidity and temperature problems. HVAC-related air quality problems originate in either the design of the system or the maintenance and operation of the system. Factors that are believed to contribute to the problem are the adequacy of ventilation and the quality of that ventilation as well as the accumulation of dust and microorganisms in ducts, diffusers, and humidification systems.

Air of an acceptable quality contains no contaminants at concentrations that are harmful to human beings. The definition, however, begs the question: At what concentrations do these contaminants become irritating, uncomfortable, or harmful to people, and how can they be reduced or eliminated from the indoor environment?

Indoor air can be assessed by an indoor air study to identify contaminants and sources of contamination. Human- or building-caused pollution is virtually

---

- Soil gases
- People
- HVAC systems
- Water coolers
- Office equipment
- Cleaning substances
- Tobacco smoke
- Microbial growth
- Outside air
- Inorganic volatile compounds from furniture and furnishings

Figure 6.1. A few of the main sources of indoor air contamination.

impossible to eliminate, so treatment focuses on methods of dilution and removal of contaminants. HVAC-generated pollution can virtually be eliminated by proper systems design, maintenance, and operation. Measures to ensure acceptable indoor air quality include:

- High-quality outdoor air
- Proper air distribution
- Proper filtering
- Use of sound traps or duct silencers rather than acoustical duct liners
- Proper humidity controls
- Selection of construction materials and furnishings that reduce the amount of VOCs used in the office

Basic HVAC System Design

Fundamentally, heating systems provide heat to the indoor environment through electricity or by burning fossil fuel. That heat is then distributed through a medium of water or air. Cooling systems remove heat from an indoor environment by transferring the heat from indoor air and ventilation to a transfer medium such as water or refrigerant and then rejecting that heat to the outdoor environment. Both ventilation (fresh air), which is considered *primary air,* and *secondary air* (air in the indoor environment) are mixed during this process to supply the necessary volume of air to the conditioned space. In most systems, the ventilation is taken in, filtered, and then heated or cooled. It is then humidified or dehumidified before it is distributed throughout the space. That air is referred to as *supply air.* Secondary air is then exhausted from the conditioned space and replaced with supply air.

Originally, HVAC systems were designed simply to provide warm-air heat and ventilation from central equipment located outside the conditioned space through ducts into the space to be conditioned. Subsequently, the capability to cool and humidify was added to the system. This approach was effective as long as the heat loads throughout the space were fairly uniform. Increasing use of office equipment, however, created varying heat loads throughout the space and established a need for systems that could accommodate those varying loads. As a result, spaces were divided into zones, and additional equipment, which could be independently controlled, was used to augment the central system.

The selection of an HVAC system is based on performance characteristics, system capacity, and the availability of space in the building to accommodate the equipment. These parameters alone will normally narrow the options to a few systems. Further evaluation of each system is based on the following requirements for the space to be conditioned:

- Heating/cooling loads
- Humidification/dehumidification requirements
- Zoning requirements (each space that requires a different control zone to maintain a constant temperature)
- Ventilation requirements

- Architectural constraints of the space (structure, size, and appearance considerations)
- Noise level created by the system

Ultimately, the system must meet these selection criteria and must provide the required flexibility to meet changing requirements through the life of the system. It must also meet the constraints for initial cost as well as operating and maintenance costs.

Typically, two systems are actually selected and used in conjunction: a primary system that converts energy from fuel or electricity and provides capacity to a secondary system, which then distributes the heating or cooling to the occupied space.

The primary types of HVAC systems are:

- Basic central system
- All-air systems
- Air and water systems
- All-water systems
- Unitary refrigerant-based systems
- Heat pump systems
- Heat recovery systems

Basic Central System

The basic central system is an all-air, constant-volume, single-zone system (Figure 6.2); that is, only air is used for heating and cooling. *Constant volume* refers to the fact that a constant volume of air is always delivered to the space. Adjustments to the air delivered to the space are made changing temperature of the supply air or balancing the system. The central system is typically housed outside the area to be conditioned in a penthouse, core area, or basement. A central system has several applications:

- As a source of conditioned air for spaces where the heat gains and losses are uniform, such as general office areas in open plan, auditoriums, or theaters. In these large, open spaces, the lack of partitions or use of low-height partitions allows greater and more even distribution of the air and equalization of the temperatures throughout the space.
- As a source of conditioned air for isolated spaces requiring precision control of temperature, humidity, and cleanliness.
- As a primary source of conditioned air for secondary systems.

All-Air Systems

All-air systems, as described under basic central systems, provide heating and cooling to the conditioned space through the use of air only. These all-air systems are of two basic types:

- Single-path systems, in which airflow for both heating and cooling coils uses a common duct distribution system and a common air temperature
- Dual-path systems, in which the heating and cooling coils are located in

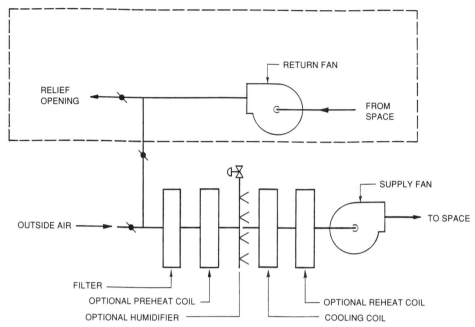

Figure 6.2. The basic central system is a constant-volume system.

separate, parallel, cold- and warm-air duct distribution systems or a single supply duct to each zone with a blending of warm and cold air

Reheat Systems. A modification of the single-zone system, a reheat system applies heat to either preconditioned primary air or recirculated room air. The medium for heating can be hot water, steam, or electricity.

The applications for the reheat system are situations requiring cooling for the interior of the space throughout the year, as well as seasonal heating and cooling for the perimeter. Since three of the four requirements are for cooling, it is less expensive to provide heating on the perimeter through the reheat unit than to provide central heating.

The advantage to the reheat system, therefore, is that it allows zoned control for areas of unequal heat loading and allows heating or cooling of perimeter areas with different exposures. The disadvantage is the high energy consumption of this type of system.

Variable Air Volume System. A variable air volume (VAV) system accommodates load variations by regulating the volume of air supplied through a single duct (Figure 6.3). That is, the temperature of the supply air remains constant. The load variations in each space are managed by delivering different quantities of air (at that constant temperature) to each area. Special zoning is not required because each space supplied by a controlled outlet is a separate zone.

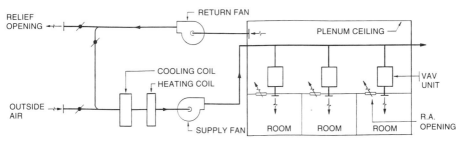

Figure 6.3. Simple variable air volume system.

The variable air volume system has several advantages. Initial cost is low because the system requires only single ducts and simple controls. Operating costs are also the lowest among the all-air systems. The disadvantage is that although it is capable of providing heating, it is primarily a cooling system and is best suited to situations in which cooling is required most of the year.

With the dual- or double-duct system, the central station supplies warm air through one duct run and cold air through another. The temperature in each space is then controlled by a thermostat that mixes the warm and cool air in proper proportions.

The advantage of the dual-duct system is that it allows great flexibility in satisfying multiple loads and in providing temperature response. Space or zone thermostats can be set once to control year-round temperature conditions. The disadvantage of the dual-duct system is that it is high in energy consumption. As a result, few of these systems are now utilized.

Multizone System. In a multizone system, a thermostat controls each zone or area requiring individual temperature control. The system mixes warm and cold air at the central station and provides air through a single duct to each zone at the temperature indicated by the thermostat. The multizone system provides flexibility and lower cost than does the dual-duct system. Its disadvantage is that it is limited by the number of zones that can be provided with each central station.

Air and Water Systems

Air and water systems distribute both air and water to a space to perform the cooling function. Both cooling and heating occur by changing the air or water temperature (or both). The air side of the system typically supplies primary, cooled air to each area at a constant volume. The water is pumped through distribution pipes within each conditioned space and runs over coils where the heat exchange occurs. The room temperatures are controlled by varying the capacity of the coils or by regulating the water flowing over or through it.

These systems are categorized as one-, two-, three-, and four-pipe systems. The two-pipe system provides one supply and one return pipe (Figure 6.4). Three pipe-systems provide cold-water supply, warm-water supply, and a

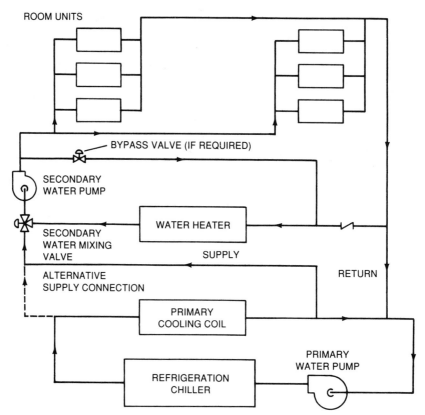

Figure 6.4. Air and water two-pipe system.

common return. The three-pipe system is rarely used today because of excess energy consumption. The four-pipe system has separate supplies and returns for both cold and warm water (Figure 6.5). The four-pipe system is more flexible and responsive to varying loads than is the two-pipe system; it is also simpler to operate and more efficient. Although the initial cost of the four-pipe system is greater than that of the two-pipe system, the four-pipe system costs less to operate.

In addition to flexibility, one of the primary advantages of the air and water system is that it requires less physical space to accommodate the system than does an all-air system. This is a result of the greater density of water to allow the same heat exchange as the all-air system, yet with smaller distribution systems (pipes) than the ductwork required for the all-air system. The application of these systems is primarily to exterior spaces of buildings with high loads and where close control of humidity is not required.

Air–Water Induction Systems. In the air–water induction system, centrally conditioned primary air is supplied to the unit plenum (area between the slab and the dropped ceiling) at high pressure. The air flows through a series of induction nozzles and induces secondary air from the room through

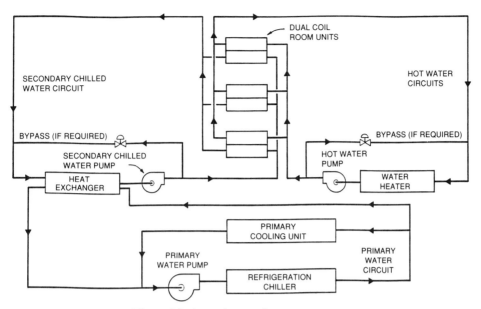

Figure 6.5. Air and water four-pipe system.

the secondary coil. The secondary coil is either heated or cooled (Figure 6.6). Induction units are usually installed under a window at a perimeter wall.

The advantages of the induction system are individual control at relatively low cost and less space for the distribution system. Its primary disadvantage is that it is limited to perimeter space applications and therefore requires the use of another system for interior spaces. The system is also very energy intensive.

Air–Water Fan-Coil Systems. The air–water fan-coil system is similar to the induction unit system. The primary difference is the substitution of a fan-coil unit for the induction unit. The advantages and disadvantages of the induction unit are similar to those for the fan-coil unit. Additionally, the fan-coil system requires no primary air system.

All-Water Systems
All-water systems heat and cool by transfer between water and air. Hot-water systems deliver heat to a space by water that is hotter than the air. All-water systems rarely used in new buildings include baseboard and free-standing radiators (Figure 6.7).

Fan-Coil Units. All-water systems can also be used for cooling. These systems move air by forced convection through the conditioned space, filter the circulating air, and introduce ventilation. Terminal units with cold-water coils, heating coils, and blowers are used. Chilled and hot water flows to the fan-

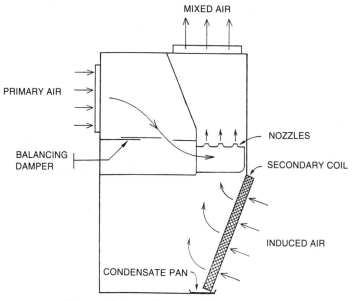

Figure 6.6. Air and water induction system.

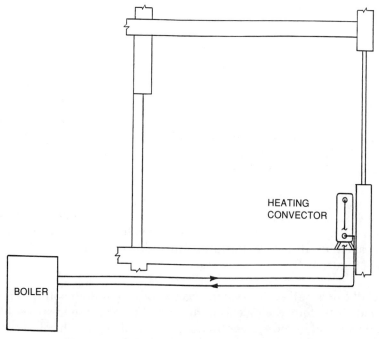

Figure 6.7. All-water freestanding radiator system.

coil unit through a two-pipe or four-pipe distribution system. The two-pipe system supplies either cold water or hot water (Figure 6.8).

The advantage of the all-water system is that it allows shutoff to local areas that are not in use. A primary disadvantage of the system is that it requires more maintenance than central all-air systems and that maintenance must occur in the occupied areas of the building in which the system is in use.

Unitary Refrigerant-Based Systems

Unitary refrigerant systems are similar to room air conditioners. They are self-contained units installed and operated as a package, requiring no additional apparatus (Figure 6.9). The applications for the system are as supplemental cooling in a small rooms, such as computer rooms, and as primary conditioning of perimeter spaces. For a small load, the advantages of a unitary refrigerant-based system are that it is relatively inexpensive, flexible and portable. The disadvantages are that it only cools, has limited capacity, and can be noisy.

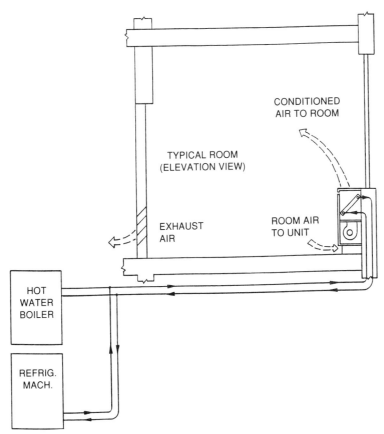

Figure 6.8. All-water fan-coil unit.

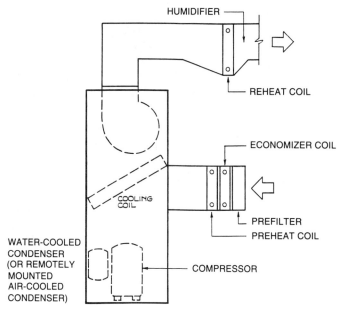

Figure 6.9. Unitary refrigerant-based system.

Heat Pump Systems

Heat pump systems takes heat from the outside air and draws it inside. This primary air flows through refrigeration equipment, where, when heating is desired, the heat is taken from the outside air and given up to the conditioned space and when cooling and dehumidification are desired, is removed from the space and rejected to the outside (Figure 6.10).

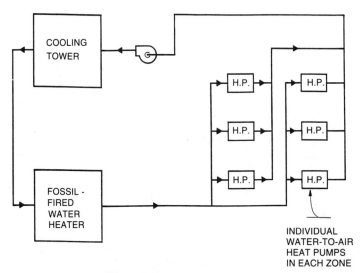

Figure 6.10. Heat pump system.

A heat pump system is particularly effective in temperate climates that create moderate loads, circumstances in which the system is relatively efficient. The disadvantage of a heat pump system is that it can be costly to operate and maintain.

Heat Recovery Systems

Heat recovery systems recover heat generated by equipment such as computers and internal building systems from conditioned air before that air is exhausted outside (Figure 6.11). For example, a heat recovery system would capture the heat produced by a computer room or cafeteria equipment and transfer that energy for the purpose of heating or cooling. The primary advantage of a heat recovery system is energy conservation. The disadvantage of a heat recovery system is its high initial cost. Generally, to cost justify the system, the internal heat source must be constant and extreme.

POWER DISTRIBUTION SYSTEMS

The responsibility for the design and specification of power distribution systems in the office building is that of the electrical engineer. The electrical engineer designs these systems to meet current and anticipated power requirements for the building users. This includes the design of the base building power distribution system as well as the distribution on each floor of the building into the office environment. Electrical systems are considered life safety systems and therefore must be designed within the parameters of local and state codes and the National Electrical Code.

Main Service

The local utility is responsible for delivering power to the general office building through service feeders or wires located above ground on power poles or buried underground (the more typical distribution method). The utility transmits the power at a highly efficient voltage. The utility terminates service and responsibility for the power at the point of entry into the office building, the main service switch, also referred to as a current transformer (c/t cabinet). Here the power is metered and transformed down to a lower and less efficient standard service voltage for use throughout the building.

From the main service switch to individual floors of the building, power is distributed in one of two ways: bus duct or feeder and conduit (Figure 6.12). A *bus duct* is a large duct containing copper or aluminum ducts. The bus duct runs vertically through the building carrying the service standard voltage to each floor. At each floor the bus duct contains plug-in ports, allowing a tap to the power to feed that floor. One of the primary advantages of a bus duct system is that it provides flexibility for the design of future power distribution.

Feeder and conduit refers to power distribution by running copper wires called feeders carrying the electrical current in metal tubes (conduit) for safety and protection of the wires. The feeder and conduit runs from the main service switchboard to branch circuit panel boards on each floor. When the power

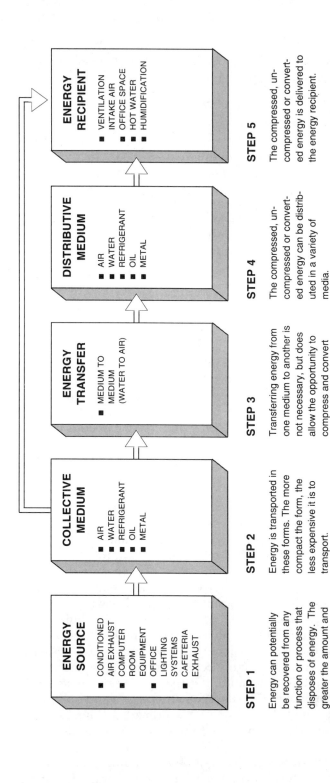

ENERGY SOURCE
- CONDITIONED AIR EXHAUST
- COMPUTER ROOM EQUIPMENT
- OFFICE LIGHTING SYSTEMS
- CAFETERIA EXHAUST

COLLECTIVE MEDIUM
- AIR
- WATER
- REFRIGERANT
- OIL
- METAL

ENERGY TRANSFER
- MEDIUM TO MEDIUM (WATER TO AIR)

DISTRIBUTIVE MEDIUM
- AIR
- WATER
- REFRIGERANT
- OIL
- METAL

ENERGY RECIPIENT
- VENTILATION
- INTAKE AIR
- OFFICE SPACE
- HOT WATER
- HUMIDIFICATION

STEP 1

Energy can potentially be recovered from any function or process that disposes of energy. The greater the amount and consistency of the energy from the source, the greater the probability that the recovery system will be successful.

STEP 2

Energy is transported in these forms. The more compact the form, the less expensive it is to transport.

STEP 3

Transferring energy from one medium to another is not necessary, but does allow the opportunity to compress and convert the energy into a smaller volume for transporting it at a lower cost.

STEP 4

The compressed, un-compressed or convert-ed energy can be distrib-uted in a variety of media.

STEP 5

The compressed, un-compressed or convert-ed energy is delivered to the energy recipient.

Figure 6.11. Heat recovery system.

150

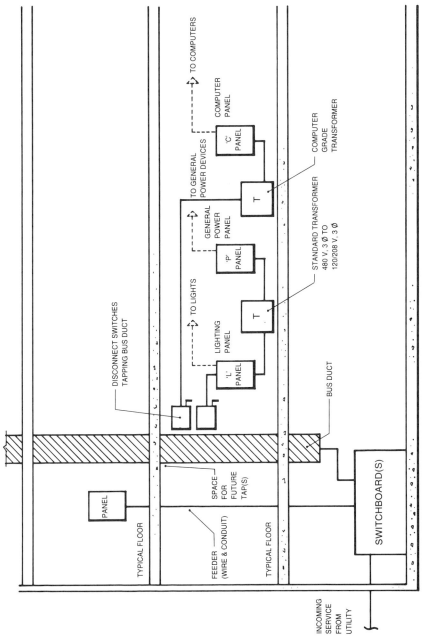

Figure 6.12. This diagram illustrates the distribution of power in a building from the main service switch to the general office areas.

151

distribution requirements of the tenant are known at the time of the base building design and construction or retrofit, a feeder and conduit distribution system can be designed specifically to meet the requirements on each floor. The feeder and conduit system is a less expensive distribution system but provides less flexibility than does the bus duct.

Power runs from the bus duct or feeder and conduit to a panel board on each floor. From the panel board, the wiring carried to the tenant floor into the office environment is called the *branch circuiting*.

Wire Management (Branch Circuiting)

Wire management is the effective handling of branch circuiting for power, voice, and data distribution systems throughout office floors. The emphasis on effective wire management results from the extensive use of open-planning concepts and increased use of office automation.

In closed plan, distribution occurs above the ceiling or below the floor and through walls, to terminate as close to the point of use as possible. Almost all of the distribution system is concealed and is not a safety or aesthetic concern. In open plan, however, wiring can be distributed in the ceiling, floor, and wall only to the point where the wiring enters the open-plan area. At that point, coordination and management of the distribution systems become complicated.

Distribution systems are categorized as either ceiling or under-floor systems. In either case, all power wiring is located in conduit or raceways to provide protection from physical or fire damage and to prevent the spread of fire caused by the power cables. Voice and data cables are not typically installed in conduit or raceways unless security or the threat of physical damage to the cables are of concern. This allows flexibility of relocation and reduces the cost of installation. The cabling is treated, however, with fire-resistant materials to prevent damage as well as the spread of flames, smoke, and toxins through the mechanical air system.

Ceiling Systems

The most common location for the distribution system is above the finished ceiling. Wiring runs from the core closets above the ceiling through the plenum (open area between the slab and the ceiling) and either down through fixed walls and columns or through power poles.

In a fixed-wall system, the wiring runs from the ceiling plenum down walls or furred-out columns (columns that have been built out to create a space) to the outlets (Figure 6.13). If the space is open plan with no existing walls, it is possible to locate hard wall areas such as closets and file enclosures in the open space. Wiring is easily redistributed without damage to ceiling or walls to implement changes.

Power poles present an inexpensive distribution method in open plan where no walls exist. Wires from the ceiling plenum run through power poles into the furniture system (Figure 6.14). Power poles, however, are not preferred as an aesthetic solution and therefore are not commonly used anymore.

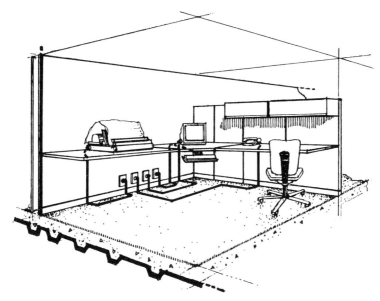

Figure 6.13. Fixed wall wire management system.

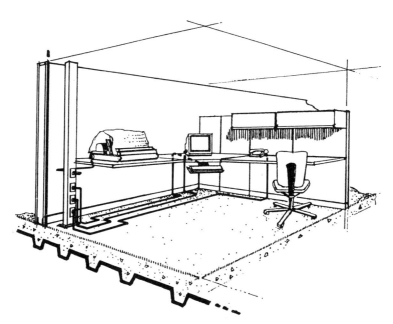

Figure 6.14. Power pole wire management system.

Under-Floor Systems

The under-floor distribution system offers more flexibility and ease of coordination and is located closer to the point of use than is the above-ceiling system, yet it is a more costly alternative. Wiring is distributed from the core closet through one of the following systems:

- Cellular system
- Poke-through system
- Flat wire
- Raised access floor

Cellular Systems. The cellular system, compared with above-ceiling distribution systems, is relatively inflexible and for that reason is rarely used in today's office environment. The system comprises a trench header duct running through the slab from the core closet throughout the office floor and incorporates a series of closed ducts with access points at regular intervals that are perpendicular to the trench header duct (Figure 6.15). This duct has a removable cover and is fully accessible over the entire length of the system. Wires are pulled through separate compartments within the ducts, and outlets are located on the floor at the access points as needed. The outlet, often referred to as a *monument*, is mounted on the surface of the floor.

One of the reasons for the cellular system's lack of flexibility is that it must be installed when the building is constructed. Consequently, installation

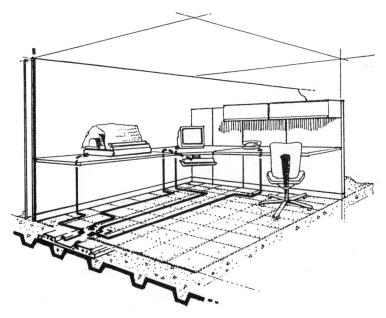

Figure 6.15. Cellular wire management system.

typically occurs without information on user requirements. Additionally, the system restricts planning options. To access the system, the areas above the trench header duct must remain open and therefore can be used only as circulation paths. Also, the monument locations must be determined prior to furniture installation. As a result, monuments frequently interfere with furniture system panel placement.

To allow access to the ducts, carpet must be installed with a quick-release adhesive in a direct-glue-down application. In a broad loom carpet installation, seams remain untaped, thus establishing a weak point in the carpet installation that can create a safety, aesthetic, and maintenance problem. When monuments are relocated, the original access point must be covered by patching the carpet, again leaving a vulnerable and unattractive point in the carpet. For these reasons, modular carpet is normally used with underfloor systems.

Poke-Through System. A more costly under-floor system, but one frequently used, is the poke-through or core drilling method. Cabling runs from the core closet down to the ceiling plenum space of the floor below and back up through a hole drilled in the slab. The cabling then runs up through walls to a location near the floor or into outlets located in the floor (Figure 6.16). The poke-through method is not typically used for slab-on-grade conditions or with some types of slab structures because of the increased installation cost. The poke-through wire management system is one of the most common methods of running wiring into a floor when no partitions or columns can be used for distribution and access floor is not a reasonable alternative.

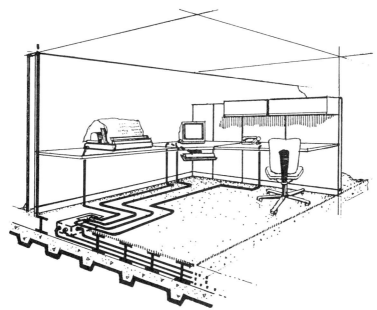

Figure 6.16. Poke-through wire management system.

Flat Wire. Flat wire is literally a flat cable that can be used for power, voice, and data distribution. The wire is distributed over the slab under the carpet to the desired outlet or floor monument location (Figure 6.17). It is most applicable in new or older buildings where open plan is used and slab-to-slab dimensions prevent the use of a raised access floor.

Although flat wire is a relatively recent development in wire distribution, it is not a popular application, for several reasons. The primary reason is the inability to flatten voice and data cabling successfully. Although voice cables have been flattened to accommodate flat wire distribution methods, the transmission suffers. Data cabling has never been flattened as successfully. Secondarily, carpet tiles must be used with the system for accessibility to the wires, and carpet tiles are often eliminated as an option, for aesthetic reasons.

Raised Access Floor Raised access floor is a floor constructed of pedestals and panels installed on top of the structural slab to create a cavity for the flexible distribution of wires and mechanical systems (Figure 6.18). The floor is typically raised from 6 to 8 inches above the slab in office areas and 12 to 24 inches above the slab in computer rooms.

Wiring runs from the core closet beneath the access floor to a junction box to a connector (pigtail) and then to an outlet. The outlet is usually mounted on the building slab and accessed through a box or grommet in the floor panel or directly in the floor panel (Figure 6.19).

Raised access floor is the most flexible wire distribution system. It is typi-

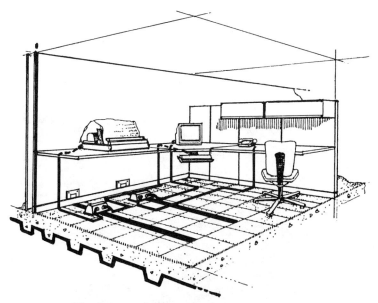

Figure 6.17. Flat-wire management system.

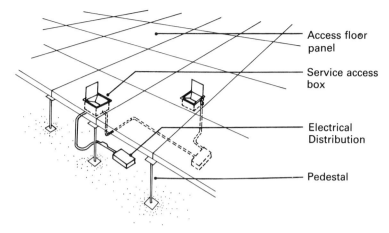

Figure 6.18. This illustration details the junction box connection to a pigtail and outlet.

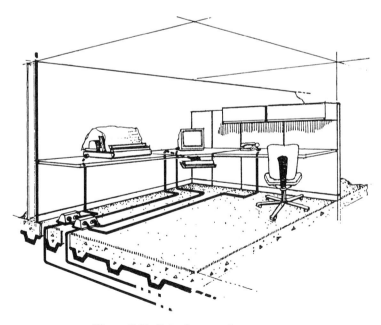

Figure 6.19. Raised access floor system.

cally installed in new buildings, but may be retrofitted in existing buildings if the slab-to-slab dimension is sufficient and the slab structure can handle the additional load. In all raised-floor installations, carpet tiles must be used for accessibility.

Segregation of Loads

One of the current issues in the distribution of power in the office environment is the segregation of what are called *dirty* and *clean loads.* General office equipment such as copiers create fluctuations in voltage that can cause damage to sensitive electronic equipment such as computers. The load created by this general office equipment is referred to as a dirty load. To protect sensitive equipment (clean load) from dirty loads, power distribution must be segregated.

The separation of wiring for clean and dirty loads affects branch circuiting in the office environment. It is a particular issue if power is distributed through the wire management capability of a furniture system. In these circumstances, the capacity of the furniture system to handle the wiring requirements must be evaluated.

Third Harmonic Distortion

Third harmonic distortion is a complex engineering issue related to the use of computers and other solid-state electronic equipment within the same power distribution system as non-solid-state electronic equipment. Although it is not necessary to understand the details of the phenomenon, it is important to understand that it is a key consideration in the design of power distribution in today's office environment.

Third harmonic distortion is created when solid-state electronic equipment creates an imbalance in electrical currents. This imbalance, in turn, causes an overload in a situation in which neutral conductors are shared by multiple current-carrying conductors. That is, the neutral conductor is shared by both solid-state and non-solid-state electronic equipment.

To prevent an overload, the neutral conductor in the panel board and wiring serving non-solid-state electronic loads must be sized appropriately to accommodate the non-solid-state electronic loads. Additionally, the transformer serving the panel board must be an appropriate computer-grade type that is appropriately sized to eliminate the distortion created by the non-solid-state electronic loads.

Emergency Power

Although always a consideration for life safety loads, the use of emergency power has also become a consideration for any critical operation that requires continuous delivery of power. Emergency power has also become a critical consideration with the extensive use of computers in the office environment.

Data that have not been saved can be lost through a $\frac{1}{60}$-second loss of power. Protection against power loss is important to avoid:

- Loss of information
- Downtime with critical computer operations

Depending on which of these considerations drives the need to provide emergency power, one of two basic systems can be implemented:

- Uninterruptible power system (UPS)
- Emergency power generation.

Uninterruptible Power System

The purpose of a UPS system is to avoid a computer crash or loss of information through a loss of power to sensitive systems. A UPS is typically powered by batteries selected to provide power for a specific time frame. Such a system is a sophisticated switching unit that regulates fluctuations in power. A UPS provides instantaneous switching from utility power to battery power and maintains an uninterrupted power source for computer operation for a sufficient time to save information or data and exit the system.

Emergency Power Generation

An emergency power generator provides an indefinite supply of power in the event of power loss from the utility. An emergency generator actually works in conjunction with a UPS system. In the event of a power loss, the UPS system instantaneously switches to battery power and provides the necessary time for the emergency generator to switch on and achieve the required speed to generate the proper voltage and frequency. The UPS switch then transfers to the generator for delivery of power (Figure 6.20).

Typically, in a commercial office building, life safety equipment such as fire pump, emergency lights, and fire alarm systems are backed by an emergency generator. Any functions in the tenant offices that might require emergency power cannot be linked to the building's emergency power system. A separate system must be installed.

FIRE PROTECTION SYSTEMS

The three key elements to addressing fire and life safety are:

- Fire detection
- Fire annunciation
- Fire suppression

Fire detection and annunciation systems are electrical and therefore, the responsibility of the electrical engineer. Fire suppression systems are mechanical/plumbing systems and are the responsibility of the mechanical engineer.

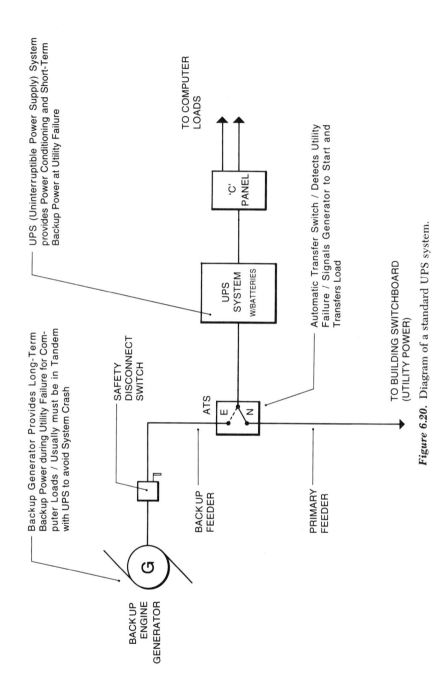

UPS (Uninterruptible Power Supply) System provides Power Conditioning and Short-Term Backup Power at Utility Failure

TO COMPUTER LOADS

'C' PANEL

UPS SYSTEM W/BATTERIES

Automatic Transfer Switch / Detects Utility Failure / Signals Generator to Start and Transfers Load

Backup Generator Provides Long-Term Backup Power during Utility Failure for Computer Loads / Usually must be in Tandem with UPS to avoid System Crash

SAFETY DISCONNECT SWITCH

ATS

E

N

TO BUILDING SWITCHBOARD (UTILITY POWER)

BACK UP FEEDER

PRIMARY FEEDER

BACK UP ENGINE GENERATOR

G

Figure 6.20. Diagram of a standard UPS system.

160

As suppression systems become increasingly complex and more closely integrated, however, knowledge of all three components becomes more critical. As a result, many professionals have chosen to cross-train in all three areas as fire protection specialists.

Fire Detection

There are three fundamental systems for fire detection: smoke detectors, heat detectors, and human detection. Some jurisdictions require the use of more than one detection system.

- Smoke detectors are actually ionization detectors. As the fire produces ions, they are detected and a signal is sent to the fire annunciation system.
- Heat detectors detect the rise of heat in the space.
- Human detection occurs when an occupant of the space detects smoke or fire and triggers the annunciation system from a pull station.

The location of detectors is dictated by local codes and requirements of the National Fire Protection Association (NFPA). Additionally, the presence of a suppression system affects the placement of detection devices. Also, suppression systems typically have integral detection systems. In the suppression systems, the detection device triggers the release of the suppressant, which, in turn, activates the annunciation system.

Fire Annunciation

There are three types of annunciation systems: bells or horns, speaker with voice, and flashing lights. The requirements for these systems have changed significantly in recent years with the enactment of the American with Disabilities Act (ADA). The ADA has established new standards for the location of annunciators as well as the use of lights and audio annunciators. These standards address:

- Bells or horns
- Location and decibels
- Speakers
- Flashing lights

Figure 6.21 illustrates a fire annunciation system that is activated by a manual pull station or sprinkler system activator.

Fire Suppression

Fire suppression systems comprise two components:

- Standpipe and hose system
- Automatic sprinkler system

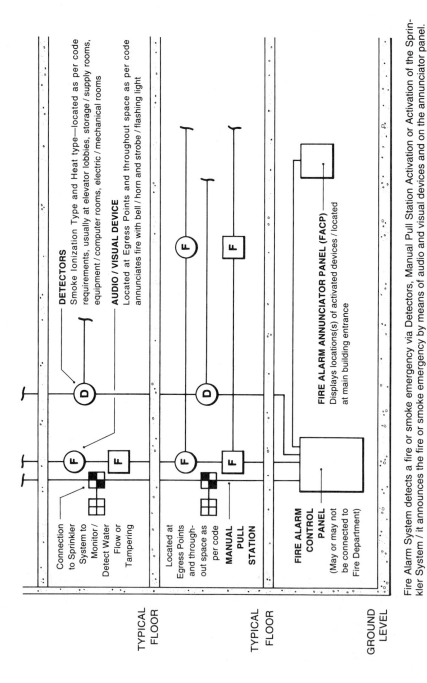

DETECTORS
Smoke Ionization Type and Heat type—located as per code requirements, usually at elevator lobbies, storage / supply rooms, equipment / computer rooms, electric / mechanical rooms

AUDIO / VISUAL DEVICE
Located at Egress Points and throughout space as per code annunciates fire with bell / horn and strobe / flashing light

FIRE ALARM ANNUNCIATOR PANEL (FACP)
Displays locations(s) of activated devices / located at main building entrance

Connection to Sprinkler System to Monitor / Detect Water Flow or Tampering

Located at Egress Points and through-out space as per code

MANUAL PULL STATION

FIRE ALARM CONTROL PANEL
(May or may not be connected to Fire Department)

TYPICAL FLOOR

TYPICAL FLOOR

GROUND LEVEL

Figure 6.21. This diagram illustrates a typical fire annunciation systems.

Fire Alarm System detects a fire or smoke emergency via Detectors, Manual Pull Station Activation or Activation of the Sprinkler System / it announces the fire or smoke emergency by means of audio and visual devices and on the annunciator panel.

Standpipe and Hose System

A *standpipe system* is a system of pipes traveling vertically in buildings over a specific height or horizontally in warehouse, manufacturing, or shopping mall facilities to deliver water to remote locations throughout the building. The purpose of a standpipe system is to provide a water supply for manual firefighting with hoses. The location of these water supplies through the building provides a source of water at heights beyond the reach of ladders and eliminates the need to carry extemely long, cumbersome hoses up stairs and throughout the building.

Standpipe and hose systems are designed for use by both building occupants and professional firefighters. The National Fire Protection Association (NFPA) classes these systems based on this use.

- *Class I:* fire department or trained personnel use
- *Class II:* occupant use
- *Class III:* fire department, trained personnel, or occupant use

Those systems designed for use by occupants are composed of both standpipe and hose. These systems are designed for a user who is not professionally trained in manual firefighting techniques. Typically, systems intended for use only by the fire department involve only the standpipe and fire department hose connection.

Systems are also classified based on the water supply features. These basic systems are described below.

- Systems that maintain water pressure at all times (wet pipe system)
- Systems that allow water into the system automatically by opening a hose valve or through the operation of remote control devices located at each hose station
- Systems that require a fire department connection or fire pump to initiate the flow of water (primed systems)
- Systems with no permanent water supply (dry pipe systems)

Water supplies to a standpipe system vary depending on the location of the building. Sources are public or private water supplies, including water mains, pressure tanks, gravity tanks, and fire department connections.

- Public and private water mains provide direct connection to water mains and are the most common source of water for a standpipe system. Although in many buildings the water pressure from the main is adequate, pumps are often required to provide the necessary pressure for structures of more than 10 stories.
- Pressure tanks are enclosed water tanks with air pressure maintained within the tank to provide for the discharge of the water. Preferably located on the top floor, or in buildings without the structural capacity, in the basement.
- Gravity tanks are installed on roofs or freestanding towers. Their advan-

tage is the ability to provide a constant source of pressure to the standpipe or sprinkler system.

- Fire department connection is mandatory for all standpipe systems and is recommended for sprinkler systems. In dry pipe systems, the fire department is the only means for providing water to the system.

Automatic Sprinkler System

An *automatic sprinkler system* is a system of pipes, tubes, or conduits with heads or nozzles that disperse water or other fire extinguishing materials throughout a fire area. The system is automatically activated by the light, heat, or combustion produced by fire.

Although the automatic sprinkler system was originally developed for the protection of buildings, their contents, and property, the outstanding record of these systems focused attention on the development of systems for life safety applications.

A typical system incorporates an underground supply main to a vertical sprinkler riser. The riser usually extends the full vertical height of the building or is zoned on high-rise buildings. The water supply mains from the risers feed the branch lines, which are the pipes extending throughout each floor. Sprinkler heads are located along the branch lines to dispense water into the space. The primary types of fire suppression systems used in the office environment are:

- Wet pipe automatic systems
- Dry pipe automatic systems

Wet Pipe Automatic Sprinkler System. A wet pipe automatic sprinkler system is designed for use in heated buildings. It is the most effective and efficient automatic sprinkler system and is prevalent in office buildings.

The design of this type of system is relatively simple, consisting of a series of pipes and sprinkler heads. The pipes, which are filled with water at all times, are connected to standpipes or risers traveling vertically through the building. The standpipes or risers are connected to an appropriate water supply.

The system is activated by operation of the automatic sprinkler head, which is triggered by a rise in temperature. Activation of the sprinkler head allows water to be dispensed into the fire area. The flow of water, in turn, activates an alarm valve on the main supply rise to the system. The alarm valve activates an alarm device. Often, this alarm is connected to the fire department. The advantages of a wet pipe sprinkler system are its reliability and its ability to extinguish or control more fire with fewer sprinkler heads.

Dry Pipe Automatic Sprinkler System. The dry pipe system evolved from the wet pipe system and was created to respond primarily to a need for sprinkler systems in unheated buildings. The design of a dry pipe system is similar to that of a wet pipe system. The primary difference is that the pipes in a dry pipe system contain air or nitrogen under pressure, rather than water. As with a wet pipe system, the rise in temperature triggers the sprinkler head, which then activates a valve to release water into the pipe.

For these building support systems described above to function effectively, they must be designed in the context of concepts developed for interior architectural elements, furniture, and furnishing components of the office. Chapter 7 delineates the options related to these design elements.

Chapter Seven

Interior Design Elements

===============

The systems and products identified in this chapter are the interior design elements that the interior architect must integrate successfully to create a design solution for high-quality work environments. These solutions must respond to functional and aesthetic program requirements as well as challenges presented by an increasingly complex workplace, including:

- Barrier-free assess
- Environmental compatibility
- Energy efficiency
- Code requirements
- Changing composition of the workforce
- Changing trends in management styles

The elements that are identified in this chapter include:

- Furniture (systems and general use)
- File systems
- Shelving systems
- Relocatable wall systems
- Ceiling systems
- Lighting
- Color
- Acoustics
- Finish materials (flooring, wall covering, and window treatments)

FURNITURE

Furniture for the office environment is typically selected based on two sets of criteria. As a functional component, furniture is chosen for performance characteristics, and cost. As a primary aesthetic element, furniture is chosen for its design features and style. In addition to meeting the criteria identified above, other key issues which are normally considered in selecting furniture are: required maintenance, durability and anticipated life of the item(s), inventory management, and flexibility of use.

Office furniture can be categorized as either a furniture system or general-use furniture. A furniture system is a generic term which refers to collection of components such as desks, bookshelves, and storage units that are meant to be used as an integrated group. Some furniture systems are designed with dimensionally-compatible components that can be physically assembled into larger units. Other systems do not have dimensionally-compatible components and, therefore, cannot be assembled. These systems are designed so that components can stand alone or be located next to each other. General-use furniture refers to individual, free-standing conventional pieces such as desks, chairs, conference tables, and sofas.

Furniture Systems

Prior to the development of furniture systems, two planning approaches were employed in the office environment: the "bull pen" plan using conventional desks in large open areas, and drywall-enclosed private offices. The concept of furniture systems was introduced to the open plan environment to achieve greater planning flexibility and efficiency as well as increased communication among personnel.

Initially, these systems were referred to as modular, that is, they were floor-standing components that could be assembled to create larger planning units. An example of this type of modular furniture was ADP furniture, designed to accommodate computer equipment (Figure 7.1). Separate free-standing panels and interior landscaping (plants) were used to enclose clusters of modular or free-standing furniture to provide some visual and acoustical privacy.

Panel-hung systems, commonly called "systems furniture" were the next evolution in furniture systems. Systems furniture represented an attempt to integrate the modular and free-standing furniture with the independent panels. In a panel-hung system, most of the components including horizontal worksurfaces, storage, and file elements, are hung from the panel (Figure 7.1). The use of the panel-hung systems increased the flexibility to tailor workstations to meet the needs of the individual and it also increased the capability to accommodate the task in a smaller amount of space, a development which resulted in more efficient space utilization.

Panel Hung System

The section that follows describes briefly the primary components of the panel-hung system, which include:

- Panels
- Panel connectors
- Work surfaces
- Overhead storage

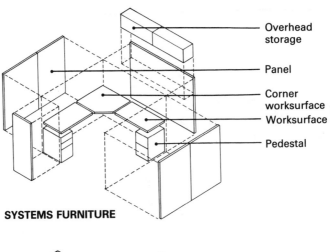

SYSTEMS FURNITURE

- Overhead storage
- Panel
- Corner worksurface
- Worksurface
- Pedestal

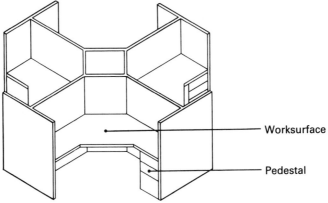

ADP FURNITURE

- Worksurface
- Pedestal

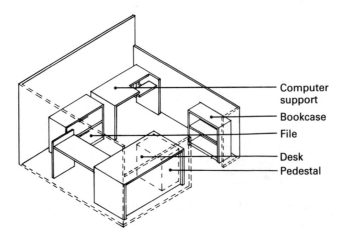

MODULAR FURNITURE

- Computer support
- Bookcase
- File
- Desk
- Pedestal

Figure 7.1. Early evolution of primary types of furniture systems.

168

- Under-work-surface storage
- Task and ambient lighting
- Integrated power distribution systems

Panels. In a panel-hung system the work-surface and overhead storage components are hung from the panel. Under-surface storage components are usually hung from the work surfaces or are sometimes floor-standing (Figure 7.1). Panels consist of a panel frame and panel surface. Panel frames are typically constructed of wood or metal. The primary distinction among panel types is in the panel surface. The panel surface can be upholstered (covered with fabric) or nonupholstered. Typically, nonupholstered panel surfaces are wood, vinyl or plastic laminate. The panel can also be tackable or non-tackable. Acoustically treated panels are also available. An acoustical panel is constructed with a sound-absorbent inner material which is attached to the panel frame and then covered with fabric. Upholstered panels are not necessarily acoustically treated panels, however, the current trend is the use of panels that are upholstered, tackable and acoustically treated.

Depending on the requirements of the systems furniture workstation, panels may also be obtained in different heights, typically ranging from 36 to 42 inches (partially seated privacy), 48 to 54 inches (total seated-height privacy) and 66 to 80 inches (standing-height privacy).

Panels also vary in width from 1 to 5 feet and are typically manufactured in standard whole-foot dimensions. The panels achieve stability through the placement of two panels or other floor-standing components at right angles; at intermittent points in the "run" of the panels.

Panel Connectors. All systems panels are joined by connective hardware. The hardware varies by manufacturer, system, and often with specific planning conditions, such as the angle at which the panels are joined. It is critical in planning to be knowledgeable about the specific product hardware and to understand the impact of the hardware on the workstations. The type of connector and the conditions at the connection substantially affect the workstation configuration, panel, and component dimensions, stability, and ease of installing and dismantling the system.

The connective hardware dimension is the cause of a planning phenomenon called *systems creep*, which is the difference in dimension between the nominal workstation dimension (usually, the inside dimension of the workstation) and the actual dimension of the workstation in the plan. The actual dimension in the plan is usually a center-to-center dimension or outside dimension plus any additional ease space that is allotted for the imperfections of the actual installation.

The undesirable result of planning with the nominal dimension rather than the actual dimension is that the workstation cluster will actually be larger than the amount of space available. In large workstation clusters, the difference can be substantial.

Work Surfaces. Systems furniture allows greater variation in work-surface type, configuration, and relationship of surfaces than does conventional furniture. This flexibility allows for greater user task adaptability.

Standard system work surfaces range from 18 to 36 inches deep, distances that are accessible and functional to the user. Rather than utilizing additional work-surface depth for storage space, storage is located either above or below the work surface. The work-surface depth can be manipulated to accommodate equipment that must be located on the work surface. Normally, however, desktop equipment such as a computer is located on a corner work-surface component.

Minimum work-surface width for primary work surfaces is usually 4 feet. The work surface that is located adjacent or perpendicular to the primary work surface is the secondary work surface and is normally a minimum of 3 feet wide. Additional work surfaces opposite the primary work surface are usually provided for additional equipment or conferencing requirements.

Overhead Storage. Storage bins with doors or shelves can be located above the work surface. Providing storage overhead and using vertical rather than horizontal space allows for greater storage capacity with less floor space. Dimensions of overhead storage components must be coordinated with the panel dimension width. For example, a 4-foot-wide panel would typically carry a 4-foot-wide overhead storage unit although some systems are designed to allow the overhead unit to span two panels. Overhead storage components should be mounted at consistent levels and be sufficiently high to allow the user adequate headroom when seated.

Under-Work-Surface Storage. Both files and drawers can be located under the work surface. These components can either be suspended from the work surface or be floor-standing units. In planning under-work-surface storage units, it is particularly important to allow for kneehole space under the work surface. Kneehole space should be a minimum of 30 inches wide. With adjacent work surfaces at right angles to each other, the kneehole space for both surfaces should be continuous through the corner. Placing the kneehole space at the work-surface corners also eliminates the potential of placing floor-standing units adjacent at right angles where drawer pull space would interfere.

Task and Ambient Lighting. Furniture-integrated lighting systems provide both task lighting to provide the proper lighting level on all task surfaces and ambient lighting directed up at the ceiling to provide general lighting in the office space. Task lighting can be suspended from overhead storage components or can be a work-surface-mounted fixture. Ambient lighting is usually accommodated in troughs built into the system or directly on top of overhead storage components.

Integrated Power Distribution Systems. Systems in which power, voice, and data cabling distribution are handled within the system workstation are called integrated power distribution systems. Not all systems have an integrated power distribution system, and where they do exist, they usually differ in design from manufacturer to manufacturer.

Generally, in integrated power distribution systems, wires are run from the ceiling or floor distribution system into the furniture and through a system of raceways, or channels, within the panels (Figure 7.2). Horizontal distribution occurs within the panel at the base line, belt line (work-surface height), or panel top. Separate vertical raceways provide a path for distribution between each of the horizontal raceways.

The furniture system's power distribution components offer a variety of circuit options with the capability for several separate circuits. It is critical to evaluate the system's capacity to handle the required number of circuits, including clean circuits for computer terminals. The distribution components are modular and are consistent with the panel widths of the system. The components plug together in a predetermined configuration, including designated circuit outlets that plug into the wireway.

Work-surface components have grommet options that permit coordination with equipment and base outlet locations. If properly coordinated, the equipment cable passes through the work surface immediately behind the equipment to an outlet in the panel base below the work surface.

Integrated Furniture Systems

As the furniture industry responds to the changing needs of its customers, the options for systems and the design of those systems are numerous. The options might best be described as flexible hybrids of free-standing furniture, modular and panel-hung (systems furniture) components. Users now have the flexibility to use panel-hung systems in circumstances in which there is a need for the

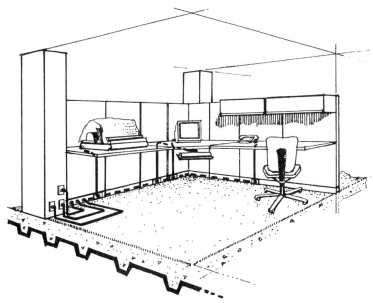

Figure 7.2. Furniture-integrated power distribution system.

visual and acoustical privacy, as well as the power and data wire management inherent in panel-hung systems. When these capabilities are not required, the user can achieve visual privacy, storage capacity, and tailored workstation configuration by integrating free-standing and modular components, therefore avoiding the cost of the panel-hung system when the specific advantages of that system are not required.

The diversity in products available with these new furniture systems is substantial. Each of the following is designed to provide options in sizes, heights, finishes, and configuration:

- Portable file cabinets
- Portable storage components
- Portable tables
- Screens
- Panels (acoustical, non-acoustical, and with vision panels)
- Adjustable worksurfaces and worksurfaces in a variety of configurations
- Stackable bookshelves
- Stackable storage components

Although the selection of components allows tremendous flexibility for meeting individual user needs, the diversity can also lead to problems in inventory management. The use of accessories such as those listed below can provide an alternative to tailoring workstations to user requirements without substantial deviation in workstation configuration from user to user:

- Paper trays
- Files/organizers
- Tool trays
- Lighting fixtures
- Equipment stands
- Power receptables
- Shelves

Selection, Inventory Control, and Maintenance

Flexibility is one of the primary advantages of the use of systems furniture. With the variety of components and potential configurations available, proper consideration must be given to planning and maintenance of the systems to prevent a chaotic, diverse appearance as well as an inventory and maintenance problem.

Selecting a system is a significant management decision. Selecting a system should be based on how well the system's capabilities meet functional workstation requirements and budgetary parameters. The development of a minimum number of workstation standards, with few variations in componentry and component finishes, also minimizes inventory and facility maintenance problems.

General-Use Furniture

General-use furniture is a term used to describe nonsystems, conventional-use furniture consisting of the following major types:

- Work surfaces
- Seating
- File cabinets
- Shelving

Work Surfaces

General-use furniture work surfaces include (Figure 7.3):

- Desks
- Tables
- Credenzas
- Computer support worksurfaces
- Wall-hung units

Desks. Desks are the primary type of general-use work surface. Desks are available in standard sizes of 30 inches by 60 inches and in larger sizes at 6-inch increments up to 36 inches by 72 inches. They are standard in one- or two-pedestal models. The term *pedestal* refers to the drawer units on either side of the desk. Double-pedestal desks are generally larger than single-pedestal desks, a result of the additional space required for the kneehole.

Single-pedestal desks are also used with *returns*, L-shaped configurations in lengths of 36 to 48 inches. The return, commonly referred to as a *right-hand return* or *left-hand return* for its location in relation to the user when seated at the desk, is at a standard desk height in an executive model and at a lower equipment height in secretarial models.

Tables. Tables are used within workstations as desks or as small conference tables. They are also used as work surfaces in workrooms and in more temporary settings for additional work space, such as training tables in a training room.

Credenzas. Credenzas normally are used in conjunction with desks as secondary work surfaces and storage units. They are placed against the wall behind the desk and are selected to match the desk in length and finish. Credenzas are manufactured with optional drawer pedestals, storage cabinets, and kneehole spaces.

Computer and ADP Support. Computer and ADP support work surfaces are similar to desks or tables and are designed to support one type of computer hardware. These pieces provide computer-specific support features, such as wire grommets, casters, and paper slots, which would not be offered on a conventional desk or table.

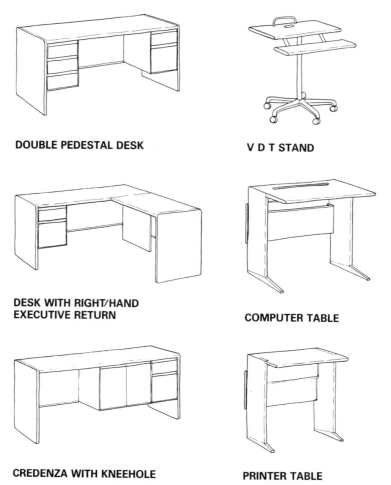

DOUBLE PEDESTAL DESK   V D T STAND

DESK WITH RIGHT/HAND
EXECUTIVE RETURN   COMPUTER TABLE

CREDENZA WITH KNEEHOLE   PRINTER TABLE

Figure 7.3. Standard worksurfaces.

Wall-Hung Units. Panel-hung work surfaces also may be used in offices as a general-use application. The unit is suspended from a partition on hanger strips or in a floor-supported configuration rather than from a systems furniture panel. These applications can also be used for counter space in workrooms and copy rooms.

Seating

The primary types of seating for the office environment, illustrated in Figure 7.4, are:

- Desk chairs
- Pull-up chairs
- Conference chairs
- Lounge seating

Desk Chairs. As one of the most important nonsystems elements in the office environment, desk chairs should be evaluated carefully to support the user task, provide personal comfort, and create a consistent, pleasing aesthetic appearance.

Chairs should also be selected for their ergonomic features. The term *ergonomic* refers to a design created specifically to fit human dimensions and respond to functional requirements. Theoretically, an ergonomic chair provides increased user comfort, which should improve task performance when sitting is required for an extended period. The primary features of an ergonomic chair relate to the degree of adjustability of body position achieved by altering the following characteristics of the chair:

- Height
- Back height, tilt, and support
- Arm height and width
- Seat tilt

The leading seat edge is also designed to avoid decreased circulation in the lower legs.

Ergonomics has become a very popular design criterion, stemming from concern for maximizing human resource efficiency through a high-quality environment. Chairs should be evaluated to determine whether the chair is truly ergonomic, or simply height, tilt, and swivel adjustable. Because desk chairs are used extensively, finishes and materials should be chosen for durability and ease of cleaning. Generally, the arms of these chairs should not be fabric-upholstered.

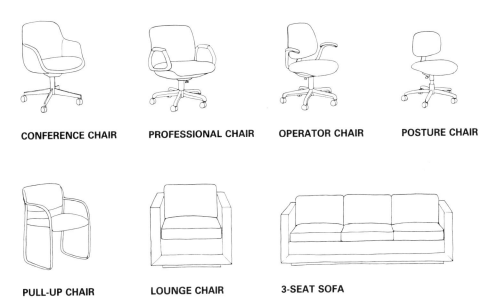

CONFERENCE CHAIR   PROFESSIONAL CHAIR   OPERATOR CHAIR   POSTURE CHAIR

PULL-UP CHAIR   LOUNGE CHAIR   3-SEAT SOFA

Figure 7.4. Standard types of seating for the office environment include desk and lounge seating.

Pull-Up Chairs. A pull-up or guest chair is a chair that is placed opposite the desk for visitor seating in a typical office plan. This seating is usually light in scale and easy to move. Pull-up chairs should be selected to match or complement the desk chair.

Conference Chairs. Conference chairs are slightly heavier in scale than desk or pull-up chairs. Conference chairs are selected for comfort at long meetings and therefore can be slightly more lounge-like than a desk chair. Pedestal-base chairs with casters are particularly well suited for this purpose, to allow the user to pull directly away from the table. Tilt-swivel chairs are also an appropriate application for conference seating.

Lounge Seating. Lounge seating is used in reception areas or other ancillary waiting areas and executive offices for informal conference areas. Lounge seating generally refers to fully upholstered sofas and chairs. Finishes for lounge seating are generally selected to enhance the image of the space.

File Cabinets

File cabinets are available in standard vertical and lateral types as well as high-density systems.

Standard Vertical and Lateral Cabinets. File cabinets are available in vertical and lateral types (Figure 7.5). The vertical file is standard in two widths—letter (15 inches) and legal (18 inches)—and in two- or four-drawer heights. Other less typical sizes are manufactured for materials with alternative widths. The drawers on the vertical file pull from front to back so that the width is less than the depth, which is always 28 inches.

The lateral file is a standard 18 inches deep. It is standard in widths of 30, 36, and 42 inches. A 48-inch width is also available but is used primarily as a system furniture component. The depth and width of lateral filecases are standard, but drawer height and internal drawer hardware vary to accommodate different materials. Because of this case size uniformity, lateral files have become on office standard.

Lateral file cases are available in two- to five-drawer heights. The drawer heights are available in 3-inch modules to accommodate material sizes from 3- by 5-inch cards (6 inches) to computer printouts (15 inches). Letter and legal drawers are 12 inches high. Any combination of drawers can be used within the same-size file case.

The lateral file drawer pull is from side to side, which requires less pull and stand space for the amount of material stored. A lateral file case 36 inches or wider is also more efficient than a vertical case in its use of space and is easier and more efficient to plan.

High-Density Systems. High-density filing is designed to maximize file storage in minimum floor space. High-density files are used for controlled-access, centralized filing needs. Floor loading capacity is a consideration with

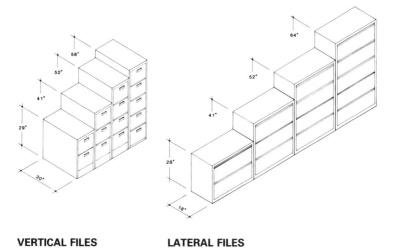

VERTICAL FILES   **LATERAL FILES**

Figure 7.5. Standard vertical and lateral file cabinets.

the use of high-density filing. In most instances, structural reinforcement is required to accommodate these filing systems in most office buildings.

Depicted in Figure 7.6, the three types of high-density systems are:

• Movable aisle system
• Sliding system
• Rotary system

Movable aisle systems consist of shelving mounted on carriages that roll on tracks. The layout of the system is identical to conventional rows of shelving, or stacks, except that there is only one aisle for a group of stacks. The stacks roll back and forth to relocate the aisle at the stack to be referenced. The movable aisle system can be driven manually or automatically.

Sliding systems usually have two or three stacks directly in front of each other against a wall. The shelving units slide on a track from side to side to allow access to the rows behind them.

Rotary systems consist of back-to-back units in cases that rotate between two positions 90 degrees to each other. When the shelf unit is in one position, the shelf openings are exposed (open). In the other position, the end of the shelf units are exposed (closed). This system achieves both neatness and density.

Automatic systems are analogous to a large automatic file cabinet. File drawers are suspended from chain drives in a case. The chain drives carry the drawers past an access door where the operator is seated.

Shelving

Extensive book or binder collections are generally stored on shelf units. Shelving is usally wood or steel construction in common depths of 10, 12, 15, 18, and 24 inches, and widths of 24, 30, and 36 inches.

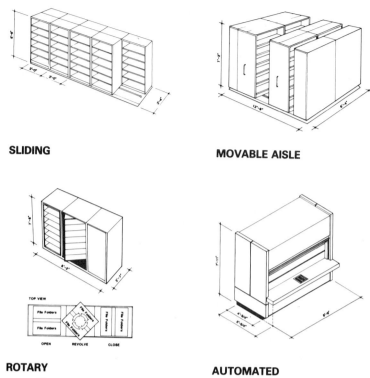

SLIDING   MOVABLE AISLE

ROTARY   AUTOMATED

Figure 7.6. Four distinct types of high-density filing systems.

Because wood can sag over extended lengths, it is generally used only for relatively small, short-span bookcase units. Steel shelving is generally available in two quality types: general utility and high-quality steel shelving.

Inexpensive *utility shelving* is often referred to as *nut-and-bolt shelving*. This shelving is constructed of prepunched angle standards and metal panel shelves, which are assembled with exposed bolts. These are serviceable units typically used when appearance is not important.

Higher qualities of steel shelving are available for libraries. The shelving is reinforced with steel bars to support high-density storage. This shelving is available with a variety of finished appearances, including wood end panels.

RELOCATABLE WALL SYSTEMS

Relocatable walls, often referred to as *demountable partitions* or *movable walls*, are utilized as an alternative to drywall partitions when ease of reconfiguration is an objective. The relocatable wall can be used to create private offices or to divide open-plan areas. The relocatable wall system eliminates the disruption, cost, and time associated with the demolition and reconstruction of drywall construction. As with systems furniture, the initial cost of a relocatable wall system is higher than that of drywall construction. The life-cycle cost, however, may be comparable, depending on the frequency of reconfiguration.

Relocatable wall systems vary from manufacturer to manufacturer in their distinctive features. There are, however, two different types of systems. One type, frequently referred to as *movable walls,* are independent, individual units. These systems are custom built and are completed to specifications at the factory. Each panel is self-contained and therefore can be replaced without disrupting the adjacent panels. The other system is commonly called the *demountable wall system.* Demountable wall systems normally require some modification or assembly on site. Both wall systems are installed in floor and ceiling tracks with clips to hold them in place. Unlike the movable wall system, in which each panel is independent, demountable wall construction relies on a vertical spline that connects the panels (Figure 7.7). Consequently, a single panel cannot be removed without affecting adjacent panels.

The frames of both types of systems are normally constructed of steel. Panels can be specified with inserts of wood, glass, fabric-wrapped, acoustical, or tackable surfaces. Doors, hardware, and base or other moldings are also integral options for these systems.

CEILING SYSTEMS

Suspended ceilings with acoustical tiles, drywall, and plaster ceiling materials are used most frequently in the office environment. The advantages and applications of these systems are identified in Figure 7.8.

Suspended Ceilings

The most commonly used ceiling treatment in the general office environment is the *suspended ceiling.* A suspended ceiling is constructed by suspending a metal grid from the structural slab. Tiles, typically acoustical, are inserted into the grid to form the finished ceiling. The advantage of using a suspended ceiling is that wire distribution and HVAC systems as well as light fixtures are easily accessed in the plenum space above the ceiling. The suspended ceiling is easily modified and has acoustical characteristics that are an advantage in general office areas. The most commonly installed suspended ceiling systems are (Figure 7.9):

- T-bar grid
- U-channel grid
- Concealed spline

T-Bar Grid System
The T-bar grid system is the least expensive suspended ceiling system. Tiles are laid on top of the inverted T in the grid, leaving the grid exposed below the tiles. *Tegular edge* ceiling tiles may be used with the same T-bar grid system. With this type of ceiling the edge of the tile is routed so that the tile face drops below the grid level. The grid is more pronounced, creating a slightly different look to the ceiling, which is considered superior to regular lay-in tile. The tegular edge ceiling is more expensive than the lay-in ceiling.

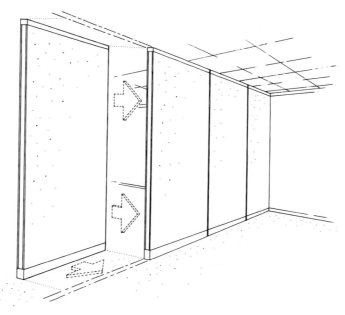

MOVABLE WALLS

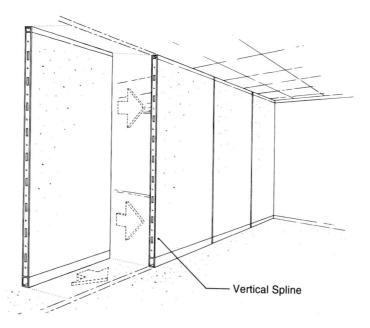

DEMOUNTABLE WALLS

Figure 7.7. Two primary types of relocatable wall systems.

CEILING TYPE	ADVANTAGES	DISADVANTAGES
SUSPENDED CEILINGS T bar grid U channel gird Concealed spline	Access to wire distribution and HVAC Easily modified Acoustical properties	Access with concealed spline more difficult
DRYWALL	Create specific design elements such as bulkheads and coves Acoustical properties	Accessibility to above ceiling systems and lighting fixtures Cannot be modified easily Acoustical properties
PLASTER	Create specific design elements such as bulkheads and coves Superior surface quality Durability	Access to above ceiling systems and lighting fixtures Cannot be modified easily Cost

Figure 7.8. The advantages and disadvantages of the three types of ceiling systems.

U-Channel Grid System

The U-channel grid system is a modified T-bar grid system with a narrower profile. The U-channel in the grid forms a reveal above the finished ceiling line. The acoustical tile is laid into the grid and fits flush with the face of the U-channel, so the ceiling has a flat appearance with a less obtrusive grid. In all other respects this system is similar to the lay-in ceiling. The U-channel grid system is more expensive, however.

Concealed Spline System

The concealed spline system is a more expensive alternative than the two systems described previously. In this system, although the tiles are routed and placed in a T-grid, they are routed in such a way that the T-grid fits into the edge of the tile. Each tile butts the adjacent tile and conceals the grid, creating a monolithic look in the ceiling.

The concealed spline system does have disadvantages. Access to the plenum space is more limited because the ceiling tiles fit together tightly. Only certain points in the ceiling are accessible. Also, over time, as the building vibrates, the tiles shift and the joints come apart. What were straight lines when the ceiling was installed can become crooked.

Grid and Tile Sizes

Grids and tiles are compatibly sized in 1 foot by 1 foot (available only in concealed spline), 2 feet by 2 feet, and 2 feet by 4 feet sizes. Grids are available in various colors and finishes. Tiles are available in a variety of materials, patterns, textures, and finishes.

Considerations in selecting tiles include reflectance for lighting efficiency, acoustical qualities, and general construction to prevent sagging and to enhance durability over time.

Drywall

Drywall ceilings are normally used in special and public areas that require a more upgraded appearance than can be achieved with a suspended ceiling.

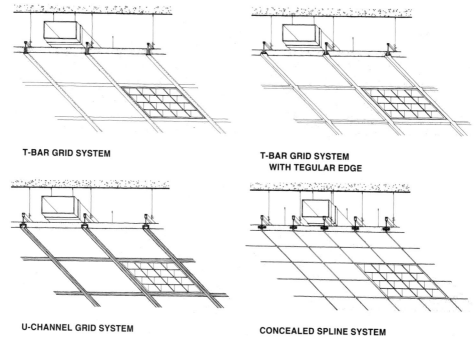

T-BAR GRID SYSTEM

**T-BAR GRID SYSTEM
WITH TEGULAR EDGE**

U-CHANNEL GRID SYSTEM

CONCEALED SPLINE SYSTEM

Figure 7.9. Suspended ceiling systems are typically used in general office areas to provide flexibility, ease of access, and acoustical properties.

Drywall can be used to create specific design elements in the ceiling, such as bulkheads, coves, and stepped configurations. The difficulties with drywall ceilings are acoustics and accessibility to mechanical systems and lighting fixtures. Drywall is a more permanent installation and cannot be modified easily.

Plaster

Plaster ceilings are relatively expensive and are used only in special or public spaces. They can be used to achieve formed curves, shapes, patterns, textures, and figures in the ceiling for a sculptured effect. Plaster has a superior surface quality to that of drywall, and it is harder and more durable. As with drywall, plaster ceilings make access to mechanical and lighting systems difficult. They are also permanent and cannot be modified.

LIGHTING

Lighting is a functional component of the office environment because it is necessary for vision. Yet it is also a design element, creating a sense of volume, form, and shape. It is an art form, with the potential to create drama and response: to excite, to motivate, and to please. It is a complex subject dealing with the physics of electricity and light as well as the science of human vision and psychology. It affects office aesthetics and employee motivation and creates substantial energy demands. For these reasons, the effective design and installation of high-quality, energy-efficient lighting systems is a priority in the office environment today and will continue to be in the future.

The primary objective in the design of lighting systems for the office environment is to achieve the desired level of illumination efficiently with the most appropriate and highest-quality light. Through the years, this objective has been approached differently as the availability and technology of artificial lighting has improved.

In the early office environment, daylight was the primary and, frequently, only method of lighting, due to the limited availability, poor quality, and expense of artificial lighting. To maximize the use of daylight to illuminate office interiors, architects designed their buildings in configurations that increased the perimeter office area and also created designs that incorporated light wells and atria.

Although these architectural designs achieved the desired lighting results, they also increased the solar heat load in these buildings. Later, when air-conditioning systems were introduced to the office environment, the daylight increased heat loads, which, in turn, created higher energy demands to cool the additional solar load. In addition to increased energy consumption, daylight was not reliable as a primary light source. The availability, intensity, and quality of daylight all vary based on exposure, season, time of day, and amount of cloud cover. Daylight is also not a lighting option before sunrise or after sunset.

For all of these reasons, as the technology for artifical lighting improved and the availability of power increased, artificial lighting systems became the primary method for lighting the office environment. In fact, until the energy crisis in the early 1970s, most architects, engineers, and lighting consultants virtually ignored daylight as a component in lighting design for the office environment.

The energy crisis focused research efforts on reducing the energy consumption related to powering lighting systems and to cooling the heat load created by them. This research resulted in several discoveries which, once again, changed the approach to lighting for the office environment. First, it was determined that overall energy consumption could be decreased using daylight to reduce the amount of artificial light needed to achieve desired lighting levels. This reduction in consumption included power for lighting as well as cooling. Second, it was determined that a higher *quality* of artificial light reduced the required *quantity* of light and, consequently, resulted in energy savings. Third, the development of fluorescent dimming systems provided the necessary flexibility in controlling artificial light levels, so that artificial light could be used to supplement daylight as needed. Fourth, it became commonly accepted that the use of daylight as a lighting design element was a positive impact on employee morale and productivity.

While advances in lighting technology continue to provide increasing flexibility, efficiency, control, and quality in lighting systems, the architectural profession has become better educated and more sophisticated in its approach to lighting design. In the past, the approach to lighting was functional, and the focus was on what was being illuminated. Today, both daylight and artificial light are used in combination to create effective lighting concepts that begin with a sensitivity toward people, what they must see, and how light affects them. These factors form the basis for two of the primary considerations in lighting design: quantity and quality.

Quantity and Quality of Light

Quantity of *artificial light* is measured in intensity, which is most commonly expressed in lumens at the source of the light or in footcandles on the illuminated area. Quantity of *daylight*, however, is often expressed as a ratio representing that fraction of the total light available in the sky to the amount that reaches the area in which the task is being executed. Although quality of light is also measurable, it is more difficult to define because it is affected by so many different factors, such as source and placement.

Quantity and quality of light must always be considered in tandem because one affects the other. Overall, the higher the quality of light appropriate for the situation, the better, for two reasons. First, human vision is better at fewer diffused footcandles than in more nondiffused footcandles. Second, the higher the quality of the light, the less light is needed. Using a lower quantity of light results in reduced power requirements, for two reasons: less energy is needed to power the lights themselves, and the additional cooling requirements that accompany higher light levels are eliminated.

The key in approaching lighting is in understanding that each situation typically requires a distinct solution. For example, providing general lighting for an open office area calls for a very different approach than that for lighting a conferencing facility. Lighting artwork in a building lobby is different from lighting work surfaces. In today's environment, a successful lighting design for any requirement should support the function and desired atmosphere of each space, maximize the use of daylight, support employee productivity and morale, and maximize energy efficiency.

Methods of Lighting

Lighting in the office environment is achieved through a combination of methods:

- Ambient lighting
- Accent lighting
- Task lighting
- Task and ambient lighting

Each of these methods of lighting has a specific purpose and is achieved through a variety of sources and fixtures.

Ambient Light

Ambient light is the general light in a space. It is categorized as direct or indirect. With *direct* ambient lighting, the source of the light is visible, located above the space being illuminated, and delivers light directly down. With *indirect* lighting, however, the source is not visible and delivers light upward onto a surface (typically, a ceiling), where it is reflected back onto the space being illuminated.

Because direct lighting is more efficient, it was the preferred means of providing ambient light in general office areas until computers became prevalent and the glare and veiling reflections created by direct ambient light became a problem. *Veiling reflections* are the reflected image of a light source which obscures the reflecting surface of work surfaces (particularly, computer screens). This problem spurred an increased use of indirect ambient lighting. The popularity of indirect ambient lighting faded rather quickly, however. Because it is the less efficient way to use ambient light, as the quality of direct ambient lighting reduced the problem of glare and veiling reflections, direct ambient lighting regained its position as the favored method of providing ambient light.

Accent Lighting

Accent lighting is focused light, directed to illuminate specific objects or small areas at levels higher than those of ambient lighting.

Task Lighting

Task lighting illuminates a task area and is located relatively close to the task surface. A desk lamp is a example of a task light. A task light is a direct source of illumination and must be shielded from the viewer. The light should also be located and lensed to prevent veiling reflections on the task.

Task and Ambient Lighting

Task and ambient lighting was developed as an energy-efficient method of creating both task and ambient light utilizing only one light source. That one source would focus an appropriately high level of illumination on a task surface as well as create the necessary level of ambient light in the surrounding areas. Over time, however, variations of the concept resulted in the common and less efficient two-source approach to task and ambient lighting: one source directed down onto the work surface for task lighting and one source directed up for ambient lighting. Task and ambient lighting became particularly popular as computers pervaded the workplace and indirect lighting applications were used to minimize the glare and veiling reflection problems associated with direct lighting methods.

The term *furniture-integrated lighting* refers to task and ambient lighting systems in which all fixtures with the exception of accent lighting are integrated into the furniture system. In furniture-integrated systems, the task light source is typically located above the work surface mounted under the overhead storage components. The ambient light source is located on top of furniture overhead storage components or in troughs in the panel components. One of the advantages of this type of lighting system is that it moves with the furniture as the furniture system is reconfigured and therefore requires no modification of the ceiling.

Lighting Sources

Illumination of the interior environment is produced by two sources: the sun, and manufactured lamps (bulbs) which create artificial light.

The Sun

The use of daylight in the office environment reduces energy consumption and positively affects worker morale and productivity. It provides changes in the environment during the course of the day as the sun moves across the sky and creates a sense of progression through the day.

The objective in using the sun as a source of light in the office environment is to distribute light evenly over a large working area. This is best accomplished with skylights rather than windows where the position of the sun substantially affects the distribution of light in the interior space. However, the use of artificial light in combination with daylight can be effectively integrated so that throughout the course of the day, as the sun's position changes, the artificial light can supplement lighting levels and fill in gaps in the daylight.

Lamps

Three basic types of lamps are used in the office environment:

- Incandescent
- Fluorescent
- High-intensity discharge (HID)

Each of these lamp types and lamps by different manufacturers varies in output (quantity), cost, energy efficiency, lamp life, and amount of *diffusion* (scatter) or *point* (focus).

Each lamp type also varies in its color rendition characteristics. *Color rendition* refers to how objects appear to change in color under illumination created by different lamp sources. The difference in color appearance, which can be dramatic, is determined by the position in the light spectrum in which the lamp operates. For example, under certain fluorescent lamps, human skin appears slightly green. Yet under a different type of fluorescent lamp, the skin appears yellow. If placed under various incandescent lamps, the skin's appearance would again alter with each type of lamp. In daylight, however, the skin would appear to be its true color. Daylight is white light. It is the only light that operates across the entire visible spectrum and therefore does not alter the color appearance of the objectives it is illuminating. For this reason, daylight is referred to as having *true color rendition* properties.

True color rendition, however, is often not the objective. Light sources are always selected for specific lighting schemes, in part based on their color-rendering properties. The finishes and objects that will be illuminated should be viewed under the actual light source to determine how they will appear in the installation. By changing the lamp source, the interior architect or lighting designer can achieve distinct lighting effects. For example, a lamp that renders reds well might be selected to light artwork that contains strong red elements.

In the past, when a relatively limited selection of lamps was commercially available, color rendition qualities in lamps were labeled warm white, cool white, and daylight. Today, with the development of new lamps with very slight distinctions in rendering quality, they are labeled in kelvin, a measure of temperature that is reflective of where in the light spectrum the lamp operates.

Incandescent Lamps. Incandescent lamps comprise a wire filament that is mounted within a glass bulb. The bulb contains a gas or a vacuum. The electrical current that passes through the filament creates resistence. The power created by the resistance heats the filament until it glows or, rather, becomes incandescent.

There are two basic types of incandescent lamps:

• Standard incandescent
• Halogen

Standard Incandescent. The most widely recognized incandescent bulb is the A *lamp.* The A lamp is used commonly in residential applications and in commercial applications for selected ambient and accent lighting. The configuration of the A lamp does not actually direct the light generated by the filament. As a result, much of the light is lost upward or in the fixture, causing the lamp to be extremely inefficient. For the wattage required to operate the lamp, the quantity of light is very low. Therefore, the A lamp is characterized by a short lamp life of only about 2000 hours, high heat generation, and inefficiency (low light output related to energy consumed).

Heat generation is a consideration with incandescent lighting, a problem that is accentuated when the fixture is used in close proximity to a person for general illumination or in significant quantity. When incandescent lighting is used in these circumstances, the mechanical system must be designed for adequate offset of the heat load.

The primary advantage of the A lamp, and one of the reasons for its continued use in the home and office, is its warm color rendition, which is flattering to the way people appear in the light. The purchase price is also lower than that of other lamps currently on the market. However, for incandescent the life-cycle cost, which considers the cost of maintenance and replacement lamps and additional cooling required, for most applications is frequently higher than that of other lamp options.

The *R* and *ER reflector lamps* are refinements of the A lamp. R and ER lamps reduce the inefficiency of the A lamp with a slight modification in bulb shape and the addition of a reflective coating on the upper portion of the bulb. As a result, the lamp is slightly more pointed (directional and focused) and slightly more efficient than the A bulb, with approximately the same lamp life.

The most appropriate applications for the incandescent lamp in the office environment are for accent lighting and areas in which color rendition is critical to the success of the space.

Incandescent Tungsten Halogen and Quartz. The tungsten halogen and quartz lamp differs from the incandescent in filament configuration and in the gas used in the bulb. Tungsten halogen and quartz lamps provide a much whiter light than that of incandescent and for that reason provide much truer rendition. The lamps' reflectors provide a high degree of directional control. These lamps are much more efficient than the incandescent lamp and have a much longer lamp life. They are used, as is the standard incandescent lamp, for accent and ambient lighting and in areas in which color rendition is a consideration.

Low-voltage Halogen. The low-voltage halogen lamp works with the same types of filament configurations as those of the tungsten halogen and quartz lamps. This type of lamp operates at a much lower voltage, however, which creates more light. The lamp burns at a much higher temperature than that of the incandescent and therefore is a very white light. The application for these lamps is in accent lighting when brighter lighting with more focused control is required with greater energy savings.

Fluorescent. Light is created in the fluorescent lamp through an electric discharge device which utilizes a mercury vapor arc (with small amounts of other gases, such as neon or argon) to generate ultraviolet energy. This energy is absorbed by a phosphor which coats the inside of the glass tube. The phosphor converts the invisible ultraviolet light into visible light. The composition of the phosphor in the tube determines the wavelength of the light—that is, where in the spectrum the light operates. The bulbs can be straight, circular, or U-shaped tubes.

A fluorescent lamp creates light that is highly diffused, generates very little heat, and is much more efficient than the standard incandescent lamp. It also has a much longer lamp life (approximately 20,000 hours) than that of the standard incandescent, whose life is approximately 2000 hours. Based on these characteristics, fluorescent lighting has been the most commonly used source for ambient lighting in general office areas.

In the past, however, the one criticism of the fluorescent lamp was its poor color rendition properties because it operated in the blue range of the spectrum, creating a very cool white light. Typically, the fluorescent was not used in areas where aesthetics or color rendition were critical. Today, however, the tri-phosphor lamp provides greatly improved color rendition, through the use of three rare-earth phosphors.

The improvements in the quality of the fluorescent's light, in addition to the refinement of the compact fluorescent, have diversified the practical application of the lamp. The compact fluorescent can be used in areas where previously only the incandescent was appropriate. Fluorescent lights are now used in general office areas for ambient lighting and in support areas such as conference, pantries, and libraries, in addition to public spaces such as corridors and lobby areas.

High-Intensity Discharge. High-intensity discharge (HID) comprises a family of lamps that includes mercury vapor, sodium vapor, and metal halide.

Light is generated by movement of an electric current through a gas or vapor under pressure. These sources are noted for their high efficiency. In fact, they generate such tremendous amounts of light and heat for their size and power consumption that they must be shielded from sight and touch.

Mercury has the longest life of the HID lamps, 24,000 hours and upward. Although it is characterized as a very blue source, color-corrected lamps are now available. Mercury is not dimmable. Applications for mercury are more common in institutional and industrial projects than in offices. Typically, this lamp is used in areas with very high ceiling heights, such as warehouses or gymnasiums. The only practical office application for the mercury HID is with the use of color-correcting lamps and lenses in a space such as a building lobby with very high ceilings.

The sodium HID, a yellow/green lamp, is in common use for street lighting. Its lamp life is approximately the same as that of mercury, about 24,000 hours. The sodium lamp can be used for lighting large areas around buildings where color rendition is not a priority. Typically, the sodium HID is not used in offices.

Although the metal halide lamp has a lower life expectancy than that of the mercury or sodium HID lamps, only about 10,000 to 20,000 hours, and is also the least efficient, it does have better color rendition properties. Yet its color tends to change over the life of the lamp. The applications of this lamp are in large spaces with high ceilings where color rendition and low mainte-nance are priorities. Examples are public spaces such as building lobbies and building atria. These light sources and their typical application are shown in Figure 7.10.

Lighting Fixtures

The term *fixture* refers to the equipment that houses the power source for the lamp, the lamp itself, and any devices that manipulate the light, such as lenses or reflectors. The fixture functions to control the light to reflect, diffuse, or direct. Fixtures are selected based on the following considerations:

- Type of lamp to be used
- Placement of the source
- Function of the lighting
- Amount of direction or diffusion required
- Amount of flexibility required in control
- Design requirements for the fixtures and the office space

Fixtures are manufactured in a variety of types and styles. The most com-monly used in the office environment as represented in Figure 7.11 include:

- Downlights
- Wallwashers
- Sconces
- Pendants
- Fluorescent lay-ins

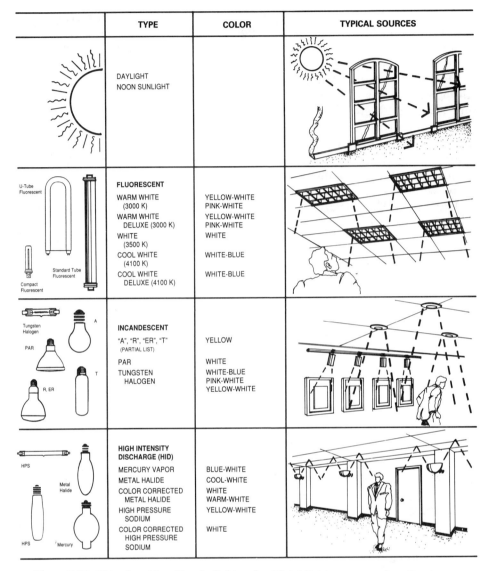

Figure 7.10. This chart identifies daylight and artificial-light sources and applications.

- Surface mounted
- Track
- Strip

Downlights

Downlights are used with standard incandescent and incandescent halogen lamps. They are most frequently used for accent lighting or for ambient lighting in spaces that require dramatic lighting or high-quality color rendition. A downlight can be used in suspended acoustical tile or drywall ceilings. The

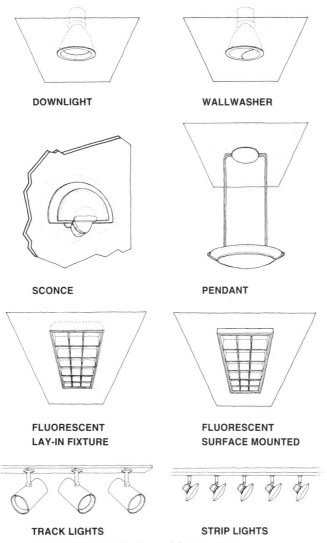

DOWNLIGHT   WALLWASHER

SCONCE   PENDANT

FLUORESCENT   FLUORESCENT
LAY-IN FIXTURE   SURFACE MOUNTED

TRACK LIGHTS   STRIP LIGHTS

Figure 7.11. Typical lighting fixtures.

fixture is a cylinder mounted in the ceiling so that the bottom or face of the fixture is flush with the ceiling and the light beam is directed straight down from the source. The downlight contains either a metallic reflective lining or a black baffle lining. The black baffle lining reduces the reflection created by the lamp and makes the sources less noticeable in the ceiling.

Wallwashers

The wallwasher is also used with a standard incandescent and incandescent halogen lamp. The application for the fixture is, as the name suggests, to wash the wall with light. A common type of wallwasher is similar to the downlight.

The fixture is a cylinder located in the ceiling adjacent to the wall. Unlike the downlight, however, which directs the light straight down, the inside of the wallwasher is reflective on one side of the interior and has a cover over the bottom of that same portion of the fixture to direct the light toward the wall. Another common type of wallwasher is a fixture suspended from the ceiling. This type of fixture allows flexibility in the adjustment of the direction of the light.

Sconces

Sconces are used for accent lighting or ambient lighting in areas that require special lighting. Typically, incandescent lamps are used in sconces because color rendition is a primary consideration. The fixture is mounted on the wall and can provide nondirected light or light that is directed upward or downward. The sconce usually constitutes a decorative element in the space.

Pendant

The pendant fixture is a decorative fixture suspended from the ceiling to provide accent ambient light to achieve a specific design result. Although the pendent fixture was typically used only with incandescent lamps, the refinement of compact fluorescent makes it possible to use fluorescent lamps in these fixtures. The pendant fixture is a nondirectional fixture.

Fluorescent Lay-Ins

The fluorescent's characteristics make it an exceptional lamp for use in general office areas to provide ambient lighting. As a diffuse light, it cannot be used effectively for directional lighting. Fluorescent is generally used in a lay-in fixture, a box that is installed in the suspended ceiling. The lay-in fixture is manufactured and labeled in standards sizes that refer to the dimensions of the fixture in inches: 1 by 1, 1 by 2, 1 by 4, 2 by 2, and 2 by 4. Each of these fixtures typically contains three to four lenses and louvers, or parabolic louver fixtures are available to diffuse the light to different degrees. The deeper the cell in the louver, the greater the diffusion. Louvers are available from $\frac{1}{2}$ to 6 inches deep.

Surface Mounted

Surface-mounted fixtures are fixtures mounted directly on the ceiling. These fixtures are normally selected for one of two reasons: either there is a lack of space above the ceiling to allow the fixture to be recessed, or the appearance of the fixture is preferred for decorative reasons. Although Figure 7.11 illustrates a fluorescent surface-mounted fixture, surface-mounted fixtures can accommodate a variety of lamp types.

Track

Track lighting integrates directional fixtures attached to a powered track that is typically mounted on the ceiling. The use of track lighting allows significant control in the location of the fixture (typically, the fixtures can be located at any desired point on the track) as well as the focus and direction of the light. Track fixtures can also accommodate a variety of lamp types, depending on the desired results.

Strip

Strip fixtures are multiple sockets located in linear housing. The housing may be open or enclosed. Open housing is normally used when the source is hidden, in recessed ceiling coves, for example. With enclosed housing the lamps may be located in tubes or in channels. Enclosed strip fixtures are often used for decorative applications and to highlight specific forms and architectural details.

Lighting Controls

In addition to the manipulation of light through the use of lamps, lenses, or fixtures, lighting can be manipulated and even orchestrated through the use of lighting controls. These controls range in complexity from the simple toggle switch to computerized systems. Typical lighting controls are illustrated in Figure 7.12.

A toggle switch has only two positions, on and off. Although it is the most economical type of lighting control, it is also most limiting.

Dimming systems allow the user to control voltage and therefore light levels. Flexibility is the primary advantage to the use of dimming systems. The components of dimming systems are as follows:

- *Wall Box:* These dimmers replace the toggle switch and are actually located on the wall. They provide varying degrees of dimming by regulating the voltage from the branch circuit to the lamp. This reduces the ability of the filament to glow. The wall box dimmer makes it possible for a person to establish the light level by manipulating the wall control. This dimmer is limited by its capacity to carry voltage.
- *Preset Systems:* A preset dimming system consists of a central control panel wired to a computerized dimming control system. The computer commands the panel board or boards required to power the lights controlled by the system. Rather than manually manipulating lighting levels with wall box units, the preset dimming system allows recall of preestablished lighting levels with the touch of the control panel. One of the advantages of the preset system is its ability to control an unlimited number of lights because the voltage to power the lights does not run through the control system itself. A second advantage of the preset system is that is allows a qualified lighting professional to determine complex and alternative lighting scenarios and program them into the system. Users of the space can implement appropriate light setting for different requirements without lighting design training or training on the use of the system.

Dimming systems were typically used only with incandescent lamps. Now fluorescent lamps are also dimmable as the result of new technology (the electronic ballast) that allows the fluorescent to be dimmed.

COLOR

Color can be used as a design element in conjunction with light, form, scale, and texture to create a desired response on the part of the observer. When

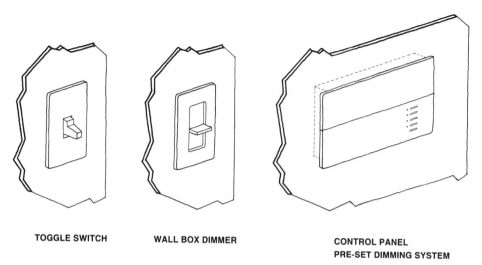

TOGGLE SWITCH   WALL BOX DIMMER   CONTROL PANEL
                                                         PRE-SET DIMMING SYSTEM

Figure 7.12. These types of lighting controls allow the effective integration of artificial and natural light in the office environment.

skillfully selected and applied in the office environment, color can raise employee morale and create an inviting and interesting interior space.

Color is actually only a perception or sensation. The sensation of color is created when light waves strike an object and the waves are absorbed, transmitted, or reflected. When the light rays that are reflected reach the observer's eye, they stimulate the light-sensitive nerves in the eyes and brain, creating the sensation of color. Where in the visible light spectrum those reflected rays operate determines the perceived color of the object. For example, a red object appears red because the rays operating in the red portion of the visible light spectrum are reflected.

To work effectively with color as a design element, the designer manipulates the light source as well as the surface and color of the object, based on an understanding of the human response to color. To better understand and use color in design and art, theorists have developed several color models graphically illustrating the interrelationship of colors. This interrelationship is represented in its simplest form by a color wheel (Figure 7.13), which illustrates primary and secondary colors. *Primary colors* (red, blue, and yellow) are the only true colors—that is, colors which cannot be further divided. When any two of these three colors are mixed with each other, they create *secondary colors* (purple, green, and orange). When the colors are placed in the color wheel, they form a continuous spectrum of color. If the color theory is extended further, the model of the interrelationships becomes a sphere containing every visible color (Figure 7.14). In the color sphere, the colors located around the sphere are called *hues*. The color progressing from lightness to darkness (white to black) are called *values*. The colors that run from neutral gray to hues are called *chroma*. Chroma is also referred to as *saturation*. From this model, the theory becomes increasingly complex, to include tints, tone, shades, and subhues.

This system and others are used to develop color approaches that aid in the selection of colors appropriate for distinct applications: for example, the selection of a work-surface color that will reduce glare significantly, or the selection of a color to increase the perceived brightness in a room.

Although styles affect color selections and approaches, there are no right or wrong color solutions. Color research has substantiated that colors do elicit consistent responses. Because color is such a personal experience, however, creativity with color will always be a valid approach.

ACOUSTICS

Acoustics, the science of sound production, control, transmission, reception, and effects, has always been a clearly recognized priority in specialized spaces such as theaters or auditoriums when excellent sound control and performance is of preeminent concern. To achieve acoustical excellence in these interior spaces, the project architect and interior architect work with an acoustical consultant, a specialist in the physical science of sound.

In the typical office environment, however, the responsibility for acoustical design often rests with the interior architect, frequently because the finances are not available for an acoustical consultant and, perhaps more frequently, because acoustics is an afterthought. Yet the need for acoustical excellence in the office, although less evident, is certainly no less important where the acoustical objective is to support a comfortable and productive workplace. This

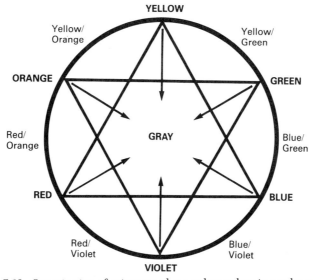

Figure 7.13. Organization of primary and secondary colors in a color wheel.

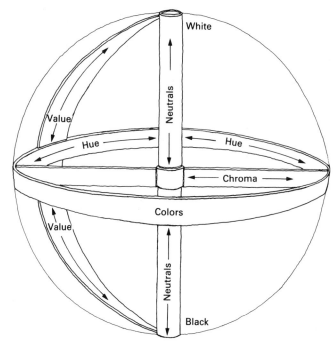

Figure 7.14. Extended model of color, the color sphere, illustrates hue, chroma, and value.

objective is accomplished through the application of fundamental principles of natural acoustics as well as the use of electronic sound systems. These methods are used to control noise and to enhance speech privacy and speech intelligibility.

The achievement of these objectives has never been more challenging than in today's office, an environment characterized by the extensive use of open-planning concepts, the need for flexibility or interchangability in the use of space, and the common use of sophisticated teleconferencing and audiovisual equipment. In the face of these complex requirements, however, major developments in the study of the physics of sound and the physiology of the listener now make it possible to effectively address acoustics for the general office environment.

Sound Generation

The internal sources of sound generation in the office environment are people, furniture, and equipment. People generate sound primarily in the form of speech. Furniture and other inanimate objects in the office generate intermittent sounds when they are in use, such as the movement of a chair or the opening and closing of file drawers. Similarly, equipment such as copiers, computers, and building mechanical systems also generate sound in the office environment. All of these sounds must be controlled to achieve a reasonable sound level in the environment, to avoid an intolerable or distracting noise level, and to promote speech privacy and intelligibility.

Sound Transmission and Absorption

As sound waves, which are generated by people, furniture, and equipment, move through a room and interact with the room components, they are transmitted, absorbed, and reflected back into the room (Figure 7.15). Sound is transmitted through barriers such as floors, partitions, ceilings, and doors. It also travels or leaks around barriers such as partitions. As sound waves travel through a barrier, a portion of the sound is absorbed by the materials. The amount of sound absorption or reflection of the sound wave is a function of thickness, density, and porosity of the materials. Generally, materials that are thick, porous, and soft absorb more sound than do those that are thin, dense, and hard.

Sound is also reflected from surfaces much as light bounces off glass. The harder the surface, the greater the reflection. As sound is reflected, it behaves with certain characteristics, such as reverberation and echo. *Reverberation* is the reflection of sound from surfaces in a confined space with decreasing energy over time. The larger the room, generally, the greater the reverberation. Excess reverberation results in impairment to speech intelligibility. An *echo* is a long-delayed reflection or repetition of sound that is at a sufficient level to be heard clearly as distinct from the original sound. Echoes can also be disruptive and impair speech intelligibility.

Materials and Treatments for Acoustical Control

The acoustical designer attempts to control sound transmission from one room to another as well as the patterns of sound within a specific room. To accomplish this, the acoustical designer treats the sound source, the path, and the

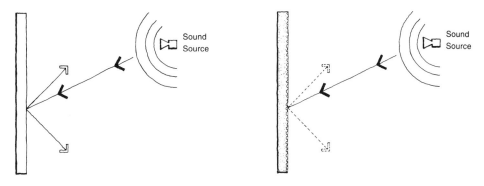

HARD SURFACE REFLECTION   **SOFT SURFACE REFLECTION**

Figure 7.15. The reflection of sound waves is diminished here with a soft, sound-absorbing surface.

receiver to enhance or diminish the sound. Examples of treatment of the sound source include the use of a microphone in a presentation room to enhance a speaker's voice, and the use of isolation techniques to reduce the sound generated by building mechanical equipment. To treat the path, the acoustical designer manipulates the air or building materials. For example, sound that leaks around a full-height partition through a ceiling plenum into the next room can be reduced by sealing the space between the partition and the slab. A partition that allows the transmission of sound by vibration can be constructed with greater attenuating characteristics to reduce the transmission level. The acoustical designer can also treat the receiver of the sound: for example, applying sound-absorbing materials to surfaces in a room that receive sound from an adjacent room.

Essentially, the acoustical design must create the correct reflection patterns to enhance sound as required, while eliminating unwanted transmission or sound, such as reverberation and echo. To accomplish this, the acoustical designer uses the sizing, shape, and angles of the room and room surfaces in conjunction with the selection and application of building materials and finishes to angle, direct, absorb, and reflect the sound.

All building materials have specific acoustical characteristics. Although many people assume incorrectly that a higher level of sound absorption in all materials results in better acoustics, certain surfaces in fact should be sound reflecting, to enhance the intelligibility of speech. Wood and glass are highly reflective surfaces.

Sound-absorbing materials should be applied only to appropriate surfaces to eliminate reverberation or echoes, to control noise, and to assist in achieving speech privacy. Fibrous ceiling tile, carpet, and fabric such as curtains are sound-absorbing materials.

Two standard rating systems evaluate the acoustical properties of various surfaces. To identify the absorptive properties of building materials, the acoustical industry has established a standard rating system, the *noise reduction coefficient* (NRC). The NRC rates materials on a scale of 0.1 to 1.0, based on their ability to absorb sound. The highest number indicates the greatest absorption. The *sound transmission class* (STC) identifies the ability of the surface or structure to reduce or attenuate sound. The higher the STC rating, the more effective the construction will be in reducing sound transmission. Figure 7.16 lists standard acoustical ratings for typical office areas.

Closed-Plan Acoustical Considerations
Primary considerations for acoustical design in a closed-plan environment are the construction of the ceiling, partitions, doors, floors, and mechanical systems.

Ceilings. Ceilings are constructed of plaster or drywall or of suspended acoustical tiles. A drywall or plaster ceiling should be used to reflect sound, for example, in a conference room over a conference table. Suspended tile ceilings should be used in private offices to absorb sound. Ceiling tiles should be selected based on their NRC ratings.

Partitions. Partitions are typically constructed of two materials: drywall and glass. Glass partitions are highly reflective surfaces and should be used where sound reflection is desired or does not created disruptive noise. The construction of a drywall partition can be altered to meet desired levels of sound attenuation. For example, a partition that should be sound attenuating can be designed to produce a higher STC rating than that of a standard drywall partition. The wall is constructed from slab to slab and sealed at the top and bottom of the partition. The partition is constructed with additional layers of drywall and insulation.

Doors. Doors act as sound transmitters. To attenuate sound effectively, the door must be constructed of heavy, dense material and must be gasketed around the perimeter to create an airtight seal.

Floors. Floors reflect airborne sounds just as does any other surface in the room, and floors also generate impact sounds such as the sound of heels hitting a hard surface. Carpet provides sound absorption for both airborne and impact sounds.

TYPE OF OCCUPANCY	NRC Noise Reduction Coefficient	STC Sound Transmission Class
Adjacent Offices		
Confidential	over .75	52
Normal	.60–.75	45
Open Plan Office	over .75	
Mechanical Equipment	over .75	37-60
Corridors and Lobbies	.60–.75	45
Washrooms and Toilets	.60–.75	45-52
Conference Rooms	.60–.75	45-60

NOTES

1. This table lists general conservative recommendations. An acoustical consultant should be involved for highly complex applications.

2. Noise Reduction Coefficient: An arithmetic average of sound absorption coefficients of the four middle frequencies (250, 500, 1000, and 2000 Hz).

3. Sound Transmission Class: A measure of the effectiveness of a partition in reducing airborne sound transmission, not impact noise, low frequency noise sources, or amplified sound. (i.e. related to speech privacy potential.)

Figure 7.16. Standard acoustical ratings for typical office areas.

Mechanical Systems. Building mechanical equipment should be isolated to prevent airborne sounds as well as vibration. The distribution system is also a source of sound. The transmission of sound in supply and return distribution systems is affected by fan noises as well as air sounds resulting from the acuteness of turns or the abruptness of change in duct sizing. This can be remedied through the design of the ductwork as well as its treatment with sound-absorbing linings (although all sound-absorbing treatments should be reviewed for potential air contamination) or sound traps.

Open-Plan Acoustical Considerations

The objective in acoustical design in the open-plan environment is freedom from noise and distraction from intruding speech. Partial-height panels should be located between workstations. Sound-absorbing finishes should be applied to the ceiling, partitions, furniture panels, and other surfaces. In addition, an electronic sound-masking system should be utilized.

Sound-Masking Systems

Sound masking is a means of achieving speech privacy primarily in open-plan situations. Sound masking is often referred to as *white* or *pink sound*, names for standard frequency spectrums generated for masking sound. Essentially, the masking sound raises the sound level in the space to one that interferes with normal speech intelligibility without becoming intrusively audible. To achieve this effectively, the masking sound must be evenly applied throughout the space while remaining as inconspicuous as possible.

Sound/Voice Reinforcement Systems

Electronic voice reinforcement systems can be installed in conference or board room ceilings and are used to maximize the flexibility and interchangeability of spaces used on an as-needed basis for conferencing and training purposes. Large spaces can be subdivided by partition wall, allowing simultaneous use of divided areas, and the system can be designed to create a zone to allow presenters to move freely without carrying or wearing a microphone.

FINISH MATERIALS

Flooring Materials

Flooring materials are categorized as nonresilient (hard) and resilient (soft). Nonresilient floors are hard and durable surfaces. Resilient floors are soft and pliable under foot.

Nonresilient Flooring

The most frequently applied nonresilient flooring materials used in the office environment include:

- Stone
- Agglomerate

- Wood
- Paver tiles and ceramic mosaic tiles

Stone. Natural stones such as marble, granite, and travertines are selected for use in public spaces for their elegance, durability, and long life.

Marble is a metamorphosized recrystallized limestone that is a result of geological evolution. The heat and pressure to which marble is subjected result in a high level of durability. Minerals and dissolved vegetation are credited with lending marble its diverse veining and color characteristics. Although marble is durable and has a long life, it should be properly finished and conditioned. Polished marble has a glossy surface that reflects light and emphasizes the color and marking of the marble. Polished marble is not typically used as a floor finish because it can become slippery, but rather, is used on walls and furniture tops. A honed finish is a satin surface with relatively little light reflection, used for floors and thresholds to eliminate a potentially slippery surface or where traffic would create wear patterns in the finish. Honed finishes are typically more susceptible to soiling than is a polished finish, but a honed finish is more easily restored.

Granite is a hard, moisture-resistant building stone. The stone's high density resists absorption. Like marble, granite can be polished or honed. Granite can also be finished with a thermal or rough texture created by application of a high-temperature flame to the surface of the stone. Sealers and impregnators can be used with certain surfaces to increase resistance to soiling and staining.

Agglomerates. Agglomerates are composition flooring materials produced from small stone chips called aggregates, bonded together in a matrix, then ground and polished. Metal strips are used to divide areas, prevent cracks, and create designs and patterns. An example of an agglomerate is Terrazzo, which is created from marble, granite, onyx, or glass chips suspended in a cement or resinous matrix. Agglomerates can be poured in place or precast. They have an aesthetic appeal, with similar durability, life, and maintenance characteristics as those of natural stone, but at less cost.

Wood. When image is a consideration, hardwoods such as oak, maple, birch, ash, walnut, and cherry are commonly used as flooring materials. These woods are typically used in strips, both tongue-and-grooved and parquet. Parquet flooring is made up of small blocks of hardwood pieced together in patterns of light and dark colors. Although wood flooring is relatively durable, it is more costly to maintain than stone.

Paver Tiles and Ceramic Mosaic Tiles. A paver tile is a glazed or unglazed porcelain or natural clay tile that is formed by a dust-pressed method. Paver tiles are defined by size as having a facial area of 6 square inches or more.

A ceramic mosaic tile is a paver tile of either porcelain or natural clay composition with a plain or abrasive mixture throughout. A ceramic mosaic tile is dense, impervious, fine grained, and smooth. Mosaic tiles are usually $\frac{1}{4}$ to $\frac{3}{8}$ inch thick and have a facial area of less than 6 square inches. These paver tiles are applied in situations that require a very durable, low-maintenance floor where a high image is not required. Paver tiles are less costly than stone or agglomerates and require the lowest level of maintenance of any flooring surface.

All of these nonresilient flooring materials are of greater dimensional thickness than are resilient flooring materials; therefore, they are finishes that should be considered in the context of the architectural detailing of the building for which the additional dimension can be compensated by depressed slabs.

Resilient Flooring

The three predominant types of resilient floor used in the office are:

- Carpet
- Vinyl
- Linoleum

These resilient materials are used in general office, support, and circulation areas where comfort under foot and acoustics are a primary consideration.

Carpet. Carpet is the most common floor finish used in general offices, circulation, and support areas. Carpet improves the acoustics and aesthetics of the space and is relatively easy to maintain. When carpet is used in an office space, it is generally installed throughout the space. Other flooring is installed only when function or image requires it, such as in reception areas, computer rooms, or back-of-house support spaces such as copy rooms, storage, and work areas accommodating office equipment.

Carpet is constructed of synthetic fibers or natural fibers. Synthetic carpet and rug fibers are selected for their durability, stain resistance, cost, and antimicrobial characteristics, that is, carpet fibers that do not promote the growth of microbes, which contribute to poor air quality.

Natural carpet and rug fibers include cotton, cellulosics (hemp, jute, sisal, and grasses), and wool. Although inexpensive, cotton and cellulosic fibers have limited durability and are not commonly used in the office environment. Wool fiber, however, has an excellent appearance and texture and good resistance to soil. Wool is more expensive than synthetic fibers, and although it has excellent wear retention, it is not as durable as most synthetics.

The two types of carpets used in the office environment are modular (carpet tiles) and broadloom carpet. *Modular carpet* is manufactured and installed in small units 1 to 2 feet square (18 inches square is standard). It is constructed primarily of nylon or other synthetic fibers. Modular carpet is used most commonly in conjunction with open-pln systems installations because it is easily removed to access under-floor wire distribution systems or to accommodate frequent reconfigurations of systems furniture. *Broadloom carpet* is manufactured in continuous rolls in widths from 27 inches to 18 feet and is constructed of synthetic fibers or wool.

Both modular and broadloom carpet are constructed in velvet weave, tufted, or fusion-bonded construction. With a velvet weave construction, yarns and backing materials are woven in an interlocking pattern. Yarns are inserted through a premanufactured backing in a tufted carpet. A latex is applied to the backing to lock the loops into place. In a fusion-bonded construction, yarn is embedded into a viscous vinyl paste that hardens to a single element of fiber and backing. Fusion-bonded construction is frequently used for modular carpet because it is dimensionally stable. The fusion-bonded product is also stable at the edge, which eliminates raveling (Figure 7.17).

For office applications, broadloom carpet is available in velvet weave and tufted constructions. Due to the cost of the woven product, the tufted product is far more common in general office applications.

Three common methods are used for installing these carpets:

- Tackless over pad
- Free lay
- Direct glue down

Of these three installation methods, only the tackless over pad does not require the use of an adhesive. The issue of adhesives is a concern as a result of the off-gassing of the chemical from the adhesive into the office environment. As a result, water-based adhesives, which are more environmentally sound, should be used during installation rather than organic solvent-based adhesives.

Tackless-over-pad installation is used with broadloom carpet over a pad or cushion to extend carpet life and increase comfort. The carpet is attached to tack strips along the floor perimeter. The term *tackless* refers to the fact that tacks are not used to attach the carpet to the floor across the general carpet area, the original method of installation for broadloom carpet.

Since most of the contemporary carpet fiber (nylon) used in the general office results in a product that will far outlast its appearance, the use of a pad to increase the life of the carpet is less of a consideration. The carpet stretches with use and should be restretched 3 to 6 months after installation. This type of installation is now normally used for office spaces where the carpet is of high quality and the space demands the plush aesthetic and feel that this type of installation provides.

With free-lay installation, modular carpet is laid directly on the floor. Quick-release glue is applied to the edges of the carpet tile area and in a grid pattern across the floor to prevent movement of the tile. This method of installation also allows the carpet tiles to be pulled away from the floor for easy access to under-floor systems and replacement without damage to the carpet or reapplication of the glue.

Using the direct-glue-down method, the carpet is glued directly to the floor. No pad is used in this installation method. Both broadloom and modular carpet can be installed with the direct-glue-down method. If modular carpet is used, a quick-release glue should be applied.

Vinyl. Vinyl tile is an inorganic compound used when an inexpensive finished floor is desired and acoustics and aesthetics are not a primary consideration. Vinyl tile is also used in heavy work areas or pantries where carpet

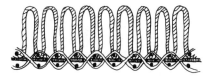

Surface yarns and backing materials are woven in an interlocking pattern.

VELVET WEAVE

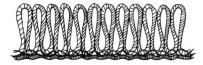

Face yarn tufts are inserted through pre-manufactured backing. A heavy layer of latex is applied to the underside, to firmly lock the loops into place.

TUFTED-LOOP PILE

A secondary backing material may be bonded over this to add body and dimensional stability.

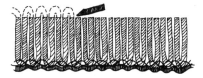

Constructed as tufted-loop pile. Final step shears tips of yarn to create a smooth face finish.

TUFTED-CUT PILE

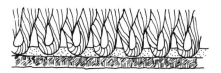

Pile yarn is imbedded into a viscous vinyl paste which hardens into a single element of face fiber and primary backing. A second piece of vinyl is then heat fused to the primary backing.

FUSION-BONDED

Figure 7.17. Standard methods of carpet construction.

could not endure the heavy traffic. Vinyl tile is also resistant to surface moisture, which makes it an inexpensive substitute for ceramic flooring.

Vinyl composition tile (VCT) is the primary vinyl flooring used in office spaces. VCT is a composition of compounds which results in a through-color product, that is, a product in which the color goes through the product from surface to bottom and does not wear off. Generally, VCT is used in a mottled or grained color pattern to hide the marking that occurs under normal wear conditions.

Other types of vinyl flooring are backed and homogeneous sheet vinyl. The backed sheet vinyl is a layered product with a vinyl sheet surface and backing layer. It is used infrequently in commercial applications. Homogeneous sheet vinyl is a nonlayered, nonbacked, solid vinyl product. It is used for highly specialized, seamless applications such as hospital operating rooms.

Vinyl floors provide good wearing surfaces which are relatively abrasive resistant. They are more susceptible to damage from cutting or punctures, certain chemical solvents, and heat such as cigarette burns. These agents are less of a problem with VCT than with sheet products. Vinyl floors are maintained by dust and damp mopping with mild detergents, buffing, and polishing.

Linoleum. Vinyl as an inorganic compound is frequently being replaced with linoleum for office applications. Linoleum is enjoying a resurgence because it is considered environmentally sound. Linoleum is manufactured from organic materials: linseed oil, resins from pine trees, wood flour, ground cork, and jute. Linoleum is available in sheets and tile and is extremely durable and long lasting. It is resistant to chips, stains, and scratches. It is also antistatic, antibacterial, and resistant to indentation.

Figure 7.18 summarizes the characteristics of the floor systems described above.

Wall Covering Materials

Wall covering options include paint, fabric, and ceramic tile.

Paint

Paint applied over gypsum wallboard (drywall) is the most frequently used wall treatment for the office environment. The painted wall is relatively inexpensive, easily maintained, easily changed, and aesthetically clean. Paint is manufactured in flat, eggshell enamel, semigloss, gloss enamel, and modified acrylate copolymer finishes.

Flat Finish. Flat finish (flat latex) is inexpensive and easy to apply. The flat finish is also excellent for hiding the imperfections common to drywall work. The disadvantage to the flat finish is that it is easily marked, quickly soiled, and difficult to clean. Cleaning usually results in additional staining. As with all painted finishes, it is possible to repaint the wall or portions of the wall for a clean appearance. Application to drywall is the most appropriate use of a flat paint finish. It should not be used for doors and trim because it is not durable, is easily marked, and is not cleanable.

Eggshell Enamel. Eggshell enamel is a finish between flat and semigloss. It has a higher luster than the flat finish and has a subtle stipple, giving an appearance very much like that of an eggshell. The finish is not lustrous and consequently, does not highlight drywall imperfections. A combination of flat and semigloss paint, eggshell is resistant to soil and easily cleaned. Eggshell enamel walls must be repainted from corner to corner, however, to prevent

FLOOR TYPE	APPLICATION	COST	ADVANTAGE	DISADVANTAGE
NON RESILIENT	Image spaces	Moderate to high	Beauty, image, durability, low maintenance	Cost, hard under foot, high noise level
Ceramic Tile	Toilet rooms, kitchens or pantries, public corridors	Moderate	Durable, low maintenance, water resistant, cleanable	Cost, hard under foot, high noise level
Terrazzo	Building lobbies, public corridors	Moderate	Durable, cleanable, water resistant, less expensive stone substitute	Hard under foot, high noise level
Stone (marble, granite)	Building lobbies, public corridors, toilet rooms, walls	High	Beauty, durable, high image, low maintenance, cleanable	Cost, hard under foot, high noise level
Wood	Image spaces	High	Beauty, durable, if maintained	Cost, high maintenance, hard under foot, high noise level
RESILIENT	General office	Low to Moderate	Relatively inexpensive, soft under foot, acoustical properties	Less durable than nonresiliant floors
Vinyl Tile	Heavy use areas, wet floor areas	Low	Durable, low maintenance, acoustical properties	Aesthetic quality
Carpet (broad-loom)	General office	Moderate	Soft under foot, acoustical properties, aesthetics	High maintenance: must be cleaned, stretched, repaired, not water resistant
Carpet (modular)	Open plan areas, raised access floor areas	High moderate	Easily repaired, replacement can be isolated, easy access to under floor systems	Cost

Figure 7.18. This chart of flooring materials identifies the applications and relative costs of nonresilient and resilient flooring.

a patchy appearance. For the same reasons as those for flat finish, eggshell enamel should not be applied on doors and trim.

Semigloss Enamel. Semigloss enamel is very durable but highlights imperfections and therefore is rarely used as a wall finish. It is, however, a standard finish for doors, door trim, and miscellaneous metal trim.

Gloss Enamel. Gloss enamel is not used for walls and is occasionally used for trim because it is easily cleaned. Most glossy finishes used in interiors—polyester and polyurethane enamel, for instance—are shop finishes created under controlled conditions.

Copolymers. Copolymers are nonblended mixes of several colors that are close enough to be seen as blending at a short distance. A very hard enamel-type finish, copolymers are resistant to soil. Any dirt that does remain on the surface is difficult to detect due to the color. Copolymers can be spot painted with no indication of the repair. The finish has a low luster with a soft appearance and is frequently used in public spaces where heavy use is expected. Copolymers are approximately twice as expensive as paint.

Vinyl is frequently used as a wallcovering, primarily because it is easily cleaned and durable. It is also perceived as an aesthetic upgrade over paint. Vinyl fabric is approximately four times the price of paint and twice that of copolymer.

The vinyl installation must be clean to avoid seam and edge curling and is used most successfully on flat surfaces. It is also important to ensure that the material meets class A fire code requirements.

Fabric

Fabric wallcoverings are applied to walls in a manner similar to paper and are used in executive or public areas for an upgraded look. For this application, almost any fabric is acceptable. Care in the selection of the texture and pattern, however, is necessary to avoid problems at the cut seams. The fabric wallcovering must also be backed with paper or double acrylic backing for dimensional stability.

Fabric is also used frequently as a wall finish applied to panels to create an acoustical surface. The fabric is stretched over the panel or frame to create a tight, flush surface emulating the direct application above. The fabric selection is more critical here and becomes more of a problem with the increase in size of the panels.

The content of the fabric applied to panels should be hydrophobic (nonabsorbent). Generally, this means that the fabric is nylon or polyester or has a relatively high content of either fiber. A fabric with a high polyester content resists bagging (stretching under high-humidity conditions to the point where it is no longer tight or even on the panel).

It is also important to have the fabric installed on-grain so that the warp (threads running lengthwise) and weft (threads running across the warp) of the fabric is even and runs vertical and horizontal. Fabric for this use should be unbacked so that it is transparent to sound and preserves the integrity of the panel's acoustical properties. It is important to use fabric wallcoverings that meet the appropriate fire safety code requirements.

The applications as well as costs associated with each type of wall covering material is summarized in Figure 7.19.

Ceramic Tile

Various types of ceramic tile are applied to walls for decorative and durability reasons. Due to cost, this covering is usually reserved for rest rooms, kitchens, and dining rooms. Ceramic tile is washable and can be wet continuously without damage to the material. For this reason, it may be advisable to use a water-resistant gypsum board with a ceramic tile covering.

Bases and Applied Trim

All walls should have an applied base element. This element functions as a trim piece at the juncture of the wall and the floor. It also functions as a

WALL MATERIALS	APPLICATION	COST	ADVANTAGE	DISADVANTAGE
PAINT				
Flat Finish (flat latex)	General office walls	Low	Easy to apply, hides drywall imperfections, can be spot painted for repair	Easily marked, quickly soiled, not cleanable
Eggshell Enamel	General office walls	Low	Resistant to soil, does not highlight drywall imperfections as enamel does, durable	Entire surface must be painted for repair
Semigloss	Doors, door trim, metal trim	Low	Durable, cleanable	Entire surface must be painted for repair highlight imperfections
Gloss Enamel	Panels, trim, often applied as shop finishes under controlled conditions	Low	Durable, cleanable	Not easily applied, entire surface must be painted for repair, highlight imperfections
Co-polymers	Public spaces	Moderate	Resistant to soiling, hides soiling, can be spot painted for repair	Cost
FABRICS				
Vinyl Fabric Wall Covering	General office walls	Moderate to high	Durable, cleanable, slight aesthetic upgrade over paint	Must be replaced if damaged
Fabric Wall Covering	Executive or image public spaces	High	Aesthetic quality, can be applied to panels for acoustical properties	Not durable, not cleanable, must meet fire code requirements, cost
CERAMIC TILE	Toilet rooms, kitchens or pantries, dining areas	High	Decorative, durable, cleanable	Cost, high noise levels

Figure 7.19. This chart of wall-covering materials identifies the applications and relative costs of the finishes.

protective bumper for the wall at the floor level. If this element is not present, the wall will be marked and damaged by vacuum cleaners, mops, furniture, and shoes.

The most common and least expensive base used in office space is the vinyl base applied to the wall with adhesive and trimmed to fit. The standard height of these bases is 4 inches. They are available in cove, a curved edge that sits down onto the floor and is used for installation over tile. They are also available straight for installation with carpet. Figure 7.20 depicts these standard base types. The vinyl base is available in a wide range of colors to coordinate with the general color scheme.

Other bases used are ceramic tile, which is also available coved or straight, and wood. The ceramic tile base is normally used only with ceramic tile floors. The wood base, the traditional option, offers a more finished and expensive base than the vinyl (Figure 7.20). Wood base is typically painted in general office space.

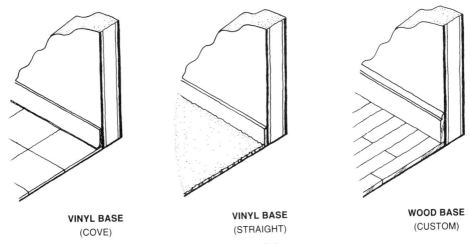

VINYL BASE
(COVE)

VINYL BASE
(STRAIGHT)

WOOD BASE
(CUSTOM)

Figure 7.20. Typical wall base types.

All bases are most effective if a medium-to-dark tone is used to make markings less visible. Painted bases, as with all painted trim, should be finished with at least a semigloss enamel finish to resist wear.

Traditional or upgraded spaces may also be designed with trim elements such as chair rail, door trim, or crown moldings in addition to the base. The finishes of these elements are treated in much the same manner as the base. Their color often varies from the wall in a tone-on-tone type of coloration or a contrasting color.

Window Treatments

Window treatments are used in the office environment primarily for temperature (solar heat load) and light control. Blinds, roller shades, and draperies are the typical window treatments. Figure 7.21 summarizes each of these window treatments, which are described further in the following section.

Blinds

Venetian and vertical blinds have become the most popular window treatments for a number of reasons. They are relatively inexpensive and can lend a feeling of uniformity to the exterior of the building. They are also an excellent solar screening device, offering a range of transparency and shading options to the occupant.

Blinds offer a clean, uncluttered appearance and are relatively easy and inexpensive to maintain. Consequently, they are frequently used as the basic and only window treatment in the office space. Although other sizes are available, blinds are standard in the narrow 1-inch slat version and are available

WINDOW TREATMENT	APPLICATION	COST	ADVANTAGE	DISADVANTAGE
Venetian Blinds	General office	Low	Inexpensive, durable, cleanable, variable control, consistent, neat appearance	Collect dirt, user controlled
Vertical Blinds	General office	Low to Moderate	Inexpensive, durable, remain clean, variable control, consistent, neat appearance	Some mechanical difficulties, user controlled
Roller Shades	General office	High	Durable, remain clean, variable control, neat appearance, passive control possible	Cost, user controlled
Draperies	Executive or public spaces, audio visual areas	Moderate to High	Decorative, blackout capabilities	Cost, Maintenance

Figure 7.21. Comparison of the standard types of window treatment for the office environment.

in a variety of colors to match the office color scheme. They are manufactured in standard elements but must be sized to match the individual window requirement.

Roller Shades

Commercial roller shades are also available as a primary solar screening device. They are generally equipped with woven vinyl fabrics (screen) that vary in transparency. Roller shades are used on the interior or exterior and can be equipped with a solar clock for passive solar control. Roller shades are a more expensive option than blinds. Shades are manufactured with standard mechanisms but must be specified by width and length.

Draperies

Draperies are not frequently used in general office space for a number of reasons. Draperies are more expensive than blinds, which may already be provided as a standard in the building. This makes the drapery an unnecessary decorative device and expense. Draperies are also less durable, as well as more expensive and difficult to maintain, than are the blinds or shades. Because draperies collect dirt and dust, they must be removed, cleaned, and rehung regularly. This often results in a faded drapery and one that might not hang properly. For these reasons, draperies are best utilized in those locations where they are justified for their decorative value or as a blackout element. Blackout draperies are given a special opaque (blackout) lining so that, when closed, they completely block out the light from the window.

This chapter has identified the major design elements of the office environment. This diversity of systems and products provides the interior architect with an incredible tool with which to design an environment responsive to the needs of the organization, and providing a safe, human, and inviting place to work.

Resources

Akers, Herbert W., *Modern Mailroom Management.* New York: McGraw Hill Book Company, 1979.

Alvich-LoPinto, Marie, "Freestanding Furniture Offers Flexibility in Office Design." *Today's Office*, June 1991, pp. 22–26.

Anderson, Donald L., Maryrose T. McGowan, and James A. Hunt, "Preventing Unauthorized Access." *Progressive Architecture*, March 1987, pp. 137–167.

Armero, Marcy Bruch, "Is Greater Privacy the Key to Better Employee Morale?" *Office*, June 1991, pp. 18–22.

Becker, Franklin, *The Successful Office.* Reading, Mass.: Addison-Wesley Publishing Company, Inc., 1982.

Behrends, Jeanette D., "Security-Conscious Site Design." *Progressive Architecture*, March 1987, pp. 137–167.

Birren, Faber, *Color and Human Response.* New York: Van Nostrand Reinhold Company, Inc., 1984.

Birren, Faber, *Light, Color and Environment,* revised edition. New York: Van Nostrand Reinhold Company, Inc., 1982.

Brauer, D. C., and G. Naadimuthu, "Office Facilities Planning Considering Organizational Constraints." *Computers and Operational Research*, 1990, pp. 273–281.

Bryan, John L., *Automatic Sprinkler and Standpipe Systems.* Quincy, Mass.: National Fire Protection Association, 1985.

Burnacz, Joanne G., "A Furniture User's Forum: Tuned into Today's Workplace." *Today's Office*, June 1990, pp. 25–35.

Burton, D. Jeff, "Physical, Psychological Complaints Can Be a Result of Indoor Air Quality." *Occupational Health and Safety*, March 1991, p. 53.

Carlson, Jennifer A., "Defense Productivity Rockets 20 Percent with Open Plan Booster." *Facilities Design and Management*, July/August 1986, pp. 72–75.

Carstairs, Eileen, "Flat Cable: Hidden Solution?" *Interior Design*, August 1986, pp. 214–215.

Clough, Richard H., *Construction Contracting*, 5th Edition. New York: John Wiley & Sons, Inc., 1986.

Clough, Richard Hudson, and Glen A. Sears, *Construction Project Management*. New York: John Wiley & Sons, Inc., 1979.

Cody, Angela, "Dressing Your Office for Success." *Today's Office*, December 1990, pp. 31–35.

"Construction Industry Management." *Aberdeen's Concrete Construction*, February 1992, pp. 170–173.

DeGoff, Robert A., and Howard A. Friedman, *Construction Management: Basic Principles for Architects, Engineers and Owners*. New York: John Wiley & Sons, Inc., 1985.

Dieffenbach, Bruce, and Don Sandberg, "An Ergonomic Chair: One of the Most Important Office Tools; Choosing Chairs to Fit the Job." *Telemarketing Magazine*, February 1991, pp. 52–57.

Dietsch, Deborah, "Picking the Brain of the Intelligent Building." *Interiors*, April 1985, pp. 13–14.

Dubin, Fred S., "Integrated Building Systems: Adding the Human Element." *Consulting-Specifying Engineer*, July 1990, pp. 56–72.

Eby, Robert W., Jr., and David Mahone, "How to Use Ergonomics as a Loss Control Tool." *Risk Management*, March 1991, pp. 42–47.

Economic Analysis of Office Design's Role in Organization Effectiveness. Buffalo, N.Y.: BOSTI (Buffalo Organization for Social and Technological Innovation, Inc.), 1991.

Edwards, Sandra, *Office Systems: Designs for the Contemporary Workspace*. New York: PBC International, 1986.

Egan, M. David, *Architectural Acoustics*. New York: McGraw-Hill Book Company, 1988.

The Environmental Resource Guide. Washington, D.C.: The American Institute of Architects, 1992.

Everest, F. Alton, *The Master Handbook of Acoustics*, 2nd edition. Blue Ridge Summit, Pa.: TAB Books, 1989.

Fleming, G. Ross, "Taking Office Lighting to Task." *Modern Office Technology*, August 1991, pp. 36–38.

Foulkes, Timothy J., and Gregory C. Tocci, "Sound Isolation in Floors." *Progressive Architecture*, March 1991.

Galer, I. A. R., *Applied Ergonomics Handbook*. London: Butterworth & Company (Publishers) Ltd., 1987.

Gardner, James B., "Daylighting Cuts Energy Use to 19,600 Btu per Sq. per Year." *Architectural Record*, January 1984, pp. 139–143.

Hahn, Kathleen, "The Eyes Have It: Workers See That Lighting Counts." *Personnel*, November 1990, p. 14.

Haworth, Richard G., "Human-Friendly Offices to Impact Employee Health and Productivity." *Telemarketing Magazine*, August 1991, pp. 60–61.

Head, George, "Fitting the Job to the Worker." *National Underwriter*, August 6, 1990, pp. 7, 19–21.

Henderson, Justin, and Peter Barna, "New Research That Puts a Fresh Perspective on Lighting Spaces." *Interiors*, June 1986.

Honeycutt, Alan, "Creating a Productive Work Environment." *Supervisory Management*, November 1989, pp. 12–16.

Horowitz, Janice M., "Crippled by Computers." *Time*, October 12, 1992, pp. 70–72.

Hund, Robert, "Marble Care." Unpublished article, Marble Institute of America, Farmington, Mich.

The Impact of the Office Environment on Productivity and Quality of Working Life: Comprehensive Findings. Buffalo, N.Y.: BOSTI (Buffalo Organization for Social and Technological Innovation, Inc.), 1982.

Joyce, Marilyn, "Ergonomics Will Take Center Stage During the 90s and into New Century." *Occupational Health and Safety*, January 1991, pp. 31–37.

Kantor, Aileen, "Making the Workplace a Fit Place." *Business and Health*, July 1991, pp. 70–72.

Katzel, Jeanine, "A Common Sense Approach to Controlling Indoor Air Quality." *Plant Engineering*, April 18, 1991, pp. 32–38.

Katzel, Jeanine, "Introduction to Ergonomics." *Plant Engineering*, June 6, 1991. pp. 48–55.

Kaufman, John E., *Illuminating Engineering Society of North America: Lighting Handbook*. New York: Illuminating Engineering Society of North America, 1990.

Kleinschrod, Walter A., "Office Space Planning: Finding the Right Balance." *Today's Office*, May 1991, pp. 36–40.

Kruk, Leonard B., "Meeting the Challenges of Designing the Automated Office." *Interior Design*, October 1986, pp. 76–82.

Kwiecinski, Gordon F., "What the Automated Office Needs: Planning." *Office*, June 1989, pp. 78–79.

Labs, Kenneth, "Acoustical Dimensions of Design." *Progressive Architecture*, April 1991.

"Lighting: An Art Supported by a Technology." *Architectural Record*, April 1985, pp. 156–163.

Lindo, David K., "It's Time to Emphasize Ergonomics." *Supervision*, May 1991, pp. 14–16.

Magliano, John U., "Access Flooring: Can It Solve the Wiring Problems of the Electronic Office?" *Interior Design*, March 1986.

Marberry, Sara O., "Updated Color Progress for Systems Manufacturer Is a Marketing Response to Designer Demand." *Contract*, March 1986.

Maren, Michael, "Productivity Palace: The Surprising Science of Workplace Effectiveness." *Success*, September 1991, pp. 30–36.

Marshall, John S., "Designers Get a Grip on Gripes: Choose Top Ten Lighting Mistakes." *Contract*, September 1986.

Marshall, John S., "Task Lighting Improves Productivity in Open Plan Workstations." *Contract*, July 1986.

Martinez, Michelle Neely, "Work Space: In Search of a Productive Design." *HR Magazine*, February 1990, pp. 36–39.

Maserjian, Karen, "Products That Are Environmentally Benign." *Interior Design*, August 1991, pp. 108–112.

McMillan, Lorel, "Carpet Backs: The Underside View of Your Carpet Selection." *Facilities Design and Management*, July/August 1986.

Mudgett, John G., "Building Freedom into Designing Office Interiors." *Office*, December 1988, pp. 47–49.

Mutchler, Robert C., "New Directions in Project Delivery." *Architecture*, August 1992, p. 19.

Myerson, Jeremy, "Health Is Wealth in the Workplace." *Management Today*, June 1991, pp. 82–84.

"Notes: On the Greening of Interior Design." *Interior Design*, August 1991, pp. 77–91.

Novitski, B. J., "Controlling Direct Sunlight." *Architecture*, June 1992, pp. 110–113.

Olin, Harold A., *Construction Principles, Materials and Methods*. Chicago: The Institute of Financial Education and Interstate Printers and Publishers, Inc., 1983.

Olin, Harold B., John L. Schmidt, and Walter H. Lewis, *Construction: Principles, Materials and Methods*. Chicago: Institute of Financial Education, 1975.

Overman, Stephanie, "Work Space: In Search of the Ideal Environment." *HR Magazine*, February 1990.

Parsons, Robert R., *1991 HVAC Systems and Applications, ASHRAE Handbook*. Atlanta, Ga.: American Society of Heating, Refrigerating and Air Conditioning Engineers, 1991.

Paznik, Megan Jill, "Ergonomics Isn't Last Year's Fad—It's This Year's Profits." *Administrative Management*, December 1987, pp. 12–13.

Rand, George, "Designing Healthy Interiors." *Interior Design*, October 1986, pp. 76–82.

Reznikoff, Sivon, "Design for Life Safety/Public Health and Welfare." *Interior Design*, October 1986, pp. 76–82.

San Luis, Ed, *Office and Office Building Security*. Los Angeles: Security World Publishing Company, Inc., 1973.

Smith, William, "Computer Accessories Decrease Health Hazards and Increase Productivity." *Telemarketing Magazine*, February 1991, pp. 50–51.

Sopko, Sandra, "Open Plan Offices: An Investment in People." *Office*, December 1988.

Stafford, Jan, "Is Your Office Making You Sick?" *Today's Office*, October 1990, pp. 29–33.

The Steelcase Study of Office Environments: Do They Work? (conducted by Louis Harris & Associates, Inc.). Grand Rapids, Mich.: Steelcase, Inc., 1980.

Stein, Benjamin, and John S. Reynolds, *Mechanical and Electrical Equipment for Buildings*, 8th edition. New York: John Wiley & Sons, Inc., 1992.

Tetlow, Karen, "Innovative Power Base Is the Latest in Wire Management Systems." *Interiors*, September 1986, pp. 31–32.

Thomas, Marita, "Is Your Office Air Fit to Breathe?" *Facilities Design and Management*, July/August 1986, pp. 68–71.

Thomas, Robert E., and Leo A. Smith, "Ergonomics According to Kipling." *Bobbin*, February 1991, pp. 80–86.

Tompkins, James A., and John A. White, *Facilities Planning*. New York: John Wiley & Sons, Inc., 1984.

Tyler, Geoff, "Design Versus Production?" *Management Accounting*, June 1991, p. 50.

U.S. Department of Justice, *Federal Register: Nondiscrimination on the Basis of Disability by Public Accommodations and in Commercial Facilities; Final Rule*. July 26, 1991.

Vonier, Thomas, "Ask Not for Whom the Alarm Rings." *Progressive Architecture*, March 1987, pp. 137–167.

Wagner, Carlton, *The Wagner Color Report*. Chicago: Color Communications, Inc., 1986.

White, Frank, and Ross E. Getman, "Indoor Air Quality: What Managers Can Do." *Employment Relations Today*, Summer 1990, pp. 93–101.

Whitehouse, Douglas, "Lighting's Contribution to the Well-Run Office." *Office*, December 1988, pp. 32–41.

Williams, James D., "Detecting Intrusions and Controlling Access." *Progressive Architecture*, March 1987, pp. 137–167.

Willson, David W., "The Control of Light, Part Three." *Interior Design*, March 1985, pp. 266–269.

Winer, Joy, "Restoring Calm to Office Space Chaos." *Management World*, May/June 1989, pp. 20–23.

Wines, James, "Inside Outside: The Aesthetic Implications of Green Design." *Interior Design*, August 1991, pp. 114–120.

Woolley, Suzanne, "Making Your Office Human-Friendly." *Business Week*, August 20, 1990, pp. 100–101.

Wormald, Karen, "Color Coding Boosts Efficiency and Morale." *Office Systems*, September 1991, pp. 64–71.

Wotton, Earnest, "Office Lighting That Works." *Canadian Insurance*, September 1989, pp. 24–27.

Woudhuysen, James, "By Design: Open and Shut Case." *Management Today*, January 1990, p. 25.

Request for Qualifications

April 15, 1996

Ms. Julie K. Rayfield
Principal
AI/Boggs
1445 New York Avenue, NW
Suite 400
Washington, DC 20005-2106

Dear Ms. Rayfield:

I am pleased to announce that AI/Boggs has been prequalified to provide interior design services for the relocation of XYZ Corporation's new regional headquarters facility.
XYZ Corporation, a leading high-tech organization with over 9500 employees across the world, is currently evaluating existing buildings in northern Virginia for its new regional headquarters facility, which will house approximately 720 local employees. In

addition to general office areas, the facility will include a data center, a library, a fitness center, training/conference areas, and a 200-person cafeteria.

The project schedule calls for occupancy of the new facility by December 1998. A preliminary construction budget of $45 per square foot has been established.

We anticipate that we will require from the selected interior design firm the following services:

- Programming
- Alternatives evaluation
- Schematic design
- Design development
- Construction documentation
- Construction administration

To assist us in our selection of a qualified firm, we request that you submit to us a qualifications statement addressing your firm's credentials to provide the required services. After a comprehensive review of the responses, we will develop a shortlist of several firms to interview and, ultimately, from which we will request a proposal.

Your qualifications statement should address the following:

Firm Description

- Background and corporate organization of the firm
- Location(s)
- Areas of expertise and associated percentages of revenue
- Staff size and composition
- In-house computer and CADD resources

Project Experience

For relevant projects for which your firm has been commissioned, provide the following information:

- Client
- Size
- Location
- Type of project (relocation, renovation, expansion, etc.)
- Project commencement/project completion
- Project budget
- Special areas
- Contact and telephone number
- Other information of interest

Project Management

- Budget control/track record
- Schedule control/track record
- Internal quality assurance program

Proposed Project Approach

- Project schedule
- Narrative project approach, including services

Proposed Project Team

For each person proposed on the project team, provide the following information:

- Proposed role
- Years of experience and year with your firm
- Educational background
- Professional registrations or licenses
- Relevant project experience
- Availability

Please forward two copies of your qualifications statement to me no later than 5:00 p.m. April 30, 1996. We will develop a shortlist

based on a comparative evaluation of firms' credentials. The
evaluation criterion is as follows: relevant project experience,
including references (40 percent), team credentials (30 percent),
project management and project approach (15 percent), and firm
credentials, including resources, location, size, etc. (15 percent).
Thank you in advance for your time and effort in responding to this
request. If you have any questions or require clarification, I can be
reached at (202) 555-1234.

Sincerely,

Joe T. Smith
Manager, Facilities and Operations

Appendix Two

Request for Fee Proposal

May 10, 1996

Ms. Julie K. Rayfield
Principal
AI/Boggs
1445 New York Avenue, NW
Suite 400
Washington, DC 20005-2106

Dear Mrs. Rayfield:

Thank you for taking the time yesterday to present your credentials to assist XYZ Corporation in its upcoming relocation project. I am pleased to announce that AI/Boggs is one of two firms from which we are requesting a fee proposal.

As you know, XYZ Corporation is currently evaluating sites in northern Virginia for its new 400,000-square-foot headquarters facility, which will house 1600 local employees. In addition to general office areas, the facility will include a data center, a library, a fitness center, training/conference areas, and a 500-person cafeteria.

The project schedule calls for occupancy of the new facility by December 1998. A preliminary construction budget of $45 per square foot has been established.

XYZ Corporation currently has planning/workstation standards; however, we anticipate that the selected interior design firm will be required to review and modify these standards. No existing furniture will be reused in the new headquarters; all furniture, which will be primarily systems furniture, will be new.

Throughout the project, the selected interior design firm will have day-to-day contact with, and will be acting under the direction of, Mr. Lyle Greene, who is a facility manager of XYZ Corporation. Approximately six other key XYZ Corporation personnel will be present during formal presentations at the completion of each phase of work, and occasionally at regular weekly progress meetings. Their collective approval is required before advancement to the next phase.

No programming information has been compiled for the new headquarters facility, although a strategic master plan study was completed for XYZ Corporation in March 1994. We anticipate that approximately 20 interviews with key personnel will be required. The following basic services will be required:

Phase 1: Programming

- Programming
- Field verification
- Preliminary opinion of probable cost
- Presentation and approval

Phase 2: Alternatives Evaluation

- Test fits
- Mechanical/electrical engineering evaluation

- Statement of suitability
- Opinion of probable cost

Phase 3: Schematic Design

- Blocking and stacking
- Workstation standard review and modification
- Schematic space plan
- Schematic design
- Opinion of probable cost update
- Presentation and approval

Phase 4: Design Development

- Final space plan
- Interior construction
- Furniture and finishes
- M/E engineering coordination
- Opinion of probable cost update
- Presentation and approval

Phase 5: Contract Documentation

- Working drawings and specifications for interior construction, furniture, and furnishings
- M/E engineering coordination
- Consulting coordination
- Bid/negotiation/award

Phase 6: Contract Administration

- Ongoing project consultation
- Weekly site visits
- Submittal review
- Move coordination assistance
- Punch list

Please provide a lump-sum fee for the basic scope of services described above. Estimate the number of personnel hours associated with each phase. In addition, estimate the reimbursable expenses for the project.

It is anticipated that XYZ Corporation might require from the selected interior design firm additional services beyond the basic scope of work. Please provide a fee for each of the following additional services:

- Mechanical/electrical engineering (indicate whether to be provided in-house or by a consultant)
- Art, interior signage, and accessories
- As-built drawings
- Executive offices
- Supplemental move coordination

Please forward one copy of your fee proposal to me no later than 5:00 p.m. May 17, 1996. We expect to make our decision by COB May 19, 1996.

Thank you again for your time and effort in preparing your proposal. If you have any questions or require clarification, I can be reached at (202) 555-1234.

Sincerely,

Joe T. Smith

Manager, Facilities and Operations

Appendix Three

Programming Questionnaire

Introduction

A planning study is currently under way to examine the current and future space requirements of XYZ Corporation. To accomplish this study, certain organizational and operational requirements must be identified and collected. This questionnaire represents the beginning of the collection of XYZ Corporation's requirements. Additional questionnaires and interviews may also be necessary.

You have been selected to identify the requirements requested in this questionnaire for your organization. Please exercise due care in providing the information in an accurate and timely manner.

Upon completion of the questionnaire, you will be interviewed by a consultant who will use your responses as a guide. You will have the opportunity to clarify and/or provide additional information at that time.

This questionnaire is divided into five sections. These are as follows:

- *Section I—Work Group Identification.* This section is provided to identify you and how you may be contacted for questions and to specifically identify the work group you are representing.

- *Section II—Staff and Shared Support Equipment.* This section requests information regarding space for staff and for the shared equipment (i.e., PC terminals, printers, files, etc.) within your work group.

- *Section III—Support Areas.* This section requests information regarding areas that your group has and can share with another group (i.e., library, etc.).

- *Section IV—Adjacency.* This section requests information regarding the desired location of your group relative to other groups and/or common support functions.

- *Section V—Conference/Training Requirements.* This section requests information regarding conference and training requirements.

Section I - Work Group Identification

Work Group Title & Code: _____

Contact Person Name: _____ Phone No.: _____

Current Location (Room #'s): _____

Department Head: _____

(List all Divisions in your Department by Title & Code)

Division/Office Title	Check Box for Divisions/Office this Questionnaire Represents
_____	☐
_____	☐
_____	☐
_____	☐
_____	☐
_____	☐
_____	☐
_____	☐
_____	☐
_____	☐
_____	☐

Remarks: _____

For Contractor Use Only

Office Code: _____ Interviewed By: _____

Date Received: _____ Date: _____

Review By: _____ Date: _____

Data Entry: _____ Date: _____

Revised By: _____ Phone No.: _____

Revised By: _____

Contact Person: _____

Abbreviation Code: _____

Date of Interview:

Section II - Staff and Shared Support Equipment

This section is requesting information regarding staff (pages 3 & 4) and the support equipment (page 5) that is located within your group and is shared.

Complete the staffing information completely. Please identify your group's staffing by position title, indicate full time or part time, supervisory or non-supervisory. Identify the category as to: Permanent (P) (includes interns), Non-MTP (N) (includes stay-in-school, summer aide, and co-op), Contractor (C) or Other (O). In the subsequent column, note the quantity of personnel currently assigned. Indicate the duration of seasonal staff and any additional comments in the remarks column. Indicate "full time/part time personnel" as full time.

Examples are provided below. Group similar positions/titles together.

STAFF

Work Group Title and Code: _____

Position/Title	FT/PT	Supvr. Y	N	Category	July 1994 Quantity	Remarks
Prog. Manager	FT	✓		P	1	
Secretary	FT		✓	P	2	

Section II - Staff and Shared Support Equipment (Continued)

STAFF

Work Group Title and Code: _____

Position/Title	FT/PT	Supvr. Y N	Category	July 1994 Quantity	Remarks

Section II - Staff and Shared Support Equipment (Continued)

List support equipment that is located within your group which is shared.

For example, a PC terminal or typewriter all secretaries access should be listed, while a PC in a secretary's station would not be identified. Another example: vertical files located in a corridor accessible to all staff would be identified on the following list, while files in an enclosed room would be identified in Section III. Include equipment that has been purchased but has not been delivered.

SHARED SUPPORT EQUIPMENT

Work Group Title and Code: _____

	July 1994 Quantity	Remarks
Equipment		
Terminal/PC		
Printer Only		
LAN File Server		
Microfiche Reader		
Typewriter		
Table Top Copier		
Copiers		
FAX		
UPS		
CADD Station		
Other:		
Storage		
Legal Vertical File		
Letter Vertical File		
Lateral Files		
Rotating Lektrievers		
Storage Cabinets		
Bookcases		
Safe		
Other:		
Worksurfaces		
Work Tables		
Desk		
Mail/Message Table		
Other:		
Coatrack		
Other:		
Other:		
Other:		

Section III - Support Areas

This section requests information regarding your group's support areas. Include any additional spaces that have been funded but not yet constructed.

Indicate the quantity of support spaces. Do not report any information that was recorded in Section II. If necessary, attach an additional page to list additional support spaces and when there are multiple requirements for a support room type (e.g., various conference rooms with widely differing functions). Please list in the Remarks column: room names, current square footage of space, special requirements, shared use of functions, frequency of use (days/week), etc. Include equipment and furniture listings for each space (e.g., a file room could have a list of 10 vertical files, 90 lateral files and a desk).

Identify special requirements above normal office environment requirements for each space in the Codes column using the legend provided (at the bottom of the page).

If you currently share a space with another organization, please cite the organization. Where applicable, note in the remarks column personnel who are located in the facility.

SUPPORT AREA

Work Group Title and Code: _____

Area	July 1994 Quantity	Total Square Footage	Remarks (Codes, Room Titles, Personnel) (List equipment in rooms)
Library			
Computer Room			
Equipment Room			
Workroom/Processing Room			
File Room			
Supply Room			
Storage Room			
Reception Area			
Reproduction Room			
Conference Room			
Duty Officer's Room			
Other			

Special Requirements Codes (Above normal office standards only)		
1. Telephone Service 2. Electric Service 3. Lighting 4. Acoustics 5. Finish Wall/Floor 6. Floor Loading 7. Raised Floor 8. Vibration Isolation	9. Air Conditioning 10. Air Exhaust 11. Water Service 12. Chemical Drainage 13. Security/Alarm 14. Freight Elevator 15. TV or Radio Antenna 16. Audio/Visual	17. Fire Detection/Suppression 18. 24-Hour Operation 19. Vault Class A 20. Vault Class B 21. SCIF 22. Teleconferencing 23. (Other - Please Specify)

Section IV - Adjacency

This section requests information regarding the importance of your group's proximity to another group or a common support element and/or space within the building. In the column, list the name of the group/area to which your group has a desired adjacency. Include "Public visitors" if appropriate. If you list Public, indicate in the remarks column how frequently (in terms of people per day), the nature of the contract, and length of stay. Check the appropriate column for preferred proximities. Add any comments in the final column.

Work Group Title and Code: _____

Divisions within XYZ Corporation	Immed. Adjacent (1)	Same Floor (2)	Adjacent Floor (3)	Remarks

Section V - Conference/Training Requirements

This section requests information regarding specific conference and training facilities hosted by your group. Identify all meetings initiated by your group in terms of number of days per month and how long each session lasts in terms of hours per day. Note how long a lead time you usually have in scheduling for these spaces. Under remarks, please list any special requirements such as classified or secret.

Please complete the following:

Work Group Title and Code: _____

Participants	Frequency (Days/Month)	Duration (Hours/Day)	Attendees (%) XYZ Corp. Other		Scheduling	Remarks
Conference						
Up to 8						
Up to 15						
Up to 25						
Up to 50						
Up to 100						
Up to 200						
Training						
Up to 15						
Up to 25						
Up to 50						
Up to 100						
Up to 200						
Other						
Other (Specify):						
Other (Specify):						
Other (Specify):						

Glossary

Accent Lighting   Directional lighting to emphasize a particular object or area.

Access Floor   A finished floor elevated approximately 6 to 24 inches above the floor slab, usually used in computer rooms. The space between the slab and the finished floor is used for cable and HVAC distribution. Access floors are usually assembled from 2-inch-square removable panels supported on adjustable-height pedestals. This allows for easy access to the electric work below the finished floor.

Acoustical Ceiling   A suspended ceiling hung with acoustical tiles for the purpose of finish, sound control, and confinement. *See also* Suspended Ceiling.

Acoustical Panels   Demountable panels constructed of sound-attenuating material, which reduces the ambient sound level in a space.

Acoustical Privacy   The degree to which sounds produced in a given area are contained within that area.

Acoustical Surface   A surface that absorbs sound.

Acoustical Tiles   Sound absorbent tiles used as a ceiling finish.

Acoustics   Science that deals with the production, control, transmission, reception, and effects of sound.

Aesthetic   Having a pleasing appearance or effect.

Agglomerate   A composition flooring material that is produced from small stone chips called aggregate.

Aggregate   Small stone chips such as marble bonded together in a matrix to create an agglomerate.

Air Balancing   The adjustment of the flow of conditioned air into a space by use of dampers, diffusers, or other control mechanisms to maintain proper air quality.

Air Conditioning   The treatment of air within a space to control temperature, humidity, and cleanliness.

Air Diffuser   A device that distributes conditioned air from a duct into a space. Adjustable vanes allow directional control of airflow.

Air Quality   The quality of the air within a space measured in terms of freshness, temperature, moisture content, and freedom from toxins.

Ambient Lighting   Lighting throughout an area that produces general illumination.

Automatic Sprinkler System   A system of pipes, tubes, or conduits with heads or nozzles that disperse water or other fire-extinguishing materials throughout a fire area.

Baffle   A single opaque or translucent element to shield a source from direct view at certain angles, or to absorb unwanted light.

Ballast   A device used with a fluorescent (electric-discharge) lamp to obtain the necessary voltage to start the source.

Building-Related Illness   A specific disease that is attributed to air quality and is accompanied by physical signs and clinical abnormalities.

Built-in   A furniture element that is usually custom fitted and bolted into place.

Bulb   A source of electrically powered light.

Cable   One or more electrical conductors (wires) inside a protective insulated covering.

Carpet Cushion   Any material placed under a carpet. Also called carpet pad.

Carpet Tiles   Uniform squares of carpet, usually 18 to 24 inches.

Ceramic Mosaic   A paver tile of porcelain or natural clay composition.

Chroma/Intensity   Color saturation brightness or dullness of a hue.

Circulation Area   That portion of the gross area, both horizontal and vertical, that is required for physical access to a space, including lobbies, ceiling-high corridors that cannot be removed or to which the public has unrestricted access, stairwells, elevator shafts, and escalators.

Circulation Factor   Circulation is conveyed as a factor which represents the percentage of the project's total area that is allotted to circulation space.

Closed Plan   A planning concept in which the available space is divided into private offices, and conference and support rooms with doors and floor-to-ceiling partitions.

Color   The characteristic of light by which an observer can distinguish between two structure-free patches of light of the same size and shape.

Color Rendering Index (CRI)   The measure of degree of color shift of an object when illuminated by a light sources and compared with the color of the same object when illuminated by a reference source of comparable color temperature.

Color Rendition   The effect of a light source on the color appearance of objects.

Column   A vertical structural support element.

Column Bay   The area defined by any four columns, usually measured from centerline to centerline.

Complementary Colors   Colors appearing opposite one another on the color wheel.

Conductor   Any material used to conduct electricity.

Conduit   A round tubelike enclosure intended to protect insulated conductors from external damage or interference.

Connective Hardware   Hardware used to connect panels to each other in a furniture system.

Conventional Furniture   Usually, freestanding furniture that is not part of a furniture system.

Conversion   Includes the redesign, remodeling, and conversion of a building from one use to another (i.e., hospital or warehouse to office space).

Copolymer Finish   A nonblended mix of enamel-like paints.

Core   The central vertical space in a building, which the elevators, fire stairs, rest rooms, and/or mechanical equipment.

Core Closet   Power, telephone, or other service closet located in a building.

Core Configuration   The layout and shape of the space occupied by the core.

Core Corridor   The circulation corridor around the building core.

Core Drill   A hole drilled through the floor slab to facilitate the access of cables.

Core Massing   Modification of a core through the adjacent placement of supply and service rooms.

Cove Base   A base with a slight curve at the bottom.

Cove Lighting   A lighting source shielded from view by a ledge or horizontal recess that lights the ceiling and wall.

Credenza   A furniture element, usually placed behind a desk, which consists of a surface over storage or file space.

Daylight Lamp   A lamp producing a spectral distribution approximately that of daylight.

Dedicated Circuit   An electrical circuit that runs independent of other circuits. This is particularly useful for computer power supplies that must remain constant.

Diffusion   The breaking up of a beam of light and the spreading of its rays in many directions.

Dimmer   A device used to control the intensity of light emitted by controlling the voltage or current to it.

Direct-Glue-Down Carpet Application   The installation of a carpet by gluing it directly to a concrete slab.

Direct Lighting   Lighting that distributes 90 to 100 percent of the light in the general direction of the surface to be illuminated. The term usually refers to light emitted downward.

Downlight   A small direct lighting unit that directs the light downward and can be recessed, surface mounted, or suspended.

Dry Pipe Automatic Sprinkler System   An automatic sprinkler system consisting of a series of pipes and sprinkler heads. The pipes are filled with air or nitrogen under pressure. Once activated, the air or nitrogen is released and a water supply is allowed into the pipes.

Drywall   A wall covering of gypsum board or other dry sheets. *See also* Gypsum Board.

Eggshell Enamel   A slightly stippled paint finish with a luster that is somewhat higher than that of flat finish paint, but not as high as that of semigloss enamel.

Egress   Exit.

Electrical Closet   A closet containing electrical panelboards.

Electric-Discharge Lamp   A lamp in which light (radiant energy near the visible spectrum) is produced by the passage of an electric current through a vapor or gas (fluorescent lamp, high-intensity discharge lamp).

Elevation   A drawing showing a vertical image of a partition or other element viewed to scale with dimensions.

Emergency Lighting   Lighting designed to supply illumination essential to safety of life and property in the event of failure of the normal supply.

Ergonomics   The science of adaptation of the work environment to suit a worker's physical dimensions and function. Also called human engineering.

Fire Rating   A system of rating materials in terms of their ability to withstand laboratory-controlled test fires for a specified period of time.

Fixture   The actual hardware device that holds a lamp in position, distributes the light, and provides a connection to the power source.

Flameproofing   Chemical treatment of a material to impede or prevent combustion or to render the material self-extinguished.

Flat Paint   A dull-finish paint.

Floor Load   The total weight of all elements supported by a floor. Usually expressed in pounds per square foot.

Fluorescent Lamp   A low-pressure mercury electric-discharge lamp in which phosphors transform ultraviolet energy into light.

Flush-Mounted Light Fixture   A light fixture that is recessed in the ceiling or a surface with the face or opening of the fixture flush with the surface.

Footcandle   A unit of measurement of light describing the amount of light falling on a surface or object. One footcandle is equal to the amount of light thrown by one candle on a square foot of a vertical surface that is one foot away.

Freestanding Partition   A prefabricated demountable panel that stands vertically, independent of the system. These are usually surfaced in fabric or plastic laminate and are capable of standing alone or being "ganged" with others of the same type. Also called freestanding screens, space dividers, privacy panels, and acoustical screens.

Furniture-Integrated Lighting   Lighting fixtures, for both task and ambient lighting, that are incorporated into a furniture system.

Furred-out Column   A column or wall that has been built out to create a space, typically for wire distribution purposes.

Gas-Filled Lamp   An incandescent lamp in which the filament operates in a bulb filled with one or more inert gases.

Gasket   A thin, flat seal placed between two joining parts to prevent the leakage of air, water, or sound.

Gauge   The distance between rows of tufts across the width of a tufted carpet.

General Lighting   Lighting designed to provide a uniform level of illumination throughout an area.

Glare   Extreme brightness or contrast in light levels that causes discomfort to the eyes.

Gloss Enamel   An enamel paint with a very shiny finish.

Grain   The direction of a piece of fabric. Selvage edges run in the same direction as the grain.

Grille   A louvered or perforated covering for air passage through a wall, ceiling, or floor. *See also* Air Diffuser.

Gross Area   The sum of all floor areas of a building [including all stories or areas that have floor surfaces and a clear standing headroom of $6\frac{1}{2}$ feet or more, including basement (except unexcavated portions), attics, garages, roofed porches, mezzanine, loading platforms, shipping platforms, penthouses, mechanical equipment, floors, lobbies, and corridors]. Gross area does not include open courts, light wells, upper portions of rooms, lobbies, or other areas that rise above the story being measured; drives, ramps, or the like extending beyond the principal exterior walls of the building; or unroofed areas such as cooling towers and unenclosed portions of ground-level or intermediate stories.

Gypsum Board   A panel consisting of a gypsum core faced with paper on the front and back. It is used as a wall or ceiling covering. *See also* Drywall.

High-Intensity Discharge (HID) Lamp   An electric-discharge lamp which may include mercury, high-pressure sodium, and metal halide.

Hue   The classification of colors, such as red, yellow, blue, or other intermediates, between a contiguous pair of colors on the color wheel.

HVAC   Heating, ventilation, and air conditioning.

Hydrophobic   A term for a material that is normally nonabsorbent, such as nylon or polyester.

Incandescent Lamp   A lamp in which lighting is produced by a filament (typically, tungsten) heated to incandescence.

Indirect Lighting   Lighting that distributes 90 to 100 percent of light upward.

Interdepartmental Circulation   Corridor or path space that allows movement between or among departments.

Intradepartmental Circulation   Corridor or path space that allows movement within a department. Also referred to as secondary circulation.

Joint-Use Space   Common space available for use by all occupants of a building, such as cafeterias, conference rooms, and snack bars. It does not include mechanical, custodial, or circulation areas.

Lamp   A generic term for a manufactured source of light.

Layout Factor   An allowance included in space programs to enable efficient location of equipment and workstation components within occupiable space, which depends on the use of existing and/or proposed furniture, various layout techniques, and anticipated or actual physical variations in the building.

Lens   A glass or plastic device used to direct and control the distribution of light.

Lessee   One who possesses the right to use or occupy a property under lease agreement.

Lessor   One who holds title to and conveys the right to use and occupy a property under lease agreement.

Linear Foot   A measurement of one foot of length measured along a line. Also called a lineal foot.

Live Load   The capacity of the building to support interior construction, furnishings, and occupants. Live load does not include the weight of the structure itself.

Load Bearing   A term describing a floor-to-ceiling wall that provides structural support to the floor or roof above.

Louver   A series of baffles used to shield a source from view at certain angles or to absorb unwanted light.

Lumen   A unit of measurement defined as the rate of flow of light radiation in a uniform solid angle from a uniform source of light.

Luminaire   A complete lighting unit, including the lamp fixture.

Mercury Lamp   A high-intensity discharge lamp in which light is produced by radiation from mercury.

Metal Halide Lamp   A high-intensity discharge lamp in which light is produced by radiation of metal halides.

Module   A standard unit of measure by which the proportions of a building or other structure are judged. A module may be structural (determined by column spacing, window size, etc.) or functional (determined by workstation or equipment size).

Monument   An electrical outlet box attached to the floor.

Noise Reduction Coefficient (NRC)   An arithmetic average of sound absorption coefficients of the four middle frequencies (250, 500, 1000, and 2000 Hz).

Nonresilient Flooring   Rigid, hard floor finish materials such as stone or tile.

Open Plan   A plan in which a majority of the personnel are placed in workstations that do not have doors or floor-to-ceiling partitions.

Outlet   The termination of an electrical circuit for connection to a fixture or device.

Panel   A demountable, prefabricated partition available in various heights and widths, and either freestanding or interconnected; acoustical or hard surface.

Panel-Hung System   A furniture system in which all elements are suspended from panels.

Parabolic   A bowl-shaped lens used to diffuse light.

PAR Lamp (Pressed Reflector Lamp)   An incandescent filament or electric discharge lamp with an outer bulb that is a reflectorized bowl and a cover for optical control.

Partition Walls Used to Divide Space.   Partitions are frequently constructed onsite, although they may also be prefabricated. Partitions can be full (floor-to-ceiling) or partial height.

Paver Tile   A glazed or unglazed porcelain or natural clay tile that is formed by a dust-pressed method.

Perimeter   The outermost wall of a building. In interior usage, "perimeter" refers to the inside of the exterior wall.

Pilaster   A column or columnlike element that is attached to a wall surface.

Pile   The upright ends of yarn, whether cut or looped, that form the wearing surface of a carpet.

Pitch   The number of surface yarn ends per 27 inches of width on a woven carpet.

Plan   An architectural drawing showing the layout or configuration of various elements and their physical relationship to each other.

Plenum   The space between a structural ceiling slab and the finished ceiling.

Ply   The number of fibers twisted together to form a single yarn.

Power Pole   Vertical metal channels, usually 2 to 3 inches square, used in open plan for wire distribution from ceiling to workstation.

Primary Circulation   Corridor or path space that allows movement between the general office space and the building core.

Primary Colors   The three base colors of red, yellow, and blue, from which all other colors are mixed.

Programming   The process of determining current and future qualitative and quantitative space requirements.

Raceway   A general term for any continuous channel or enclosure intended to house and protect voice/data and power wires.

Recessed Light Fixture   A light fixture that is mounted above the ceiling or behind another surface with the face or opening of the fixture flush with the surface.

Reflector Lamp   An incandescent filament or electrical discharge lamp in which the outer blown glass bulb is coated with a reflecting material in order to direct the light.

Resilient Flooring   A floor material such as carpet which is flexible underfoot.

Secondary Colors   Colors created by mixing together two of the three primary colors. The secondary colors are purple, green, and orange.

Section   A drawing showing a cut through a wall or other element viewed to scale, identifying critical dimensions.

Selvage   A specially woven edge that prevents cloth from unraveling. The selvage runs along the same direction as the grain.

Semigloss Enamel   An enamel paint with a moderately shiny finish.

Shades   Colors that have black mixed into them.

Sick Building Syndrome   A condition in which building occupants experience discomfort such as fatigue and headaches which are attributed to the building.

Slab   A level surface of concrete either on the ground (slab-on-grade) or supported above ground.

Sound Lining   A sound-attenuating material used to line the interior of ducts to inhibit the transmission of sound through ductwork.

Sound Masking   Also called white sound or pink sound. Sound masking uses electronically produced noise to increase the ambient sound level so that normal conversation becomes unintelligible.

Sound Reflection   The portion of incident energy that returns back to the atmosphere when a sound wave encounters a surface. The angle of reflection is equal to the angle of incidence.

Sound Transmission Class (STC)   A measure of the effectiveness of a partition in reducing airborne sound transmission, not impact noise, low-frequency noise sources, or amplified sound.

Space Layout   The arrangement of the elements of a space as shown in a plan. The specific placement of workstations, furniture, and equipment to provide maximum efficiency in terms of space usage and agency operation. *See also* Space Plan.

Space Plan   The arrangement of elements within a space as seen in a plan. The specific placement of workstations, furniture, and equipment.

Specification   Written instructions that usually accompany a drawing, which elaborate on information necessary for the completion of work.

Standpipe System   A system of pipes traveling either vertically in buildings of more than four stories or horizontally in warehouse, manufacturing, or shopping mall facilities to deliver water to remote locations throughout the building. The purpose of the standpipe system is provide a water supply for manual firefighting with hoses.

Stand Space   The space around an object that must remain clear of obstacles to allow the user access to the object.

Subdividing Partition   Floor-to-ceiling walls used to divide space or provide acoustical control, providing no structural support to the building.

Support Space   Spaces used for support functions such as files, mail, copying, storage, and libraries.

Surface-Mounted Fixture   A light fixture mounted directly on the ceiling.

Suspended Ceiling   A ceiling, hung by wire or wood framing from a floor or roof above. Suspended ceilings often consist of a grid of metal tees into which acoustical tiles are placed. *See also* Acoustical Ceiling.

Systems Creep   The difference between the nominal workstation dimension (usually the interior area) and the actual amount of space that each workstation consumes. This difference can often be accounted for by considering the thickness of the panels and the dimensions of the connective hardware.

Systems Furniture   A collection of furniture elements intended to be used together to form a space-efficient workstation in any of a number of different configurations.

Tackless Carpet Installation   A carpet installation method by which the carpet is stretched over a large area and attached to tackless strips (three-ply plywood strips containing rust-resistant pins that penetrate the carpet backing). The tackless strips are then attached to the floor surface.

Task Lighting   Light that is directed toward a work surface or task area to provide illumination for visual tasks.

Terrazzo   A nonresilient agglomerate floor finish made from aggregate of marble chips suspended in a cement matrix.

Third Harmonics   An imbalance in an electrical current created by nonlinear loads.

Tight Building Syndrome   Discomfort and illness originally associated with reduced ventilation in an indoor office environment. Tight Building Syndrome is now referred to as Sick Building Syndrome.

Tints   Colors that have been mixed with white.

Toggle Switch   An on/off switch.

Torchere   An indirect floor lamp directing light upward.

Trench Header Duct   A duct that carries a number of conductors that branch into a series of underfloor ducts running perpendicular to the trench header duct.

Troffer   A recessed lighting unit, usually long and installed with the opening flush with the ceiling. The term is derived from "tough" and "coffer."

Uninterruptiable Power System (UPS)   A sophisticated switching unit that regulates fluctuation in power.

Usable Square Footage   The square footage within a building that can actually be used by the occupants.

Value   The lightness or darkness of a color in terms of tints and shades. A tint has a lighter value than a shade of the same color.

Variable Air Volume   An all-air building mechanical system that accommodates load variations by regulating the volume of air supplied through a single duct.

Veiling Reflections   The reflected image of a light source that obscures or veils the reflecting surface.

Ventilation   Outdoor air delivered to the indoor environment.

Volatile Organic Compounds (VOCs)   Synthetic materials found in an office environment which emit harmful vapors or gases.

Warp   The threads running lengthwise in a loom which are woven with the weft to create a fabric.

Weft   Also called woof or filler yarns. The yarns carried back and forth across the warp of a loom by a shuttle to create a fabric.

Wet Pipe Automatic Sprinkler System   The most effective and efficient automatic sprinkler system, consisting of a series of water-filled pipes and sprinkler heads.

Window Mullion   A framing or vertical separating member between adjacent window sections.

Wireway   A metal wiring enclosure with a removable front or top cover for access.

Workstation   Space required to accommodate the performance of a task. A workstation may house an individual or shared equipment.

Index